Qol Tamid

The Shofar in Ritual, History, and Culture

Qol Tamid
The Shofar in Ritual, History,
and Culture

Jonathan L. Friedmann
and Joel Gereboff, editors

CLAREMONT STUDIES IN
HEBREW BIBLE AND SEPTUAGINT

Qol Tamid
The Shofar in Ritual, History, and Culture
©2017 Claremont Press
1325 N. College Ave
Claremont, CA 91711

ISBN: 978-1-946230-04-1

Library of Congress Cataloging-in-Publication Data

Qol Tamid: The Shofar in Ritual, History, and Culture / edited by Jonathan L. Friedmann and Joel Gereboff
    xii + 358 pp. 22 x 15 cm. –(Claremont Studies in Hebrew Bible & Septuagint 1)
    Includes bibliographical references and index.
    ISBN: 978-1-946230-04-1
    Subjects: 1. Bible—Old Testament—Criticism, Interpretation, etc.

Call Number: BM657.S5 Q65 2017

Cover Credit: Jason C. Mitchell

*To Elvia, Lorenzo, and Eloise, and to the glorious
animals who gave us the shofar*
-JLF

*To Avi, Reachel, Arielle, Noah, Yonah, Rami and Elan
"Praise the Lord with the sound of the Shofar"
(Ps. 150:3)*
-JG

Table of Contents

Preface — ix
    Joel Gereboff and Jonathan L. Friedmann

Abbreviations — xi

Introduction — 1
    Joel Gereboff and Jonathan L. Friedmann

The History and Ritual Uses of the Shofar — 11
    Jeremy Montagu

The Shofar in War and Worship in the Bible — 31
    Marvin A. Sweeney

The Emotional Resonance of the Shofar and the Preacher's Voice — 57
    Joel Gereboff

Of Sound and Vision
    The Ram's Horn in Medieval Kabbalistic Rituology — 83
    Jeremy Phillip Brown

Sephardic Shofar Practices
    Theology and Mysticism — 115
    Haim Ovadia

Each One Blowing its Own Horn   *139*
    Sounding the Shofar in American Maḥzorim
    Joel Gereboff

Ancient Symbols, Modern Meanings   *165*
    **The Use of the Shofar in Twentieth-
    and Twenty-First-Century Music**
    Malcolm Miller

Same Signals, Different Meanings   *221*
    **The Shofar in Compositions
    by Elgar and Berio**
    Kees van Hage

Sounding the Shofar in Hollywood Film Scores   *247*
    Aaron Fruchtman

From Stale to Silly to Sublime   *267*
    The Shofar in Comic Books
    Jonathan L. Friedmann

List of Contributors   *297*

Bibliography   *301*

Index   *325*

Preface

This book brings together original essays on previously unexplored aspects of the shofar and its uses. Some of the essays analyze religious functions and meanings of the shofar from biblical to contemporary times. Others examine the use and depiction of the shofar in music and popular culture, especially during the past century.

The editors' interest in the shofar emerges from their respective scholarly pursuits. As a historian of music in the Bible, Jonathan is fascinated by the shofar's survival (it is the only biblical instrument we can identify with any certainty); and, as a cantor, he has blown the shofar for many years. Joel's first paid position in the Jewish community was as the shofar blower in his synagogue. His larger academic focus on Judaism and the emotions, ritual, and American Jewish denominational views informs his research on the shofar in rabbinic and modern American Jewish life.

The editors would like to thank Thomas E. Phillips and the staff at Claremont Press for embracing this project and guiding it to publication

Abbreviations

AB	Anchor Bible
BO	Bibliotheca Orientalis
ECC	Eerdmans Critical Commentary
EncJud	*Encyclopedia Judaica.* Edited by Fred Skolnik and Michael Beernbaum. 2nd ed. 22 vols. Detroit: Macmillan Reference USA, 2007
FAT	Forschungen zum Alten Testament
FOTL	Forms of the Old Testament Literature
HR	*History of Religions*
HUCA	*Hebrew Union College Annual*
JAP	*Journal of Applied Psychology*
JBR	*Journal of Bible and Religion*
JJML	*Journal of Jewish Music and Liturgy*
JQR	*Jewish Quarterly Review*
JRJ	*Journal of Reform Judaism*
JRPC	*Journal of Religion and Popular Culture*
NCBC	New Cambridge Bible Commentary
OTL	Old Testament Library
YAB	Yale Anchor Bible

Introduction

Joel Gereboff and Jonathan L. Friedmann

From biblical times until today the shofar has served an array of practical purposes and communicated a range of symbolic meanings. The roughly seventy references to the shofar in the Hebrew Bible show four stereotypical functions: announcing the divine presence (e.g., Exod 19:16; Zech 9:14); accompanying sacred ceremonies (e.g., Lev 23:24; 2 Sam 6:15); proclaiming kingship (1 Kgs 1:34; 2 Kgs 9:13); and signaling on the battlefield (e.g., Judg 3:27; 2 Sam 2:28). In addition, the shofar served as a symbol for messages of joy, fear, group identity, and redemption. Many of the references to the shofar occur in narratives and liturgical poetic passages, while only a few references are of an explicitly legal nature. Leviticus 25:9-10 stipulates the sounding of the shofar on the tenth day of the seventh month to proclaim the Jubilee. Two passages, Leviticus 23:24 and Numbers 29:1, require that the first day of the seventh month, what is now called Rosh Hashanah, be a day for *teru'ah*, the sounding of a horn, generally understood to be a shofar. Although biblical passages mention two words with regard to the blowing of the shofar, *tq'* (*teqi'ah*) and *teru'ah,* the exact nature of the sound is not fully evident, nor is how the shofar should be sounded for the different occasions. No passages detail the species of animals for making a shofar.

Rabbinic texts and *halakhic* deciders (*posqim*) since the time of the Mishnah, the first rabbinic document, have developed and disagreed about various stipulations regarding the materials for the shofar, the specific character of the sounds, and the liturgical dimensions of its use. Moreover, local practices among different Jewish communities emerged. In addition to comments on the legal aspects of the use of the shofar on Rosh Hashanah and other occasions—including its sounding in the period before and after that day, and its being blown to announce fasts, communal bans, and the commencement of the Sabbath—rabbinic sages have also elaborated upon the purposes and meanings of the shofar blasts. Such views appear in the earliest homiletical midrashic documents (*Leviticus Rabbah* and *Pesiqta deRab Kahana*), and find expression in later sermonic sources, as well. Kabbalists, in particular, enveloped the shofar with extensive cosmic and personal mystical import, thereby also shaping *halakhic* aspects of the ritual of shofar blowing. Such notions found their way into various liturgical texts (*maḥzorim*), with differences among those committed to such views and those, in time, opposed to them. The never-ending production of Jewish prayer books that continues unabated today exhibits continual efforts to both detail the actual sounds for different parts of the Rosh Hashanah services, and, more so, to frame the shofar blowing with traditional and creative liturgical elements meant to impact all those listening to the sounds, including the individuals at prayer and God in the divine realm.

Perhaps equally as important to its liturgical use is the shofar's status as a national symbol. This is attested in the earliest artistic representations of the horn. From at least the Roman period, the shofar was revered as a badge of Jewish self-identification. It was woven into architectonic elements such as the capitals, stone reliefs, and mosaic floors of synagogues, as well as smaller artifacts such as oil lamps, medallions, and coins. More often than not, it appeared as part of a symbolic grouping, which typically included a seven-branched menorah, a *maḥta* (incense shovel), a Torah scroll, and/or a *lulav*. For instance, a mosaic found at the sixth-century Shalom Al Yisrael synagogue in Jericho depicts a shofar, a menorah, and a *lulav*; and a seventh-century gold Byzantine medal features a shofar, a menorah, and a Torah scroll. The shofar also appears in medieval and early modern illuminated texts, such as a fourteenth-century German manuscript depicting two shofar blowers around the word *litqo'a* ("to sound the shofar"), and the Venice Haggadah of 1609, which includes an extra-biblical image of the shofar as a shepherd's horn, similar to those found in Europe. To this day, the shofar remains a multivalent ethnic identity marker.

The shofar is the only musical instrument that has survived in Jewish practice since ancient times. Other types of biblical instruments (harps, lyres, frame drums, flutes, rattles, cymbals, etc.) are notoriously difficult to identify, both because the text reveals little about how they looked or sounded, and because they were effectively silenced after the destruction of the Second Temple and the subsequent unemployment of the Levitical musicians. A few archaeologists and instrument makers have attempted the speculative (and controversial) work of reconstructing these long-lost devices. Such labors are not needed when it comes to the shofar.

Two factors account for the shofar's remarkable preservation. First, it is a biological instrument. Unlike human-made objects, which are influenced by technological changes and cultural evolution, the undetectably slow forces of nature set the dimensions of the shofar. Second, the rabbis did not include the shofar in the prohibition against playing musical instruments on holy days.

The exclusion of the shofar from the family of instruments had a double motivation: one part aesthetic and one part pragmatic. The aesthetic position derived from the horn's limited facilities and utilitarian purposes. Its normal range of two or three pitches is not musical per se, although it is technically an aerophone (wind instrument). Rather than having the beautifying effect of music proper, the shofar functioned as a solemn and sometimes disconcerting tool of proclamation, commemoration, and alarm.

Pragmatically, the rabbis did not want to interfere with the shofar's national-cultic value. According to the Torah, the first day of the seventh month (Rosh Hashanah) was a day for blowing shofars (Lev 23:24; Num 29:1). The only other Torah-mandated action for that day was ritual sacrifice, which ended with the fall of the Second Temple. Therefore, grouping the shofar with musical instruments, and thus barring it from New Year observances, would have eliminated the holiday's scriptural basis. The same problem would have arisen on the tenth day of the seventh month (Yom Kippur), which was likewise mandated as a day for horn blasts (Lev 25:9).

Rabbinic opinions notwithstanding, historians of Jewish music are unanimous in viewing the shofar as a musical instrument. The perspective was laid out in an 1892 essay by Cyrus Adler, assistant curator of the Smithsonian Institution Collections of Oriental Antiquities and Religious Ceremonial and an editor of the twelve-volume *Jewish Encyclopedia* (1901–1906).

Adler's essay, "The Shofar: Its Uses and Origin," offers five conclusions: the shofar represents the oldest type of wind instrument used by "inland peoples" (an animal horn with a natural cavity and a mouthpiece formed by cutting off the end); it was originally a signal horn; many of those signals had religious purposes, which led to its adoption for sacred purposes; the shofar's sanctity was enhanced by its connection to sacrificial animals; and the word shofar may derive from the Akkadian *šapparu*, a species of wild goat.[1] These points informed other early Jewish musical studies, and were canonized in the influential work of Abraham Z. Idelsohn, the father of Jewish musicology.[2] Recent surveys of Jewish music likewise focus on biblical sources pertaining to the shofar and its ritualistic place in Jewish life.

The shofar came into its own as a musical instrument during the twentieth century. In 1957 Moses Asch's Folkway Records released *Kol Ha'Shofar* by David M. Hausdorff. Asch included the album in his expansive project to document music from global cultures. It features shofar demonstrations, liturgical recitations, and selections of scriptural cantillation. Concert works and film scores have taken the shofar

---

[1] Cyrus Adler, "The Shofar: Its Use and Origin," *Report of the United States National Museum for 1892* (1894): 437–50.

[2] See, for example, Abraham Z. Idelsohn, *Jewish Music in Its Historical Development* (New York: Henry Holt, 1929), 9–11.

out of the ritual context and augmented its musical capacities, beginning with Edward Elgar's 1903 composition, *The Apostles: An Oratorio*. In 2013 avant-garde experimenter Alvin Curran released *Shofar Rags* on John Zorn's iconoclastic Tzadik Records. Curran's compositions fuse innovative blowing techniques with electronics to create tonal expressions ranging from groaning agony to kinetic ecstasy.

The shofar has also expanded into the realm of fine art. It figures commonly in paintings sold by Judaica dealers, and occasionally finds its way into prominent pieces, such as Marc Chagall's *Le Shofar* (1911) and Moshe Castel's *Shofar on the Temple Mount* (1982), housed at the Israel Museum. Representations in popular culture are not unheard of, including occasional appearances in comic book illustrations. The production of shofarot has itself become a large-scale industry, as has collecting them as *objets d'art*.

This book examines the various uses, functions, and meanings of the shofar from ancient times to the present, bringing together studies from historical, theological, musicological, cultural, and ritual perspectives.[3] It is the first multidisciplinary volume

---

[3] Due to space limitations there are numerous other aspects of the shofar not discussed here, including: iconography of the shofar over the ages; later kabbalistic and Hasidic understandings; the production, purchase, and display of shofarot as art objects; the aesthetics of shofarot; and ethnographic studies

devoted to the shofar, touching on areas ranging from biblical and rabbinic texts to modern-day film and concert music.

Jeremy Montagu opens the volume with a survey of historical, liturgical, and legal discussions surrounding the construction and blowing of the shofar. Marvin Sweeney identifies the core functions of the shofar according to a range of biblical texts, drawing connections between the horn's use in war and worship. Joel Gereboff delineates early and medieval rabbinic views on the purposes of blowing the shofar, with particular attention to the emotional resonance of this ritual. Jeremy Brown turns to twelfth- through fourteenth-century kabbalistic understandings of the various aspects of the shofar and its ritual use, and provides a richly textured analysis that highlights the synesthetic phenomenology of the mystical experience. Haim Ovadia comments upon two aspects of Sephardic views on the shofar: how contentious theological perspectives found expression in a classical *piyyut* (liturgical poem), and how Sephardic legal opinions, past and present, have disagreed about the number and significance of the shofar sounds for Rosh Hashanah. Joel Gereboff examines conflicting liturgical choices for the shofar

---

of the meanings contemporary Jews ascribe to the shofar and its use.

service in American Orthodox *maḥzorim*, Ashkenazic and Sephardic, and provides brief observations on the most recent prayer books of liberal American Jewish movements.

Malcolm Miller presents an expansive survey and analysis of twentieth- and twenty-first century musical compositions showcasing the shofar and shofar-imitative sounds. Kees van Hage explores the genesis and meaning of two concert works for choir and orchestra inspired by the shofar: "The Calling of the Apostles" from *The Apostles* (1903) by Edward Elgar, and *Hör* by Luciano Berio, his Prologue to the multi-composer *Requiem of Reconciliation* (1995). Aaron Fruchtman investigates the use and symbolism of the shofar in several Hollywood film scores, including two by Academy Award-winning composer Jerry Goldsmith: *Planet of the Apes* (1968) and *Star Trek: The Motion Picture* (1979). Jonathan Friedmann concludes with a study of the evolution of shofar depictions in American comic books, and how those portrayals reflect larger trends in the comic book industry.

These eclectic contributions demonstrate the perpetual significance of the shofar in ritual and art. The horn resounds with a *qol tamid* — an eternal voice — resonating through the ages.

The History and Ritual Uses of the Shofar

Jeremy Montagu

Our first evidence for the shofar appears in the book of Exodus 19:13, 16, and 19. "Then the shofar sounded from Heaven amid thunders and lightnings; Moses spoke and God answered him with a voice." This was the first time that God had spoken to all the people of Israel; before that God had spoken with Abraham, Isaac, Jacob, and Moses, but now God spoke to the whole House of Israel, those that were standing there that day and those who were not there that day, and thus to all the generations past and to all the generations to come. So it was then that the Israelites, the Jews, really became God's people.

But was this really the first time that the shofar was heard? Many peoples around the world use animal horns for a multitude of purposes — as a signal, for alarms, for battle, for assemblies, for herding animals, and for much else. The shofar is a horn, traditionally that of a ram or a goat, and the Israelites had always been pastoralists. Jacob kept sheep and goats for his father-in-law Laban (Gen 30:32); Jacob's sons told the Egyptian Pharaoh, ignoring Joseph's warning that the Egyptians despised shepherds, that they were keepers of sheep (Gen 47:3). Thus ram's and goat's horns must always have been available in plenty. Abraham led a war party to rescue Lot (Gen 14:13ff), and there were many other occasions when it would seem that such a horn would have been useful before that occasion on Mount Sinai, when the Law was given from Heaven.

But we have no earlier biblical reference to horns or trumpets of any kind until Exodus 19, nor, other than two verses in Leviticus to which we shall return, do we have any other biblical references to any such instruments until we come to Numbers 10:1. There we have God's command to Moses to make a pair of metal trumpets, the *hatzotzerot*. Then, through the whole of the rest of that chapter, God detailed very precisely to Moses the process of manufacture, specifying their material of silver, saying how they were to be made, by beaten work (meaning that they were to be raised from sheet metal by hammering, rather than being cast), and how they were to be used. They were to be for the priests to call the people to assemblies; to signal the movement of the camps in the desert; for war; and for festivals, the days of gladness, always by the priests. It is abundantly clear, from the precision of these details that, until then, these were something that the Israelites had never used before. But these were metal trumpets, made specifically for the priests to use; surely before that time natural animal horns could have been used. The shofar must already have been known, because if it were not, would not some prescription or description have been necessary when it did appear, as it is here in Numbers 10 for the *ḥatzotzerot*?

One of the most important aspects of the shofar, in contrast with the *ḥatzotzerot*, is that it was not a priestly horn—it was for everybody, for any of the people, whether priests or anybody else, and this is why it is the only instrument to have survived from biblical times and to remain in use today. All the priestly instruments of the Temple, used by the Levites in all the ceremonies, died out after the Romans destroyed the Temple in 70 CE. From then on, there were no more Temple ceremonies, there were no more sacrifices, and therefore there was no more work for the priests; for the function of the priests, the Kohanim (the descendants of Aaron), and their assistants, the Levi'im (the descendants of other members of that tribe), was to offer sacrifices and to look after all the Temple ceremonies, all the equipment of the Temple, and indeed the Temple itself.

Other instruments that would have been used domestically or for nonceremonial music, as well as in the Temple, did survive for a time among the people, but like all musical instruments they changed character, use, and shape over the generations; only the shofar remained as it had always been, the horn of a ram or a goat, the horn of the whole People of Israel.

It is with the first reference to such an instrument in Leviticus that a trumpet or horn first appears in ritual. In chapter 23, verses 23–24, God told Moses to tell the children of Israel that on the first day of the seventh month they will have a holy gathering, a reminder of *teru'ah*, of a trumpet call. God did not say on which of the two instruments, the *hatzotzerah* or the shofar, this call was to be blown, nor by whom, nor even whether it should be blown or whether it should merely be remembered. When this injunction is repeated, slightly more elaborated, in Numbers 29:1, it is no longer "a reminder," but "a day of *teru'ah*," which does suggest that it should indeed be blown, but it still does not say on which instrument, nor does it say by whom. It is only when we reach the Talmud that we find that indeed it should be blown and on the shofar, and that what was, in the Torah, the first day of the seventh month, had by Talmudic times already become the first day of the first month of the year, Rosh Hashanah. But since the Talmud came after the destruction of the Temple, this only tells us that by then the *teru'ah* of the shofar was to be remembered and, we assume, blown; it does not tell us what actually happened in the tented sanctuary in the times of Leviticus and Numbers, nor later in the Temple any earlier than passed-on human memory might have survived.

It is in Leviticus 25:9-10 that we have the first undoubted use of the shofar in ritual, for there, on the tenth day of the seventh month, on the Day of Atonement, Yom Kippur, there was to be a proclamation by a *teru'ah* — a proclamation throughout the land on the shofar — to sanctify the fiftieth year, the Jubilee. Again, God does not say who should blow the shofar, whether it was to be by a Kohen, a Levi, or an Israel. A complication here is that in the Gemara of the Talmud, in *Rosh HaShanah* 26b, it is laid down that the shofar of the Jubilee was a straight shofar "of wild goat's horn (*yael*)." It is otherwise assumed throughout the Tanakh and the Talmud that the shofar was a ram's horn, and specifically in this same passage of Gemara, that for Rosh Hashanah it should be curved "because on that day the more a man bends his heart the better while on Yom Kippur [for the Jubilee] the more a man straightens his mind the better."

So what was the *yael*? The only wild goat in that part of the world with a straight (or almost straight) horn was the Arabian oryx, *Oryx leucoryx*. Translations of this passage normally suggest that the *yael* was an ibex, *Capra nubiana*, but an ibex's horn, though flat in one plane, is strongly curved in the other; while not quite so curved as a letter C, it is more curved than a parenthesis, "(", whereas the oryx horn is all but straight. Both ibex and oryx shofarot are available today from makers in Israel, the ibex coming from those that have died naturally in the National Parks, for both are protected species, and the oryx horn more often from southern African gemsboks, *Oryx gazella*, or the east African species *Oryx beisa*. Since we have not observed the Jubilee for many centuries if ever, neither type is really necessary today, though more recent Syrian communities have been known to use an ibex shofar for Rosh Hashanah. What complicates the story even further is that our word Jubilee is a transliteration of the Hebrew word *yovel*, a word which can mean both Jubilee and ram.

While we do not know which of the three—Kohanim, Levites, or Israelites—blew for the Jubilee, in our next reference in the Tanakh, in the book of Joshua chapter 6, it was specifically the Kohanim, the priests, who were to blow the shofar, and, to remove all doubt, in that chapter they are called ram's horns, *shofarot ha-yovelim*. It was a lengthy process, the siege of Jericho. For six days all the men of war (v. 3) were to walk around the city once with (v. 4) seven priests carrying seven ram's horns before the ark, walking around the city seven times, and the priests blowing with the shofarot. Skipping now to verse 16, because the narrative, here in the past tense, is clearer: on the seventh circuit, the priests blew (presumably a long call as specified in v. 5), and Joshua told the people to make a loud noise, and then (v. 20) when the people heard the sound of the shofar they made a great noise and the wall fell down flat.

The "great noise" is commonly translated as a great shout, but the Hebrew words are *teru'ah gedolah*, and *teru'ah* is a word normally used for trumpeting. Did the people also each blow a shofar? Or did they make some other noise? Or was it indeed a shout? We can never know, but what we do know is that it was not the sound of the priests' seven shofarot that flattened the wall, but that it was the noise that the people made.

Thereafter in the shofar's history in the Tanakh[1], the shofar appears in many roles. In Judges it was a summons (3:27 and 6:34) and again a war trumpet (7:16ff) when Gideon attacked the huge Midianite invading army with his three hundred men, each one of them with a sword in his belt, a shofar in one hand, and a dark lantern, made of a torch inside a jug, in the other hand. The sound of the shofarot, and the blaze of light when each man broke his jug, were so alarming that the Midianites broke and ran.

In 2 Samuel 6:15 it was a horn of rejoicing, for it was sounded when David brought up the Ark in its

---

[1] I am following the order of the books in the Hebrew Bible, the Tanakh, rather than that of the English Old Testament, though for simplicity I am using the English names for the books.

second stage of the journey. When this story reappears in 1 Chronicles 15:28 it manages to conflate the two halves of that journey into one, combining the other instruments of 2 Samuel 6:5 with the shofar of 6:15. Chronicles, which was written very late in the biblical canon, certainly well after the return from the Exile in Babylon, is the least reliable book of the Tanakh, often getting matters wrong and often grossly exaggerating them. The account of 120 priests sounding with trumpets (*ḥatzotzerot*) in 2 Chronicles 5:12 is surely incredible, as are the accounts of huge numbers of singers elsewhere in those two books. We do know the size of Solomon's Temple to the nearest half-meter (a cubit) and, assuming that Nehemiah's rebuild on the return from the Exile (Neh 4) was on the same footprint, there simply would not have been room for such numbers, quite apart from any other considerations.

But returning to the shofar and to the earlier books, in 1 Kings 1:34 and 39 it was the shofar that was blown for Solomon's coronation, and later for other crownings. In Ezekiel 33:3–6 it was a watchman's horn, and if anyone ignored the watchman's warning calls, their doom was to be on their own heads. For Joel (2:1) it was an alarm, as it was to be again and again in other books, right up to Nehemiah 4:12 and 14, and in Joel 2:15 it was a call to a solemn assembly. In Psalms it was an instrument of praise (Pss 98 and 150). It is in Psalm

81 that we have clear evidence of the growing use of shofar over *ḥatzotzerah*, because whereas in Numbers 10:10 Moses is told that the *ḥatzotzerot* were to be blown "in the day of your gladness, and in your appointed seasons, and in your new moons," in Psalm 81:4-5 we are told "Blow the shofar at the new moon, at the full moon for our feast day. For it is a statute for Israel, an ordinance of the God of Jacob." Incidentally, these two verses are by far the most common quotation on all those shofarot that bear biblical verses inscribed upon them.

These citations probably suffice for the history of the shofar through the biblical centuries, for most others are repetitions of these, but for a full listing of references in Tanakh, see pages 121-27 of my book *The Shofar: Its History and Use* (Lanham: Rowman & Littlefield, 2015), and for all the Talmudic, and some later, references, see pages 128-53.

Let us now turn to the pages of the Talmud, the codification of the Oral Law. There are two sets of Laws that were given by God to Moses, according to the Orthodox Jewish tradition: one was the Written Law, which we have in the Torah, the first five books of the Tanakh, and the other was the Oral Law, which was passed down by word of mouth, from one generation to the next, until it was finally written down by Judah haNasi, around 200 CE in Palestine, as the Mishnah. This became the basis of rabbinical discussion of both the Oral and the Written Laws throughout the Jewish world for another few hundred years, until once again it was written down as the Gemara, first in what was called the Jerusalem Talmud, or Yerushalmi, in about 400 CE, and then in Babylon in what was called the Babylonian Talmud, or Bavli, between 600 and 700 CE. Because much of the Yerushalmi has been lost, the Bavli is now regarded as the standard version, and it is the Bavli that will be cited here. Since then there has been a multitude of commentaries and further discussions, but few of these will concern us here. It is the Talmud, sometimes modified by the later discussions, that has become the basis of *halakhah*, Jewish religious law.

Talmudic references to the Gemara are always by the leaf (*daf* in Hebrew and *blatt* in Yiddish), by its number within each tractate, and by its recto (a) or verso (b). All editions have used this same system since it was first printed in the sixteenth century, even if extra commentaries demand that a *daf* continues over several physical pages. The Mishnah is cited by the tractate, the number of the chapter, and then the number of the paragraph.

In *Berakhot* 30a, the first mention in Talmud, the shofar was blown as preparation for a journey, but a far more historically important reference comes from *Shabbat* 35b, the second reference. Before the days of the introduction of cheap portable timepieces, from the biblical era into quite modern times, there was no way for ordinary people, particularly those working in the fields, to know precisely when Shabbat was to begin each week. That time changes week by week throughout the year and its exact observance is of great *halakhic* importance. And so we read in *Shabbat* 35b that six *teqi'ot* were blown on the Shabbat eve. The first was to stop people working in the fields; the second was for shops to close in the city. The third was the signal to light the lights, though one rabbi said it was to take off the *tefillin*, which in those days many men wore all day but which are not worn on Shabbat. Then, after the time it takes to cook a small fish or to put a loaf in the oven, three calls were blown after or during which one observed Shabbat. There was, as always in Talmud, much discussion over the details, which call was for which action, at which point in the last three calls the Shabbat actually began, how it differed in Babylon from elsewhere, and so on, winding up with a question of whether a shofar could be used to give a child a drink (the answer was "yes").

The use of the shofar for signaling Shabbat goes right back to Temple times, for a stone was found at the base of the Wall, where it had been thrown down by the Romans when they destroyed the Temple, engraved with the words "the place of the blower for the...," and there it breaks off, but the likeliest continuation is "Shabbat." Even to this day in many small communities a shofar is blown at least once to signal the arrival of Shabbat, and in some larger cities, such as Jerusalem, a siren sounds, for even now, when we all carry a watch, our attention may be elsewhere at the critical moment.

Which of the two types of trumpet, shofar or *hatzotzerah*, was used to signal Shabbat in the Temple is unknown, though by Talmudic times it was certainly the shofar. Equally, this applies to the rituals of the Pilgrimage Holy Days, for in the discussions of Pesah and Sukkot in Gemara, the names of the different calls are used but neither instrument is ever mentioned. In the Mishnah (*Sukkah* 5:4) it is stated that the *hatzotzerot* were used for the Water Libation, but not in Gemara.

It is, as one might expect, in the discussions of Rosh Hashanah that we get specific information on the use of the shofar in ritual. In Gemara *Rosh HaShanah* 16a, Rabbi Abbahu asks, "Why do we blow with a shofar from a ram? The Holy One, blessed be He, said 'Blow *teqi'ah* before me with a shofar from a ram so that I remember for you the binding of Isaac the son of Abraham and consider that you have bound yourselves to me.'" This is why there are so many references to the Aqedah, the Binding of Isaac (Gen 22), in the Rosh Hashanah liturgy, and it also harks back to the legend that the shofar that sounded from Heaven at Mount Sinai was the left horn of the ram that Abraham had slaughtered instead of Isaac, while the right horn, the larger of the two, is retained up there and will be heard "in time to come" (Isa 27:13).

Despite what R. Abbahu said, many other animals are used for a shofar, even though Maimonides said in his *Mishneh Torah*, "And any not from a ram, *pasul* (forbidden)" and Saadia Gaon in his *Siddur* was equally positive, "The shofar which we blow can only be a ram's horn and it is forbidden to alter its shape." Goat horns were more common in Europe until the mid-twentieth century, and also around the Mediterranean, and the horn of a kudu, an African antelope, with its long curly shape, is very often seen today. It is generally taken that the horn of any kosher animal whose horns are naturally hollow (thus excluding deer antlers) may be used, except those of any member of the cow family, which are forbidden because of the episode of the Golden Calf (*Rosh HaShanah* 26a). The animal does not have to have been killed by *shehita* (kosher killing) because although it is put to the mouth, it is not eaten. It does not matter whether it is thick or thinned to a wafer thickness (*Rosh HaShanah* 27a), nor whether it has been shortened, for example, due to a split in the horn, provided that enough is left to produce a call. How much was allowed to make a call? R. Simeon ben Gamliel said, "Enough that when it is held in the hand something can be seen on either side," and "If its sound is thick or thin or dry it is kosher, because all sounds produced by a shofar can pass." It is forbidden (*pasul*) if anything such as gold or silver is added to the mouthpiece or to the inside, but it is kosher if it is added elsewhere to the outside, unless the sound is changed, when again it is *pasul*. If it has a hole that has been stopped up but which alters the sound it is *pasul*, but if the sound is not altered it is kosher—other rabbis disagreed with this, R. Nathan saying that if it was stopped with its own material it was kosher, but others saying that even then it was *pasul*.

It is essential on Rosh Hashanah that both the blower and the listener blow and hear with intent (*Rosh HaShanah* 28b); if not, neither has performed his religious duty. If the hearer was merely passing by and heard the shofar, it was not valid, and besides the blower perhaps was "merely making music—perhaps he merely barks." Also discussed on that page is the clarity of the calls, forbidding any sort of amplification such as blowing into a barrel or a pit; what must be heard is the sound of the shofar itself.

On the next leaf, 29b, the rabbis go into much detail regarding who may or may not blow for a congregation. The rabbis taught that "All are under obligation to blow the shofar, priests, Levites and Israelites, proselytes, emancipated slaves, *tumtum* and androgynous, and one who is half slave and half free." A *tumtum* is someone of uncertain sex and an androgynous one who has genitalia of both genders; a half slave is one who has had two masters, one who has freed him and one who has not. However, this then is much modified. A *tumtum* cannot blow for himself nor for anyone else; an androgynous can blow for himself or a fellow androgynous but for no one else, and one who is a half slave cannot blow for anyone because a slave cannot blow, and how do we know which half is blowing, the free half or the slave half? And also a deaf-mute, a lunatic, or a minor cannot blow for a congregation. Later on the same page we read that because not all are skilled in blowing, and someone who is ignorant of the Law might have transgressed by carrying the shofar on the Holy Day, all Israel should hear the shofar rather than blow it, so leaving blowing only to those learned enough to know what they are doing.

The Mishnah, *Rosh HaShanah* 4:5, shows that the liturgy for that day at least resembled ours today, for it mentions the *musaf Amidah* and its verses of *Malkhiyot* (kingship), *Zikhronot* (remembrance), and *Shofarot*, and the rabbis of both Mishnah and Gemara (32a) discussing where one blows. Certainly these were fixed by the ninth century, for Saadia Gaon writes the instructions:

> The calls we blow are ten calls, divided into three sections. The first section is *teqi'ah*, three *shevarim*, *teru'ah*, *teqi'ah*; the second section is *teqi'ah*, three *shevarim*, *teqi'ah*; and the third

section *teqi'ah, teru'ah, teqi'ah*. The *teqi'ah* is a long drawn-out sound, the *shevarim* is three short sounds, each of which is like one third of the long sound, and the *teru'ah* is a long trembling sound as long as the first [here he inserts a diagram illustrating the sounds]....If *musaf* on Rosh Hashanah is said with a congregation one blows these three sounds in its three paragraphs which I will describe later [*Malkhiyot, Zikhronot* and *Shofarot*]....If there is a congregation they must also blow the shofar before *musaf*: thirty calls repeating each of these calls three times.

His *Siddur* must have been compiled in his lifetime in the ninth century, though this copy of it, in the Bodleian Library of Oxford, MS Hunt 448, f.149r, dates from the thirteenth century and was found in the Cairo Geniza. Also from the Geniza from the same date is an anonymous *siddur*, known as the Codex Adler, now in the New York Jewish Theological Seminary, MS 4607, whose folio 21v shows another and better graphic portrayal of the calls immediately before the *musaf Amidah*, and a shorter version of each before each of those same three paragraphs that Saadia lists. What the portrayal shows for the calls is the hand gesture that the reader would make to remind the blower of which call comes next, just as someone does to indicate the accents (*te'amim* in Hebrew, *trup* in Yiddish) for the man who is reading Torah. The *teqi'ah* is a long straight line, the *shevarim* three short straight lines, and a long wiggly line for the *teru'ah*, all vertical. The need for the gestures is that the use of someone, the *maqri*, to call out each of the calls to the blower seems to be peculiar to Ashkenazi congregations, and perhaps of fairly recent date. That is thought to be a transgression among the Sephardim because, for the first of the calls, it intervenes between the blower pronouncing the relevant blessing ("...who has commanded us to hear the shofar") and then carrying out that commandment by blowing.

From *Rosh HaShanah* 34b onwards there is much discussion of which calls should be blown, *teqi'ah* or *teru'ah*, how many, in what order, and their comparative lengths. Toward the bottom of that page, Rabbi Abbahu prescribed that there should be a *teqi'ah*, three *shevarim*, a *teru'ah*, and a *teqi'ah*. "How can this be justified? If *teru'ah* is a kind of wailing, then there should be *teqi'ah*, *teru'ah*, and *teqi'ah*, and if it is a kind of groaning, there should be *teqi'ah*, three *shevarim*, and *teqi'ah*." And then, after argument, it was agreed that to make certain all was correct, these should be combined, as R. Abbahu had said.

And thus the Talmud establishes the basis of what we do today. Between then and the Codex Adler in the thirteenth century, all the rest of our modern practice had been settled. For *Malkhiyot*, further on in the *musaf*, on f.26, the same four calls were blown; for

Zikhronot (f.29) *teqi'ah, shevarim, teqi'ah,* and for *Shofarot* (f.31) *teqi'ah, teru'ah, teqi'ah.*

The Talmud makes no mention of any longer call to end a sequence. R. Ya'aqov ben Asher wrote in his *Tur* (*Oraḥ Ḥayyim* 596), in the thirteenth century, that Rav 'Amram wrote in the ninth century, "after the service we *teru'ah* a *teru'ah gedolah* without any *teqi'ah*," and this remains the Sephardic procedure. When the Ashkenazi custom of blowing a *teqi'ah gedolah* came in is unknown; the first reference to it seems to be in the *Minhagim* of R. Ya'aqov ben Moshi Levi Moelin, published in 1536; Rashi in the eleventh century merely mentions a long sound.

Equally obscure is the origin of the total number of calls, today 100 or 102. Among the Sephardim the total of 101 or more seems to go back to Babylon, perhaps as early as Talmudic times, but among Ashkenazim 40 or so seems to have been the norm until the mid-nineteenth century, when numbers went up, group by group, until they reached the present hundred or so. The distribution of the calls and their number at different points in the service, after the initial thirty calls, as or just before *musaf* begins, varies widely. It is too complex and too variable to list here, but all such details of practices that I have been able to find are listed in chapter 3 of my book.

Nor is there any agreement of what happens at the end of the Day of Atonement (Yom Kippur). All agree that there should be a call, but whether just a *gedolah*, or a series of calls, varies from one congregation to another. Among Ashkenazim it is always a single blower, but in many Sephardic congregations it can be everyone who has a shofar. And, because the Gates of Repentance do not finally swing shut until the end of Sukkot, in many congregations, especially among the Sephardim, the shofar is blown, often by more than one person, while the Hoshanot are being processed on Hoshanah Rabbah, the last day of Sukkot, preceding the day (days in the Diaspora) of Shemini Atseret and Simḥat Torah.

What of the calls themselves, the musical notes? I can only say that I have heard many blowers, and that no two blow exactly the same. Since a shofar can only produce two or three notes, plus some modifications by mouth-shape, these variants are limited in number, but there are also wide differences in phrasing and in styles, especially in the *teru'ah*. Actual pitches vary according to the acoustics of each shofar. The different notes vary according to the tradition of each blower, and to the expectations of each congregation, who can be very firm in telling a new blower, "No, not like that."

Where else does the shofar sound in ritual? During Elul, the month preceding Rosh Hashanah, it is blown each day (not on Shabbat, nor on the last day) to warn the community to prepare, though the

Sephardim usually blow only in the late-night Seliḥot services of repentance. A custom that is growing is to blow on Rosh Ḥodesh, the new moon. This is a day especially appropriate for women, who also have a monthly cycle, and there are now many women-only services at which, in conformity with Psalm 81, the shofar is blown, of course by a woman. Now that there are no sacrifices on Pesaḥ (Passover), nor Water Libations in Sukkot, it is not blown in those services.

One final point: especially among the Sephardim but fairly universally, there is a tradition of not looking at the blower while he blows, similarly to that of not looking at the Kohanim while they pronounce the *birkat kohanim*, the priestly blessing; both that and the shofar calls come directly from Heaven, and so one bows one's head.

It is because the shofar sounded from Heaven at Mount Sinai, when God called all the generations together, that worshippers bow their heads when hearing the sound of the shofar in their synagogues on Rosh Hashanah. And it is because the shofar was the rallying call and the war trumpet of the Children of Israel in its noncultic uses throughout Jewish history that many hold their heads high when hearing its sound, *qol ha-shofar*, the Voice of the Shofar, in our daily lives, outside the synagogue.

The Shofar in War and Worship in the Bible

Marvin A. Sweeney

I

The shofar is well-known in contemporary Jewish worship as the instrument which is sounded at Rosh Hashanah to herald the New Year.[1] In Ashkenazi communities, it is blown every day (except for Shabbats and the last day of the month) beginning with the second day of Elul, to announce the approach of Rosh Hashanah on Tishri 1. It is also sounded on Rosh Hashanah itself, unless it is Shabbat, and on Yom Kippur to signal the opening and closing of the divine book of judgment for the coming year. The shofar is blown again on Hoshana Rabbah, the seventh (or eighth in the diaspora) day of Sukkot to signal the conclusion of the holiday and the onset of Simḥat Torah when the annual reading of the Torah begins anew.

Although the blowing of the shofar in the context of worship during the High Holidays is well-rooted in biblical texts and practice, the shofar was also

---

[1] For an overview discussion of the shofar and its use, see Albert L. Lewis, "Shofar," *EncJud* 18:506–08.

employed extensively for use in times of war—both to warn the people of impending danger and to signal the onset and conclusion of hostilities in times of battle. Indeed, the contemporary practice of sounding the shofar during the High Holidays, when G-d is acknowledged as the sovereign of all creation, apparently grows out of the wartime use of the shofar to signal the approach of the King or other leader to deliver the people, and the realization of his victory over the enemies of Israel and Judah. The liturgical use of the shofar then signals the security of the nation as YHWH and the King are recognized for restoring order to the world.

This paper therefore considers three dimensions of the use of the shofar in the Bible: 1) its use as an instrument of warning the nation of danger; 2) its use as a signal in time of war to commence hostilities against an enemy and to conclude them; and 3) its use in the liturgy of Israelite and Judean Temples and elsewhere to celebrate the roles of YHWH and the King in restoring order to creation by bringing peace and security to the nation.

II

The shofar is one of the more ancient musical instruments known to human beings. It is fashioned from the horn of a ram or a wild goat. Indeed, the Hebrew noun šōpār is linguistically related to the Akkadian term šapparu, which means "wild sheep."[2] The shofar is sounded when one blows into the smaller end of the horn to produce its various tones. Use of the breath, lips, and tongue enable the shofar to produce sounds ranging from long blasts to short, staccato notes.

One of the most fundamental uses of the shofar is as an instrument of warning in times of danger. A number of prophetic texts indicate such usage.

Ezekiel's self-understanding of his prophetic role provides an important illustration of the function of the shofar as an instrument of warning.[3] Ezekiel was a Zadokite priest who was born and raised for service in the Jerusalem Temple, but he was exiled together with the young King Jehoiachin as part of the first exile of Jews from Jerusalem following King Jehoiakim's failed revolt against Babylonia in 598 BCE. Ezekiel was apparently twenty-five years old when he was exiled. When he turned thirty, the year in which a young

---

[2] Lewis, "Shofar," *EncJud* 18:506.

[3] For discussion of Ezekiel, see esp. Marvin A. Sweeney, *Reading Ezekiel: A Literary and Theological Commentary* (Macon, GA: Smyth and Helwys, 2013).

Zadokite man would be ordained for holy service at the Temple altar, he apparently experienced a vision of G-d in which he was commissioned as a visionary prophet of YHWH in Babylonia who would serve as a "watchman," Hebrew ṣôpeh, in Ezekiel 3:17. Ezekiel's role is defined in Ezekiel 3:16-21 as one who would warn the people of impending judgment from G-d in cases of wrongdoing and impurity. Leviticus 10:10-11 specifies that his role as a priest is to teach the people what is holy and what is profane and what is clean and what is unclean. As a visionary prophet in Babylonian exile, his task is to teach the people holy and pure conduct.

Ezekiel 33:1-20 specifies Ezekiel's role as a watchman of G-d. In times of danger when YHWH brings a sword against the nation, the people are to appoint a watchman to warn them of impending danger. The text makes it very clear in Ezekiel 33:3-6 that the watchman's task is to sound the shofar upon sighting approaching danger. If anyone fails to take warning from the sound of the shofar, his blood is upon his own head, that is, he is responsible for his own fate. However, if the watchman fails to sound the shofar at a time of approaching danger, the watchman is responsible for the blood of those who are killed. Insofar as Ezekiel hardly functions as a watchman in time of war, the use of the watchman motif and the role of the shofar as an instrument of warning in time of war apparently function as metaphorical devices to define the prophet's responsibility to teach the people concerning their responsibilities to conduct themselves properly before G-d in the world, even when they are in Babylonian exile.

Similar usage of the shofar motif appears in Jeremiah 2-6, which is formulated as an announcement of judgment against Israel and Judah by the prophet Jeremiah.[4] Like Ezekiel, Jeremiah was born to serve as a priest, but he was not from the Zadokite line that normally served in the Jerusalem Temple. Jeremiah was from Anathoth in the territory of Benjamin, which means that he was a member of the priestly line descended from the high priests Abiathar of Jerusalem and Eli of Shiloh, and ultimately from Ithamar, the son of Aaron. When David served as King of Israel, both Zadok and Abiathar served as high priests in Jerusalem. Whereas Abiathar was of the line of Eli and Ithamar, Zadok was of the line of Phineas and Eleazar, respectively the grandson and son of Aaron. Upon his accession to the throne, 1 Kings 1-2 recounts that Solomon expelled Abiathar to Anathoth, but retained Zadok in Jerusalem as high priest, allegedly on the advice of his dying father, David. During the reign of

---

[4] For discussion of Jeremiah 2-6, see esp. Marvin A. Sweeney, "Structure and Redaction in Jeremiah 2-6," *Form and Intertextuality in Prophetic and Apocalyptic Literature* (FAT 45; Tübingen: Mohr Siebeck, 2005), 94-108.

the Davidic monarch Josiah ben Amon (640–609 BCE), 2 Kings 23 reports that Josiah invited priests from the countryside to come to Jerusalem to serve in the Jerusalem Temple at the time of his program of religious reform and national restoration. Although 2 Kings 23 alleges that no priests accepted Josiah's invitation, Jeremiah's pedigree indicates that he was one such priest who did.

Jeremiah apparently supported King Josiah's efforts to reunite the kingdom of Judah with the people and territory of the former northern kingdom of Israel during the period of the collapse of the Assyrian empire. As part of his early efforts to call for such unification, Jeremiah formulated oracles now found in Jeremiah 2:2–4:2, which were designed to call for Israel's return to Jerusalem. But following Josiah's unexpected death at the hands of Pharaoh Necho of Egypt in 609 BCE, Jeremiah was compelled to recognize that Judah would suffer judgment much like that suffered by Israel a century before. As part of his efforts to announce his views, he expanded his earlier oracles directed to Israel in 2:2–4:2, with oracles directed to Judah in 4:3–6:30, which announced that an enemy from the north, apparently Babylon, would come to invade Judah much as Assyria had invaded Israel a century before. Although Babylon was due east of Jerusalem, the lack of water in the Arabian Desert would compel the Babylonian army to travel to Judah by way of the so-called Fertile Crescent in Mesopotamia, so that it would invade Judah from the north.

Jeremiah's expanded oracles against Judah in Jeremiah 4:3–6:30 make important use of the blowing of the shofar to signal impending danger. Following an initial appeal to Judah and Jerusalem to circumcise their hearts to G-d, i.e., a metaphorical expression employed to call for Judah and Jerusalem to return to G-d, Jeremiah 4:5-8 begins, in verse 5, with the prophet's announcement to proclaim a warning to Judah and Jerusalem of impending judgment by blowing the shofar, viz.,

> Declare in Judah and in Jerusalem announce and say, blow the shofar in the land; proclaim out loud and say, Gather and let us enter into the fortified cities! Raise a signal in Zion! Seek refuge, do not stand still, because evil from the north I bring together with massive disaster!

The motif appears again in 4:21, when Jeremiah expresses his exasperation at the people's alleged failure to heed the warning, "How long shall I see the signal??!! Shall I hear the sound of the shofar??!!" And again the motif appears in 6:1 when Jeremiah announces in the face of impending invasion, "Seek refuge, O people of Benjamin, from the midst of Jerusalem! And in Tekoa, blow the shofar! And over

Beth haKerem raise the warning! For evil has appeared from the north together with great disaster!"

Likewise in 42:14, Jeremiah critiques those who would abandon Judah and Jerusalem to flee to Egypt as those who say, "No, but to the land of Egypt we will come where we will not see war, the sound of the shofar we will not hear, for bread we will not hunger, and there we will stay!"[5] Finally, Jeremiah employs the motif in his oracle against Babylon in 51:27-28 when he announces the gathering of the nations that will bring Babylon down,

> Raise a signal in the land! Blow the shofar among the nations! Sanctify against her nations! Appoint against her kingdoms! Ararat, Minni, and Ashkenaz! Appoint against her a marshal! Bring up horses like swarming locusts! Sanctify against her nations! The Medean Kings, her governors and all of her officers, and all the lands that they rule![6]

The motif of the shofar as a device for warning appears in other prophets as well. The eighth century northern Israelite prophet Hosea ben Beeri warns Israel in Hosea 8:1 about its alliance with Assyria, "Place a shofar to your mouth like an eagle upon the House of

---

[5] Jack Lundbom, *Jeremiah 37–52* (AB 21C; New York: Doubleday, 2004), 133–34.

[6] Lundbom, *Jeremiah 37–52*, 463–66.

YHWH, because they have violated my covenant and against my Torah they have rebelled!"[7] The late-eighth century Judean prophet Amos of Tekoa condemns Moab for its betrayal of Israel in Amos 2:2, "And I will send fire against Moab so that it will consume the fortresses of Kerioth. And Moab shall die in agony amid the blaring of the sound of the shofar."[8] And again when he warns of danger against Israel in Amos 3:6, he states, "When the shofar is blown in a city, do the people not tremble?"[9] Isaiah 18:3 notes that the shofar is blown in times of danger, when Judah sends emissaries to Egypt to seek help.[10] And Trito-Isaiah, an anonymous prophet from the early Persian period who writes and speaks in the tradition of Isaiah ben Amoz, warns the people against transgression in Isaiah 58:1, in an attempt to persuade them to perform G-d's will, "Proclaim with full throat, do not hold back! Like a shofar, raise your voice, and declare to my people their rebellion and to the House of Jacob their sin!"[11]

---

[7] Marvin A. Sweeney, *The Twelve Prophets* (BO; Collegeville, MN: Liturgical Press, 2000), 84–93.

[8] Sweeney, *The Twelve Prophets*, 211–12.

[9] Sweeney, *The Twelve Prophets*, 220–21.

[10] Marvin A. Sweeney, *Isaiah 1–39, with an Introduction to Prophetic Literature* (FOTL 16; Grand Rapids, MI: Eerdmans, 1996), 252–62.

[11] Marvin A. Sweeney, *Isaiah 40–66* (FOTL 17; Grand Rapids, MI: Eerdmans, 2006), 273–85.

Finally, the shofar as a device for warning of danger appears in Job 39:24-25 as part of YHWH's description to Job of a powerful horse that ignores warnings of danger as it charges into battle.[12]

III

The use of the shofar as a signal warning of impending danger has obvious implications for times of war. Indeed, a number of texts in the Bible indicate that the shofar is used to call troops together for battle and to signal the end of hostilities. Treatment of the account of the fall of Jericho in Joshua 6 will appear later, insofar as the use of the shofar there indicates a combination of battle and liturgical functions. Attention will instead turn to a number of early battle accounts in the books of Judges and Samuel to illustrate the use of the shofar in battle.

The book of Judges presents accounts of the actions of the various local leaders of the tribes of Israel who delivered the people from threats posed by various nations and tribal groups, from the time of Israel's early settlement in the land in the fourteenth to twelfth centuries BCE through the emergence of the Saulide and Davidic monarchies in the tenth century BCE. Although Judges currently stands as a major

---

[12] For discussion of Job, see Marvin Pope, *Job* (AB 15; Garden City, NY: Doubleday, 1965).

component of the Former Prophets, known to most modern scholars as the Deuteronomistic History (DtrH), it is clearly the product of several redactions, such as the Judean exilic, Josianic, and Solomonic editions of the DtrH and quite possibly the northern Israelite History of the House of Jehu, which gathered tribal traditions concerning local leaders and deliverers in an effort to present them as the Judges that ruled Israel prior to the emergence of the monarchies.[13] Although the English term "judge" suggests a judicial function, the Hebrew term *šôpēṭ*, related to the Akkadian term *šappatum*, refers more generally to a ruler who might exercise judicial power along with a broader range of political functions. In the fourteenth-century Amarna letters, *šappatum* was employed to designate the governors of the Canaanite city-states that served as vassals of the Egyptian empire.

The Ehud narrative in Judges 3:12–30 is the first example in which the shofar plays a role. Although the current form of the Ehud narratives presupposes the participation of all of the tribes of Israel, earlier research indicates that it originated as a local Benjaminite narrative in which Ehud ben Gera

---

[13] For discussion of Judges, see Marvin A. Sweeney, *King Josiah of Judah: The Lost Messiah of Israel* (Oxford: Oxford University Press, 2001), 110–24; Serge Frolov, *Judges* (FOTL; Grand Rapids, MI: Eerdmans, 2013); Jack Sasson, *Judges 1–12* (YAB 6D; New Haven and London: Yale University Press, 2014).

assassinated the Moabite King Eglon, who had taken control of the site of Jericho and used it as a base for controlling the tribe of Benjamin in the Jordan Valley and Dead Sea Basin. Archeology provides only sparse evidence of settlement during the transition from the Bronze through the Iron Ages, when Israel first emerged in the land, and so it is difficult to date the narrative. It might be dated to the premonarchic period, but it is also possible that it is a local tradition dated as late as the early eighth century BCE, when Israel began to recover lands lost to the Moabites and other Trans-Jordanian powers following the Aramean suppression of Israel during the late tenth and early eighth centuries BCE. The narrative emphasizes Benjamin's left-handedness, a trait deemed to be typical of the tribe of Benjamin, in gaining private access to Eglon with a weapon so that he might assassinate him. Benjaminite left-handedness serves as a basis to view the Benjaminites with distrust and to suggest that Ehud's victory was due to trickery. Although Ehud's victory may have been intended to illustrate his cleverness, when placed in relation to other narratives concerning the shortcomings of northern Israelite Judges, the motif serves as a basis for pointing to the need for just Davidic rule in the present form of the book. Beginning in verse 27, Ehud had escaped following his assassination of Eglon and sounded the shofar throughout the territory of

Ephraim to signal that all Israel should gather for war to drive the Moabites out of Israel. Here, the shofar functions as both a warning of danger and as a summons to battle. Once the Moabites were defeated, the land allegedly had peace for eighty years.

The account of Gideon's judgeship in Judges 6:1-9:56 likewise illustrates the use of the shofar in time of war. The present form of the narrative includes an account of the attempted *coup d'etat* by Gideon's son Abimelech, which aids in illustrating problems with Gideon's judgeship that would justify the rise of Davidic kingship. Nevertheless, the account of Gideon's judgment in Judges 6-8 gives enough justification for viewing him with suspicion due to his Canaanite association. Gideon is also known by the Canaanite theophoric name Jerubbaal, which means, "may Baal contend," and his father, Joash, was known for constructing an altar for offerings to the Canaanite gods. Nevertheless, Gideon emerges as a deliverer for his tribe, Manasseh, from both foreign threats by the Midianites, Amalekites, and Kedemites, as well as domestic threats by the Ephraimites. Although the Gideon narratives are placed in a literary framework that suggests all Israel, the conflict with Ephraim suggests that they originate in the premonarchic period when Ephraim would have attempted to solidify its control over the other northern tribes of Israel.

Once the question of Gideon's loyalty to YHWH is settled by the destruction of his father's altar and his own offerings to YHWH, the shofar makes its appearance in Judges 6:34 as Gideon summons the men of Manasseh, Asher, Zebulun, and Naftali to fight the Midianites, Amalekites, and Kedemites in the Jezreel Valley, situated in the tribal territory of Manasseh north of the Manassite hill country of Israel and south of the Galil, inhabited by the other tribes mentioned. As Gideon prepares for battle in Judges 7, YHWH advises him that he has too many men gathered to his side and that it will be more advantageous to reduce his number to 300 select men, who would engineer an ambush against the Midianites to throw them into confusion and thereby facilitate Gideon's victory. Gideon therefore observes his men as they drink from a stream and selects those who used their hands as cups to drink water as they kept a watch for danger.

He divides his 300 chosen men into three groups and equips each man with a shofar, an empty jar, and a torch. After positioning his three groups around his enemies, Gideon signals his men to sound their shofars, break their jars, and hold their lit torches aloft. These actions throw the Midianites, Amalekites, and Kedemites into confusion so that they turn their swords upon each other, thereby making it easier for Gideon's men to attack and drive them out of the land. Here, the shofars serve as an instrument of war: they are employed to suggest the gathering of a huge army and throw Gideon's enemies into a panic. Although the Ephraimites come to threaten Gideon for not calling them out to battle, a move apparently intended to assert their authority over Manasseh and the other tribes, Gideon talks his way out of the situation, defeats the remaining Midianites and Kedemites, and rules Israel in peace for forty years. His rule is marred, however, by his construction of an idolatrous ephod and by the actions of his son, Abimelech, which play into the larger literary agenda of justifying the rise of Davidic rule.

Other examples of the use of the shofar in times of war appear in various narratives in the book of Samuel.[14] In 1 Samuel 13:3, when Saul gathers the tribes of Israel for battle against the Philistines, he sounds the shofar following his son Jonathan's action in striking down the Philistine prefect at Geba. The shofar is used in this case to announce the Israelite action and thereby to signal the commencement of hostilities against the Philistines, who dominated Israel at the outset of Saul's reign. Although Samuel is now a part of the DtrH, and 1 Samuel 13–14 functions as an account of why YHWH rejected Saul as king, the narrative appears to be based

---

[14] For discussion of 1–2 Samuel, see esp. Antony F. Campbell, *1 Samuel* (FOTL 7; Grand Rapids, MI: Eerdmans, 2003); Antony F. Campbell, *2 Samuel* (FOTL 8; Grand Rapids, MI: Eerdmans, 2005).

in an early account of Saul's initial victory against the Philistines, which would have justified his role as Israel's first major king.

A second instance appears in 2 Samuel 2:28 in the context of the account of David's defeat of northern Israelite forces led by Abner at Gibeon in 2 Samuel 2. Once the Benjaminites have been defeated and forced to take defensive positions on a hill, David's general Joab asks Abner if it is necessary to continue the fight, given that Israel was clearly defeated. When Abner acknowledges Joab's point, Joab signals the end of hostilities with a shofar blast.

Other instances include the use of the shofar in 2 Samuel 18:16 to signal the end of hostilities when Abshalom ben David, who had led a major revolt against his father, is killed. When Sheba ben Bichri revolts against David, a shofar blast signals the opening of hostilities in 2 Samuel 20:1 and the end of hostilities following Sheba's death at the hands of a woman in 20:22.

A final instance of the use of the shofar in battle appears in Zechariah 9:14 to signal the advance of YHWH and YHWH's king against Israel's enemies in an allegedly proto-apocalyptic account in Zechariah 9–11.[15]

---

[15] Sweeney, *The Twelve Prophets*, 666–67.

IV

The liturgical use of the shofar in Israelite and Judean worship is dependent upon the use of the shofar in times of war. The following discussion demonstrates the overlapping understanding of liturgy and war in the account of Joshua's conquest of the city of Jericho. Insofar as the shofar plays a key role in the successful attack against the city and the collapse of its walls, the shofar signals a new Israelite political order in the land of Canaan based upon the rule of Israel's leaders, kings, and, ultimately, YHWH. The role of the shofar therefore is to announce the presence of both the Israelite/Judean kings and YHWH, the deity who authorizes human kingship. It also emerges as a signal for YHWH's role in ensuring justice in the world.

Joshua 6 presents the account of Israel's conquest of the Canaanite city of Jericho at the outset of Israel's conquest of the land of Canaan.[16] Interpreters have long recognized the liturgical character of the battle account and the role of the shofar in the liturgically formulated assault against the city. Joshua commands the people to march around the city for six days, led by seven priests, each of whom is equipped

---

[16] For discussion of Joshua, see Sweeney, *King Josiah*, 125-36; Richard Nelson, *Joshua: A Commentary* (OTL; Louisville, KY: Westminster John Knox, 1997); Thomas B. Dozeman, *Joshua 1-12* (YAB 6B; New Haven and London: Yale University, 2015).

with a shofar. The priests are to sound a long blast from their shofars on the seventh day, followed by a shout from the people, after which the walls of Jericho will collapse, thereby giving the victory to Israel. The circumambulation of the city appears to be based in the *haqqaphot* or circumambulations of the sanctuary as part of the ancient celebration of the festival of Sukkot, Tabernacles, which concludes the harvest season and inaugurates the rainy season in the fall in ancient Israel and Judah. The shofar therefore signals the onset of YHWH's rule over the world of creation for another year.[17]

Jericho is a known archeological site. Indeed, it is one of the oldest cities in the world, and it was protected by especially large walls and fortifications that were destroyed by earthquake ca. 2300 BCE. The liturgical configuration of the city's conquest was

---

[17] The shofar is not blown during Sukkot in the Ashkenazi tradition, but there is a Western Sephardi tradition in which the shofar is blown on Hoshanah Rabbah at the conclusion of Sukkot. See "Shofar," *The Oxford Dictionary of the Jewish Religion* (ed., R. J. Zwi Werblowsky and Geoffrey Wigoder; New York and Oxford: Oxford University Press, 1997), 640. The custom is mentioned in Meuhas Refael Behar's *Peri Haadamah* (Turkey, Jerusalem, Egypt, 1705–1771). *HaManhig*, by Abraham ben Nathan of Provence (b. 1155), connects the seven circles around the *tevah* on Hoshana Rabbah to the conquest of Jericho. Since in Jericho the shofar was blown, perhaps at a certain point the shofar was introduced in Hoshana Rabbah as well. Thank you to Haim Ovadia for these notes.

apparently intended to announce the inauguration of YHWH's rule or kingship over the land of Canaan, which would coincide with Israel's rule and kingship over the land.

The role of the shofar in announcing kingship is evident, for example, in the attempt to crown Adonijah ben David as king of Israel following the death of his father in 1 Kings 1.[18] Adonijah presumes himself to be David's heir at the time of his father's death and gathers a number of supporters, such as David's military commander Joab, and the high priest Abiathar, to announce his coronation at the Gihon Spring even before the death of his father. As 1 Kings 1:34, 39, and 41 indicate, the shofar would be sounded immediately following the anointing of Adonijah to announce him as Israel's new king. But when word of Adonijah's actions reach the prophet Nathan, he instructs David's wife Bath Sheba, to enquire concerning David's successor, indicating to David that he had promised that David's son Solomon would in fact succeed his father as king. Once Solomon is announced as David's successor, Adonijah's party disbands, and both he and his supporters ultimately

---

[18] For discussion of Kings, see Marvin A. Sweeney, *1–2 Kings: A Commentary* (Louisville, KY: Westminster John Knox Press, 2007).

suffer punishment from Solomon once he ascends the Israelite throne.

Second Kings 9:13 likewise indicates that the shofar is sounded when Jehu ben Jehoshaphat ben Nimshi is anointed as king on the instructions of the prophet Elisha. He then goes on to overthrow King Jehoram ben Ahab of Israel and the rest of the house of Omri and to found his own dynasty that would rule Israel for approximately a century.

The liturgical role of the shofar is therefore rooted in the declaration of kingship in Israel and Judah. Such a role is easily transferred to YHWH, who is conceived as the true king of Israel and who in turn authorizes the rule of the kings of both Israel and Judah as regents on YHWH's part. Psalm 2 demonstrates this point by identifying the King in Jerusalem as YHWH's son.[19] The conceptualization of YHWH as the true king of Israel is also evident in the architectural construction of the Temple. The Temple is constructed on the pattern of a royal palace, with a three-part structure that includes the Ulam or Entryway, the Heikhal or the Great Hall, and the Devir or the Holy of Holies, where the Ark of the Covenant resides.[20] Insofar as the Ark of

---

[19] For discussion of Psalms, see Walter Brueggemann, *Psalms* (NCBC; Cambridge and New York: Cambridge University Press, 2014).

[20] Baruch Halpern, *The First Historians: The Hebrew Bible and History* (San Francisco: Harper and Row, 1990), 46–54.

the Covenant is conceived as YHWH's throne guarded by Cherubim, over which YHWH sits enthroned, the Devir or Holy of Holies functions as YHWH's throne room. Every day, YHWH is honored with liturgical worship three times: morning, afternoon, and evening, which happen to coincide with the time for meals. Offerings of food are always a central feature of worship in the Temple at morning and afternoon worship.

The role of the Temple as YHWH's royal palace also provides the setting for YHWH's proclamations of divine justice in the world. The shofar plays a key role in such proclamations. The theophany narrative in Exodus 19 illustrates such a role.[21] Moses and the people arrive at Mt. Sinai to appear before the presence of YHWH. Mt. Sinai is covered with cloud and lightning flashes in the midst of the cloud. Such imagery is symbolic of the role that incense smoke and the lighted menorot or candelabra play in the Temple during times of liturgical worship. But another feature of the theophany in Exodus 19 is the blowing of the shofar to signal YHWH's presence to the people in 19:16 and 19. The theophany in Exodus 19 portrays the presence of YHWH as the true king of creation before the people, but it also serves as an introduction to the

---

[21] For discussion of Exodus, see Thomas B. Dozeman, *Commentary on Exodus* (ECC; Grand Rapids, MI: Eerdmans, 2009).

announcement or revelation of divine Torah to the people in Exodus 20-23.

The initial presentation of YHWH's Torah appears in two major segments: the first version of the Ten Commandments in Exodus 20 and the Covenant Code in Exodus 21-23. The Ten Commandments are not law per se because they are not adjudicable insofar as they do not announce the disposition of the case; rather, they constitute a statement of the principles of justice that inform Israelite law. The Covenant Code is the earliest known law code of ancient Israel, apparently modeled on Hammurabi's law code, mediated to Israel by the Assyrians and quoted by Amos in Amos 2:6-16. Following the revelation of the Ten Commandments and prior to the revelation of the Covenant Code, Exodus 20:13 states that the sounding of the shofar took place, apparently announcing YHWH's presence as the true king of Israel and the authority who would introduce the Ten Commandments and the Covenant Code to the nation.

The liturgical role of the shofar appears in other contexts, associated with the conceptualization of YHWH as the true king of Israel, creation, and divine justice. Leviticus 25:9 twice mentions the sounding of the shofar to announce the Jubilee year, when all land will revert to its original owners.[22] The Jubilee year marks the conclusion of seven cycles of seven weeks of years. It is based on the principle that fields in the land should lie fallow every seventh year to provide the poor with food. After seven such cycles, totaling forty-nine years, the fiftieth year is proclaimed as the Jubilee year, in which land mortgaged to pay debts is then returned to its original owners. The shofar is blown on Yom Kippur of the fiftieth year to announce the Jubilee year.

Other instances indicate YHWH's role as king on the Day of YHWH. The Day of YHWH is a day of divine theophany in the Temple, when YHWH will act against those who present a threat to the sanctity of the Temple, either foreign threat or evil perpetrated by the people themselves. Joel 2:1, 15 and Zephaniah 1:16 both portray the blowing of the shofar as a warning of the impending Day of YHWH.[23] The above-noted Isaiah 58:1 calls for the sounding of the shofar as a means to warn the people concerning their transgression at the outset of a fast to ask forgiveness from G-d.

Isaiah 27:13 calls for the sounding of the shofar when YHWH defeats Leviathan, the chaos monster, in 27:1, thereby allowing the exiles of Egypt and Assyria

---

[22] For discussion of Leviticus, see Jacob Milgrom, *Leviticus* (AB 3ABC; New York: Doubleday, 1991–2001).

[23] Sweeney, *The Twelve Prophets*, 161–71, 508–09.

to return to their homes in the land of Israel and Judah.[24] Otherwise, the Psalms announce YHWH's role as King. Psalm 47:6 calls for blowing the shofar as part of the celebration of YHWH's kingship in Jerusalem.[25] Psalm 81:4 presents YHWH's calls for the sounding of the shofar to announce the New Moon. Psalm 98:6 calls for the sounding of the shofar to celebrate YHWH's role as king of creation, particularly following YHWH's subduing of the sea and the rivers as chaotic threats against the order of creation. And Psalm 150:3 calls for the sounding of the shofar to celebrate YHWH's role as king seated in the fortress Temple, which serves as YHWH's home in ruling the world.

V

Altogether, the shofar in the Bible functions as a means to announce warnings of danger, the commencement and conclusion of hostilities in times of war, and the presence of YHWH as king in Israelite and Judean liturgical contexts. It is from such a basis that the shofar emerges in post-biblical Judaism as the means to announce YHWH's sovereignty over all

---

[24] Sweeney, *Isaiah 1–39*, 345–53.
[25] See note 19 above.

creation and humanity at Rosh Hashanah and Yom Kippur.[26]

---

[26] Although the references to the *yom teru'ah* in Lev 23:23-25 and Num 29:1-6 clearly refer to the observance of what is now known as Rosh Hashanah, the term is only used in Ezek 40:1, where it appears to refer to the tenth day of the year. The term later came to designate the Jewish New Year on the first of Tishri.

The Emotional Resonance of the Shofar and the Preacher's Voice[1]

Joel Gereboff

The blowing of the shofar on Rosh Hashanah is one of the most well-known and emotionally impactful Jewish rituals. Even today, a hush falls over the congregation when the shofar begins to be sounded.[2] All eyes, even those of children who in some congregations are brought in for this part of the long prayer service, focus with awe upon the shofar blower. At the conclusion of the sounding of the shofar, members of the congregation often break out with laughter, a sense of release, if the shofar blower is able to hold for an extended time the final note, the *teqi'ah gedolah*. While there are a number of scholarly, popular, and traditional *halakhic* studies of the shofar, no one has examined the emotional dimensions of this ritual.[3] This

---

[1] A version of this paper was presented at a conference, in February 2016, on Religious Materiality and Emotions held at the University of Adelaide under the sponsorship of the Australian Research Council Centre of Excellence for History of Emotions.

[2] Here I draw upon personal observations over many years of attending services at many congregations. This is not meant as a claim based on careful ethnographic data.

[3] Publications of the shofar include: Jeremy Montagu, *The*

paper addresses this topic and forms part of a larger discussion of the intersection of emotions and religion, a significant current topic in scholarship in religious studies and many other disciplines.[4] In particular, it explores connections between material objects, in this case the shofar, and embodied experiences, including the hearing by people of the sounding of the shofar.

Beginning with two brief passages in the Bible that simply describe the first day of the seventh month,

---

Shofar: Its History and Use (Lanham, MD: Roman and Littlefield, 2015); Sol B. Finesinger, "The Shofar," *Hebrew Union College Annual* 8-9 (1931-32): 198-228; David Wulstan, "The Sounding of the Shofar," *The Galpin Society Journal* 26 (1973): 29-46; Solomon Freehof, "Sound the Shofar—'Ba-Kesse' Psalm 81:4," *Jewish Quarterly Review* 64 (1974): 225-28; Malcolm Miller, "The Shofar and its Symbolism," *Historic Brass Society Journal* 14 (2002): 83-113; Jonathan L. Friedmann, "The Shofar and Jewish Identity," *The Shekel: The Journal of Israel and Jewish History and Numismatics* 48.2 (2015): 44-47; and various comments on the shofar in Amnon Shiloah, *Jewish Musical Traditions* (Detroit: Wayne State University Press, 1992); and Hayim Herman Kieval, *The High Holy Days: A Commentary on the Prayerbook of Rosh Hashanah and Yom Kippur* (Jerusalem: Schechter Institute of Jewish Studies, 2004).

[4] The study of emotions has emerged during the past two decades as a subject of examination in multiple disciplines. The topic chosen by the Katz Center for Advanced Jewish Studies at the University of Pennsylvania for its full-year fellowships for 2015-16, "Jews Beyond Reason: Exploring Emotion, the Unconscious and Other Dimensions of Jews' Inner Lives," indicates the emerging interest in this issue. I have written a number of articles on emotions in Judaism, including an early overview essay on "Judaism and the Emotions," *Handbook of Religion and the Emotions* (ed. John Corrigan; New York: Oxford University Press, 2009), 95-110.

the day that in time is called Rosh Hashanah, as a *yom teru'ah*, a day for blowing a blast, which also is assumed to be done by using a shofar, later rabbinic sources lay out in detail the ritual for blowing the shofar. Many of these rabbinic comments focus upon such matters as the type of animal from which a shofar may be made, the nature of the notes, and the place in the prayer service when the shofar is blown. By contrast, the exact purpose for performing this ritual and its intended audience are detailed only over the course of rabbinic thinking found in sources ranging from the earliest rabbinic texts until current works. Over time, a ritual initially performed primarily to impact either God or Satan comes to be seen as an action intended to give rise to several interiorized emotional transformations in the congregants who hear the sounding of the shofar.[5]

Nearly seventy texts in the Hebrew Bible refer to the blowing of the shofar. This sounding occurs on various occasions to accomplish different tasks, such as assembling the people, calling the forces forth to war, or announcing the coronation of a monarch. Two verbs and associated nouns, *tq'*, *taqa*, and *rw'*, especially *teru'ah*, signify the sounding of horns, and on some

---

[5] This paper deals only with biblical and rabbinic *halakhic* and moralistic texts composed up through the early modern era. It does not examine iconographic images of the shofar or comments on the shofar in kabbalistic and Hasidic works.

occasions appear without specific reference to the shofar, though in many instances it can be assumed to be the particular instrument to be blown. References in Leviticus 23 and Numbers 29, prescribing the first day of the seventh month as a *yom zikhron teru'ah*, a day for remembrance with the sounding (of the horn), are important in later Judaism, as this date becomes known as Rosh Hashanah. Only a few biblical passages explicitly note any direct emotional impact of that action. Amos 3:6, "When a shofar is sounded (*yitaqah*) in a town, shall the people not tremble (*yeḥeradu*)?" and Exodus 19:16, "On the third day, as morning dawned, there was thunder and lightning, and a dense cloud upon the mountain, and a very loud blast of the horn, and the people in the camp trembled (*yeḥerad*)" connect blowing the shofar with fear and trembling.[6] By contrast, Psalms 98:4–6 and 150:1, 3, and 6 associate the hearing of the shofar with joy. They state, "Raise a shout to the Lord, all the earth, break into joyous songs of praise. Sing praise to the Lord with the lyre, with the lyre and melodious song. With trumpets and the blast of the shofar, raise a shout (*hari'u*) before the Lord, the King," and "Hallelujah. Praise God in His sanctuary; praise Him in the sky, His stronghold.... Praise Him

---

[6] The description of the conquest of Jericho in Joshua 6 may also associate the sounding of the shofar with fear, but it is possible that the fall of the walls of Jericho were due to some other force, divine intervention or magic.

with the blast of the shofar (*beteqa shofar*); praise him with harp and lyre.... Let all that breathes praise the Lord. Hallelujah." Isaiah 27:13 and Leviticus 25:8–10 do not speak of joy per se, but connect the blowing of the shofar with what are clearly happy occasions — either the ingathering of the people of Israel after exile or the inauguration of the Jubilee year.

As noted above, Leviticus 23:24 and Numbers 29:1 are the two biblical texts that refer to a festival to be observed on the first day of the seventh month. Unlike other festivals mentioned in the surrounding passages which have specific names, e.g., Passover, Sukkot, and Day of Atonement, there is no particular name assigned to this day. By the rabbinic period this day is labeled as Rosh Hashanah, a New Year's festival. Leviticus 23:24 describes the day as a sacred occasion of *zikhron teru'ah*, that is, one commemorated with loud blasts. Neither what exactly is being remembered nor what is to be blown are specified. Over time, the shofar is taken to be the instrument to be blown, and, analogous to the description of the blowing of trumpets described in Numbers 10:1–10, the purpose of doing so is to provoke God's memory of the people. Numbers 29:1, the only other biblical passage connected with Rosh Hashanah, merely labels the day as a *yom teru'ah*, a day the horn is sounded. Exactly what sort of note is to be blown — the specific sound of a *teru'ah* — is not defined.

A number of other biblical passages that speak of sounding the shofar, though not specifically referring to the first day of the seventh month, in time contribute to rabbinic understanding of the ritual of blowing the shofar on Rosh Hashanah. These passage include Psalm 81:4 ("Blow the shofar on the new moon, on the full moon [alt. on the covering of the moon, *bakeseh*] on our festival day"); Psalm 89:16 ("Happy are the people who know the sound [of the shofar, *yodei teru'ah*]. O Lord, they walk in the light of your presence"); Psalm 47:6 ("God [*Elohim*] ascends midst the sounding [of the shofar, *teru'ah*], the Lord [*Adonai*], to the blast of the shofar"); and Isaiah 58:1 ("O Isaiah, prophet, Cry with full throat, without restraint; Raise your voice like a shofar! Declare to My people their transgression, to the house of Jacob their sin"). We now turn to rabbinic sources on the shofar.

Several passages in the earliest rabbinic document, Mishnah, edited in approximately 200 CE, are relevant to an analysis of the shofar, though none makes clear exactly what is to be accomplished through its sounding. Mishnah *Rosh HaShanah* (*m. R.H.*) 1:1-2 delineates that there are actually four new years in the Jewish calendar. Included among the purposes of the one observed on the first of Tishri, the seventh month of the year, it is "when all people pass before God for judgment." *m. R.H.* 3:3, 3:5, 4:7, and 4:9 are the specific passages that refer to the blowing of the shofar. 3:3 and 5 indicate that there are disagreements among sages about the animal from which a shofar should be made and the desired shape of a shofar. The anonymous voice of the Mishnah asserts that the shofar should be straight, while R. Judah opines that the horn should be curved. *m. R.H.* 4:7 details the place in the liturgy, in the prayer service for Rosh Hashanah, where the shofar must be blown,[7] while *m. R.H.* 4:9 discusses the nature of the notes to be sounded, an issue that is unclear due to a lack of specification in biblical sources. This passage prescribes, "The order of the [blowing of] the shofar (*seder teqi'ot*) is three sets of three blasts [i.e., *teqi'ah, teru'ah, teqi'ah*]. The length of the *teqi'ah* is like three *teru'ot*. The length of a *teru'ah* is like three *yevavot* [the interpretation of this word is unclear, though the Talmud renders it to mean "whimpers"; the actual basic meaning is blasts of some sort on a horn]." The passage refers to the two key biblical terms, *teqi'ah* and *teru'ah*. The *teqi'ah* is a single note, while the *teru'ah* is some sort of broken note.[8]

---

[7] *m. R.* 4:7 states, "The one who leads the prayer service on the festival of Rosh Hashanah, the second prayer leader [the one leading the *musaf*, the additional prayer service] causes the shofar to be blown, but on occasions when Hallel [Pss 114–18, are recited] the first one [the one leading the *shaḥarit* service] leads the Hallel."

[8] A parallel version of this text appears in the *halakhic midrash* on Leviticus, *Sifra*, and instead of the word *yevava*, it uses the term, *shevarim*, broken notes. *b. R.H.* 34a seeks to reconcile the two versions.

The final tannaitic source providing information on the use and meaning of the shofar appears in the *halakhic* (legal) *midrash* on Numbers, *Sifre Num* 77. In a comment on Numbers 10:10 this text connects various aspects of the blowing of the shofar with the liturgical units of the Rosh Hashanah *musaf* prayer. And it depicts the shofar as seeking God's mercy, leading to the freedom of Israel. It states:

> R. Nathan says, "It is said, 'You shall sound the trumpets,' lo a reference to the ram's horn; 'they shall serve as a reminder,' this [refers to sounding for] remembrance; 'I am the Lord your God,' this [refers to sounding for] God's sovereignty."
>
> If so why [in the Rosh Hashanah liturgy] have sages placed [verses referring to] the sounding of the shofar for God's sovereignty first, then for remembrance second, and finally for the ram's horns blast?
>
> The sense is: first accept Him as king over you, then seek mercy from him, so that you will be remembered by him. And with what? With the shofar of freedom [*herut*].
>
> And the shofar indicates only freedom, as it is said, "And in that day, a great shofar shall be sounded [*yitaqa*], and the strayed who are in the land of Assyria shall come and worship the Lord on the holy mount, in Jerusalem" [Isa 27:13]. But I do not know who will blow it? Scripture therefore says, "The Lord God will sound the shofar" [Zech 9:14].

The last sections of this passage assert that the shofar is a symbol of freedom and its use serves to seek mercy and deliverance of some sort from God, perhaps the final one as the citations from Isaiah and Zechariah imply. None of the above tannaitic sources makes any specific reference to a desired emotional impact of the blowing of the shofar. For such comments, or, in more general terms, for comments that begin to spell out the intended audience and desired impact of the blowing of the shofar, we must turn to amoraic and anonymous texts in the Babylonian Talmud and some in classical homiletical *midrashim*.

Several passages in the Babylonian Talmud, a work whose redaction is now dated to the sixth to seventh centuries, discuss the purpose for blowing the horn and allude to its emotional dimensions. A comment by R. Abbahu in *b. R.H.* 16a is the first expression of an idea that is repeatedly noted in rabbinic thinking about the purpose of blowing the shofar. According to this text, in commenting on *m. R.H.* 1:2,

> R. Abbahu [third generation amora, land of Israel, c. 300 CE] said, "Why do we blow with a shofar of a ram?"
> Said the Holy One Blessed be He, "Blow before me with a shofar of a ram so that I can remember in your behalf the binding of Isaac the son of Abraham, and I will consider it as if you had bound yourselves before me."

Abbahu connects the ritual of blowing the ram's horn with the story of the binding of Isaac in Genesis 22. In that passage Abraham does not end up sacrificing Isaac, but instead substitutes a ram. In this Talmudic passage, R. Abbahu explicitly claims that the blowing of the shofar should cause God to remember the willingness of Abraham and Isaac to endure the latter's being offered up as a sacrifice. As was true in some of the biblical passages, the intended audience who is to be affected by the blowing of the horn is not the congregation, but God. Abbahu's comment in no way makes clear the extent to which the blowing of the horn is meant to impact the members of the community, if at all, and, in turn, to communicate something of their feelings and commitments. While it is possible that the congregants should imagine themselves as if they were Isaac and feel his dread at his impending death and the joy of his deliverance, emotions not mentioned in the biblical text, these potential impacts of hearing the shofar and thereby recalling the biblical story are not mentioned.

By contrast to this first comment, in which God is the intended being to be moved by hearing the sounding of the shofar, a different comment in *b. R.H.* 16a and b identifies Satan as the one to be affected. It states:

> Rabbi Isaac [third generation amora, land of Israel] said, "Why do they blow the shofar on Rosh Hashanah?"...
>
> Rather [he was asking] why do they blow the *teqi'ah* and the *teru'ah* while they are sitting and blow the *teqi'ah* and the *teru'ah* while standing?
>
> In order to confound [*le'arbev*] Satan.

The anonymous voice of the Talmud interprets Isaac's question regarding blowing the shofar as seeking to explain why it is blown in two different parts of the service: while the congregation is sitting, after the Torah reading, and while they are standing, when reciting the *musaf* (second) standing prayer, the *Amidah*. The answer to this repetition of the shofar blowing is that it will confuse Satan. The meaning of this expression is not spelled out. This passage appears to assume the general depiction of Satan in early rabbinic sources, derived from several biblical books, that he is a member of the heavenly court whose primary task is to challenge God regarding God's views of the just status of human beings. Satan is the prosecuting attorney in the heavenly court. This passage in the Talmud seems to indicate that in hearing the shofar, Satan will not be able to successfully carry out his prosecution.

Another passage in the Babylonian Talmud, *b. R.H.* 26b, picks up on the previously cited comment of R. Judah in *m. R.H.* 3:3 and 5 about the required shape of the shofar, and elaborates that a curved shofar must be used so that a person sees himself as physically bent before God on Rosh Hashanah. It states:

> Said R. Levi [third generation amora, land of Israel], "The commandment of Rosh Hashanah and of [Jubilee year on] the Day of Atonement is [fulfilled] with curved horns, and for all the rest of the year with straight ones."
>
> [The Gemara asks]: But we have learned in our Mishnah: The shofar of Rosh Hashanah [should be] of a wild goat and straight?
>
> He [R. Levi] stated [his position] in accordance with that tanna [R. Judah]…
>
> On which issues do they [R. Judah and the anonymous view of the Mishnah] disagree?
>
> One master [R. Judah] thinks that the more a person on Rosh Hashanah bends over [some mss. have "bends his mind"], the better it is; and at [the conclusion] of the Day of Atonement [in a Jubilee year], the more a person straightens out, the better. But the other master [the anonymous view in the Mishnah] thinks that on Rosh Hashanah the more a person is straight, the better. And on fast days the more a person bends, the better.

The very shape of the shofar should occasion for the congregation an embodied feeling of being bent. This probably serves to convey feelings of humility and subservience, perhaps even of fear, though these emotions are not explicitly mentioned.

Two additional Talmudic passages explicitly invoke emotionally charged language in commenting on the blowing of the shofar. In these instances the sages draw upon the imagery of different types of crying to define the sound of the *teru'ah* note. Confusion about the exact sound of this note results from differing descriptions of this note in two tannaitic texts, Mishnah and Sifra, the *halakhic midrash* on the book of Leviticus. The former uses the term *yevava* to specify the sound of the *teru'ah*, while the latter invokes the word *shevarim* for this purpose. That passage reads as follows:

> Commenting on M. R.H. 4:9 (The length of a *teru'ah* is like three *yevavot*):
>
> But it has been taught [cites as a *baraita* the text from *Sifra*], the length of the *teru'ah* is three broken notes [*shevarim*]?
>
> Said Abaye [fourth generation Babylonian amora], "In this [about the meaning of the following biblical text] they [the two texts] disagree. For it is written, 'You shall observe it as a day when the horn is sounded [*yom teru'ah*]' [Num 29:1]. And the Aramaic translators render as, 'A day of *yevava*; and it is written regarding the mother of Sisera, 'Through the window she looked, and she cried [*vateyavev*]' [Judg 5:28].
>
> One master [the view in Sifra] thinks that [the *teru'ah*] is like trembling [alt: moaning] [*ganuḥei ganaḥe*, hence speaks of broken notes, *shevarim*] and the other master [the anonymous view in

the Mishnah] thinks it refers to sobbing [*yelulei yalal*, short whimpers]."

In order to explain the Mishnah's term *yevava*, Abaye observes that the Targum, the Aramaic translation of the Bible, translates the word *teru'ah* in Numbers 29:1 using the word *yevava*. While this word can simply mean "to sound a shofar or trumpet,"[9] Abaye connects it to Judges 5:28, which describes the mother of Sisera, who is waiting for the return of her son from battle with the Israelites, as "standing by the window and crying [*vateyavev*]." The last comment in this Talmudic passage then resolves the confusion between the use in different tannaitic sources of two words, *yevava* and *shevarim*, to define the nature of the *teru'ah* note by seeing each as referring to a different type of crying: moaning and whimpering. This note, then, can be seen as expressing these different types of weeping, with their associated emotions. But the text does not make explicit whether the person sounding the shofar should have these feelings, whether the congregation should, or whether it is God who should react in this way.

Drawing upon this passage, R. Abbahu on *b. R.H.* 34a expresses a solution for how the *teru'ah* note

---

[9] See Michael Sokoloff, *A Dictionary of Jewish Babylonian Aramaic of the Talmudic and Geonic Periods* (Baltimore: Johns Hopkins University Press, 2002), 521.

should be blown in light of its being associated with two different types of crying. He instituted three sets of notes: 1. *Teqi'ah, shevarim, teru'ah, teqi'ah;* 2. *Teqi'ah, shevarim, teqi'ah;* 3. *Teqi'ah, teru'ah, teqi'ah.* In doing so he aligns the type of crying connected with the *shevarim* and *teru'ah* with the normal human responses to tragedy, for a person first moans and then whimpers. Although the text does not specify that the sounding is to occasion the corresponding emotional effect in the hearers,[10] it does laden the ritual with much emotion.[11]

In sum: Talmudic statements propose three different beings, God, Satan, and humans, as the ones to be impacted by the blowing of the shofar. Although several texts may well imply that, in the case of humans, certain emotions should result from hearing the shofar, feelings connected with a sense of being bent or those that occasion tears, these are not explicitly noted. Comments in several homiletical (*haggadic*) *midrashim* restate elements of some of the above views, while also introducing new purposes and desired impacts for the use of the shofar.

---

[10] See Sokoloff, Jewish Babylonian Aramaic, 521.

[11] For discussions of *halakhic* views on how exactly to sound the shofar, see Steven Exler, "*Teki'ot* Transforming Texts: *Elul* Shofar Blasts in Medieval *Minhag*," *Milin Havivin* 2 (2000): 46-82. Mordechai Gafni, "Shofar of Tears," *Tikkun* 15.5 (2000): 46-48, offers a moving sermonic development of the symbolism of crying.

A small number of comments on the purpose of blowing the shofar appears in the parallel texts of *Pesiqta DeRab Kahana* (*PRK*) 23–24 and *Leviticus Rabbah* (*LR*) 29, documents redacted in the fifth century in the Land of Israel.[12] At least one of these texts is explicit in detailing emotional impact as the intended result of this ritual. We begin with *PRK* 23:3, a text in which God is the audience meant to be moved by the hearing of the shofar blasts. This passage is built around an interpretation of two different names for God, Elohim (God) and Adonai (Lord), in Psalm 47:6. It states:

> Judah b. R. Nahman in the name of R. Simeon b. Laqish commenced [by citing the following verse], "God [*Elohim*] ascends midst the sounding [of the shofar, *teru'ah*], the Lord [*Adonai*], to the blast of the shofar [Ps 47:6]."
>
> When the Holy One, blessed be He, ascends to take his seat on the throne of justice on Rosh Hashanah, he goes up [with the intention of judging] with strict justice. But when Israel take up their shofarot and blow them, the Holy One, blessed be He, arises from his throne of justice and sits on the throne of mercy, for it is written, "the Lord [*Adonai*], to the blast of the shofar.

---

[12] For the dating and provenance of various rabbinic texts I rely upon generally accepted scholarly views, and, in particular, upon information in H. L. Strack and Gunter Stemberger, *Introduction to the Talmud and Midrash* (Minneapolis: Fortress Press, 1992).

> [The *midrash* builds upon the standard rabbinic interpretation of *Elohim* (God) standing for God's attribute of justice, while the term, *Adonai* (Lord) symbolizes mercy.] And he is filled with mercy for them and then transforms the attribute of justice into that of mercy."

Like R. Abbahu's comment in *b. R.H.* 16a, according to which the purpose of sounding the shofar is to cause God to remember the binding of Isaac,[13] this passage asserts that God will be moved by hearing Israel perform this ritual. In this case, God will be transformed from the God of justice to the God of mercy.[14] This interpretation emerges from the frequently stated rabbinic understanding of Elohim as an allusion to the God of justice, and that of Adonai as the God of mercy.

A second *midrashic* passage, PRK 23:8 (LR 23:6) offers a different analysis of the significance of the shofar. In this case, playing on the Hebrew

---

[13] A different *midrashic* statement in PRK 23:9 (LR 29:9) dramatically portrays Abraham demanding that God remember his willingness to sacrifice Isaac. While these comments do not explicitly cite the blowing of the horn, the overall *midrashic* unit does conclude with the citation of Lev 23:24, "In the seventh month... a memorial proclaimed with the blast (of the shofar)."

[14] A comment by R. Josiah in PRK 23:4 (LR 29:4) also makes reference to the impact on God of the propitiatory sounding of the shofar.

words for the shofar and for the specification of the first day of the seventh month as Rosh Ḥodesh, the new moon festival, the passage claims that the blowing of the horn should occasion some renewal of the community and an improvement of their deeds. The text states:

> [Interpreting several words in Ps 81:4] "Blow the shofar on the new moon [baḥodesh], on the full moon [alt. on the covering of the moon, bakeseh], on our festival day" —
> The new moon [or new month, baḥodesh] — renew your deeds [ḥidshu]. Shofar — improve [shipru] your deeds.
> Said the Holy One, blessed be He, "If you improve your deeds before me, lo, I shall become for you like a shofar. Just as a shofar takes in at one [narrow] end and lets out at the other [wide side], so shall I arise from the throne of justice and take my seat on the throne of mercy and become filled with mercy for you and have mercy on you and turn the attribute of justice into the attribute of mercy."

According to this *midrash*, the purpose of the shofar is to remind Israel to transform its deeds as indicated by the words used in the verse from Psalm 81, now interpreted to signify the need to renew (*ḥadesh* and *shaper*). Doing so will lead to God, now symbolically portrayed as taking up the divine shofar and as moving from the narrowness of justice to the breadth of mercy. Although this passage focuses on transformations in human behavior, another passage in *PRK* explicitly connects the change in actions with the emotion of fear occasioned by the hearing of the sounding of shofar. *PRK* 24:1 states,

> When a shofar is sounded [*yitaqah*] in a town, shall the people not tremble [*yeheradu*]?
> [Amos 3:6]…"When a shofar is sounded in a town" on Rosh Hashanah, "and the people" — Israel—"do not tremble, then if evil befall the city, the Lord has not done it." The Holy One, blessed be He, is not pleased with the death of the wicked…. O people [of Israel], what do I require of you? "Turn back, turn back from your evil ways, that you not die, O House of Israel" [Ezek 33:11].

This is the earliest explicit articulation in rabbinic sources of the emotion of fear as the desired effect of hearing the shofar. Amos 3:6 validates the connection between fear and the sounding of the shofar. Fear in turn should lead individuals to "turn back from their evil ways." The Hebrew here is *shuvu midarkhekhem,* and while in other rabbinic sources biblical texts using the verb *shuv* are interpreted as referring to engaging in repentance, *teshuva,* in this exegetical statement the focus is on behavior, not on attitudes or self-understanding.

Many of the ideas expressed in these traditions in *PRK* also appear, but in slightly different ways, in the later homiletical *midrash, Pesiqta Rabbati* (*PR*). The date and place of redaction of this document is a matter of some dispute, with dates ranging from the fifth to the ninth centuries and proposed locations for redaction including the lands of Israel, Greece, and Italy. *PR* 40:5, like *PRK* 24:1, sees as a purpose for blowing of the shofar on Rosh Hashanah the instilling of fear, and it specifically notes that this, in turn, should lead the people to repentance. It states:

> [The unit focuses on the Ten Days of Repentance between Rosh Hashanah and the Day of Atonement].
>
> Isaiah said, "But yet for [Israel] shall be a period of ten; if it returns, then there will be removal" [Isa 6:13]. Said the Holy One, blessed be He, "On Rosh Hashanah I judge my world, and I should have on that day completed the judgment. And why do I suspend [it] for ten days? In order that you still will repent.... If Israel shall return, then there will be removal. For if you are moved to repent during these days, even if you have some sins, I will remove them and declare you innocent. But if you do not repent during them, you should know that your judgment will be rendered on the Day of Atonement. And I shall not have done it to you; rather, you shall have done it to yourselves. Why? For in ordaining for

you that you shall blow shofars on Rosh Hashanah [it was] in order that you tremble at the blowing of the shofar to prepare yourselves for repentance." [The text concludes with a citation of Amos 3:6].

A second tradition in PR 40:7 brings together the association of the blowing of the shofar with the themes of mercy, fear, and the ultimate redemption. It states:

> The Holy One, blessed be He, said, "In this world I desire to have mercy upon you by means of the shofar, so too in the future [perhaps the messianic era], I will have mercy upon you by means of the shofar. How is this known? From that which is read from the prophet [as the *haftarah*], 'Blow a shofar in Zion, sound the alarm on my holy mount. Let all dwellers on the earth tremble, for the Day of the Lord has come.'"

In this case the proof text comes from the prophet Joel 2:1. That verse alludes to the blowing of the shofar, fear, and the Day of the Lord, which by the time of this *midrash* is taken to mean the coming of the Messiah. Many of the above themes are reiterated in various medieval texts. But new elements include the desired interiorization of the battle against Satan within each person who hears the shofar.

Medieval and early modern Jewish writers — legalists, moralists, kabbalists and preachers — offered a range of views on the shofar.¹⁵ For example, Maimonides (1135–1204) presents a rationalistic interpretation of this ritual during the High Holidays in the section on the Laws of Repentance in his *Mishneh Torah*, according to which the blowing of the shofar calls for people to "Awaken, those who sleep from your slumber, and arise, those who slumber, and inspect your deeds and return in repentance and recall your Creator." Maimonides here proposes that the blowing of the shofar is meant to stimulate repentance toward God and personal transformation. Other medieval commentators take up a different purpose for blowing the shofar; the one proposed by R. Isaac — to confuse Satan. Rashi (1040–1105) interprets the blowing in a straightforward manner: upon hearing the blowing of the shofar, Satan, the prosecutor in the heavenly court, will not be able to accuse the Jews of not observing the commandments. He will see that they lovingly obey the commandments.¹⁶ By contrast, Tosafot suggest Satan will be confused and not put forward his case against Israel as he will fear that the double sounding of the shofar announces the coming

---

[15] Saadia Gaon's tenth-century list of reasons for sounding the shofar that he presents in his commentary on Lev 23:24 is preserved in the *Siddur* of Abudarham.

[16] This explanation is already found in the *Arukh*, a medieval dictionary of rabbinic/Talmudic terms composed by the Italian lexicographer Nathan b. Yechiel, 1035–1106.

of the Messiah and his own demise. Most interestingly, the Spanish commentator Shlomo ben Aderet (1235-1310) connects the blowing of the shofar with personal transformation. He remarks,

> "In order to confound Satan" — There are those who explain this to mean to subdue one's inclination, for as it is written, "When a shofar is sounded [*yitaqah*] in a town, shall the people not tremble [*yeheradu*]?" [Amos 3:6]. And Satan is the evil inclination as our rabbis said [*b. B.B.* 16a]: Satan is the evil inclination, is the angel of death.

This comment discloses an interiorization of the experience of hearing the shofar. The fear resulting from hearing the blowing of the shofar should lead to the overcoming of one's evil inclination, one of the two dispositions according to rabbinic psychology within each person.[17]

Medieval homilists also focus on the emotional aspects of hearing the shofar. For example, the fourteenth-century Spanish rabbi Yaakov ben Hananel of Sikily, in his collection of sermons in *Torah Haminha*,[18] speaks of the fear that should be occasioned by the sounding of the shofar, such that the person

---

[17] Ishay Rosen-Zvi in *Demonic Desires: Yetzer Hara and the Problem of Evil in Late Antiquity* (Philadelphia, University of Pennsylvania Press, 2011) provides a detailed examination of the development of the notion of the *yetzer* in early rabbinic texts.

[18] *Torat HaMincha*, sermon 77 on Rosh Hashanah.

should eliminate their worldly desires, their internal Satan. He states:

> For a person needs to fear, be agitated, and tremble from Yom Hadin [the Day of Judgment, Rosh Hashanah], and the blowing of the shofar awakens to be in awe and to fear, as it is written, "When a shofar is sounded [*yitaqah*] in a town, shall the people not tremble [*yeheradu*]?" [Amos 3:6]. And when a person trembles and is afraid some of the forces of worldly desire will be eliminated, and these are Satan who sinks a person into the sea of desire.

A quite different interpretation of the purposes of sounding the ram's horn is offered by a slightly later fifteenth-century Spanish preacher, Isaac Arama, in a sermon appearing in his *Akedat Yitzhak*,[19] the Hebrew term for the binding of Isaac. This preacher connects the sequence of shofar notes, each of which has a different emotional resonance, with the differing emotional impact these sounds ought to have on different types of people. Based on R. Abbahu's views in the Talmud, which by this time had become the established practice for blowing the shofar — one began with the *teqi'ah*, the long note, and then followed with the *shevarim*, three broken notes, the *teru'ah*, the nine

---

[19] Here I cite the translation of Eliyahu Munk, *Akedat Yitzchak: Commentary of Rabbi Yitzchak Arama on the Torah* (Jerusalem: Lambda, 2001), 1: 650.

staccato notes, and finally ended with the sounding of another *teqi'ah* — Isaac Arama remarks:

> If the *teru'ah* by itself signals being troubled, being sad, and the *teqi'ah* by itself signals joy, then a combination of these two notes, i.e., *shevarim*, signals a mind which is somewhere between the other two emotional states. If the assumption about the emotions represented by the sequence of *teqi'ah, shevarim, teru'ah, teqi'ah* is correct, then the custom of blowing [this sequence] during the *Malkhiyot* [sovereignty section of the *musaf Amidah*], makes sense.... *Malkhiyot*, i.e., proclaiming God's Majesty, is welcomed by the completely righteous who can afford to react to these sounds with joy and equanimity, i.e., *teqi'ah*. The completely wicked person, on the other hand, shrinks from such an encounter and is represented by the *teru'ah* sound of the shofar. The great majority of people, who fall somewhere between those two categories, view the coming of a reward for their meritorious deeds with a certain feeling of gladness, while trembling at the thought of the impending retribution for the sins they have committed [and thus respond to the *shevarim*].

These comments display a rich, emotionally coded interpretation of the hearing of the sounds emitted from the material shofar. Isaac Amora speaks to the majority of his congregation in noting that, while the few wholly righteous welcome with joy and equanimity the first *teqi'ah*, the long note, as it proclaims God's majesty, and the small in number wicked people, by contrast, experience the nine staccato notes of the *teru'ah* with great fear, the majority of people who are neither wholly righteous nor wholly wicked when hearing the note sounded between the *teqi'ah* and the *teru'ah*, the three broken notes of the *shevarim*, should experience both joy and trembling.[20]

With this comment we conclude our brief discussion of rabbinic views on the emotional impact of the shofar. From the amoraic period onwards rabbinic sources comment on the emotional resonance of the shofar, thereby underscoring the complex connections between ritual/cultural practices, materiality, embodiment, and emotions.

---

[20] The title chapter in Marc Saperstein, "*Your Voice Like a Ram's Horn*": *Themes and Texts in Traditional Jewish Preaching* (Cincinnati: Hebrew Union College Press, 1996), 1-9, analyzes how a variety of Jewish preachers interpreted Isa 58:1 to define the role of the preacher and the nature of sermons appropriate especially for the period of the High Holydays. He cites many examples of preachers who sought to move their congregations emotionally just as the shofar does.

Of Sound and Vision

The Ram's Horn in Medieval Kabbalistic Rituology

Jeremy Phillip Brown

IN MEMORIAM
Ornette Coleman (1930–2015)

The early teachers of kabbalah gained much ground for their interpretation of rabbinic Judaism in establishing mystical rationales for the traditional precepts.[1] The earliest texts dating from the twelfth century already demonstrate a profound engagement with the commandments, expositing liturgical and cultic aspects of Jewish practice in terms of their correspondence to the divine potencies. The earliest material contains episodic discussions of the secret rationales, but R. Ezra ben Solomon of Gerona's

---

[1] In preparing this study, I have benefited from conversations with Avishai Bar-Asher, Michael Centore, Matt Marble, and Leore Sachs Shmueli. I thank each wholeheartedly. For an overview of the kabbalistic literature on the commandments, see Daniel Matt, "The Mystic and the *Mizwot*," *Jewish Spirituality I: from the Bible to the Middle Ages* (ed. Arthur Green; New York: Crossroad, 1994), 367–404; and Charles Mopsik, *Les Grands Textes de la Cabale: Les rites qui font Dieu* (Lagrasse: Éditions Verdier, 1993).

commentary on the Song of Songs inaugurates a formal genre dedicated to explaining the commandments according to kabbalah. Most representative of the kabbalistic approach to the commandments is R. Ezra's bold axiom "the *mitzvot* are the *middot*."[2] Identifying normative practices and prohibitions with the very attributes of God, this onto-theological premise is basic to the kabbalistic understanding of the commandments. On this premise, the study of the precepts becomes identical with the contemplation of divinity. And their observance becomes a way for humans to seize hold of God's attributes — a concrete means of actualizing God's immanence in the world through the performance of symbolically saturated actions and the maintenance of emblematic taboos.

The Italian kabbalist R. Menahem Recanati, writing around the turn of the fourteenth century, epitomized the kabbalistic approach to the commandments in this way:

> The commandments are a single entity, and they depend upon the supernal chariot, [which manifests to] each person according to the service they perform. But each individual commandment depends upon a particular part of the chariot. This being so, the blessed Holy One is not one particular area apart from the

---

[2] *Kitvei ha-Ramban* II.538.

Torah. And the Torah is not outside Him. And He is not an entity outside the Torah. Therefore, the sages of the kabbalah teach that the blessed Holy One *is* the Torah.³

With this assertion, the Italian kabbalist intends that divinity is not something outside the lived performance of Torah, which is to say, a life of ritual engagement with the commandments. The medieval teachers of kabbalah espoused a dynamic symbolism of the commandments, a symbolism leveraging the manifestation of the supernal chariot with human action. But the medieval discourses do not impose a symbolism of the commandments in a generic, systemic, or mechanical way.⁴ Each precept, according to Recanati, is rooted in one individuated aspect of divine reality, and the performance of each draws a

---

³ Menahem Recanati, *Sefer Ta'amei ha-Mitsvot* (Basel, 1581), 3a. See Gershom Scholem, *On the Kabbalah and its Symbolism* (tr. Ralph Manheim; New York: Schocken, 1965), 44. Moshe Idel argues that this final phrase, based originally on the language of R. Azriel of Gerona, informs Jacques Derrida's famous locution: "Il n'y a rien hors de texte." See Moshe Idel, *Old Worlds, New Mirrors: On Jewish Mysticism and Twentieth-Century Thought* (Philadelphia: University of Pennsylvania Press, 2010), 178–81.

⁴ While sympathetic to the view that kabbalah and Jewish magic cannot be readily disentwined, I take issue with the blanket assessment that the medieval kabbalists imagined *"a magical mechanism* to be operative in every sacramental action, and this imagination is attended by a decline in the essential spontaneity of religious action." Gershom Scholem, *Major Trends in Jewish Mysticism* (New York: Schocken, 1946), 30 (my emphasis).

secret out of concealment: "each and every commandment has a great root and hidden meaning [עיקר גדול וטעם נסתר] which may not be discerned from any commandment but the one which reveals that mystery [המגלה הסוד ההוא]."⁵ This study addresses early kabbalistic accounts of the secrets revealed through the particular commandment of shofar.

The ram's horn receives special attention in the medieval kabbalistic literature on the commandments. In a sermon delivered some decades after the culmination of the period set for this study, R. Joshua ibn Shu'eib, the distinguished student of R. Solomon ibn Adret, speaks to the problem of why so much rabbinic legislation is dedicated to the commandment of shofar, when scripture gives it comparatively scant consideration. He reasons that this is due to the fact that the ram's horn rites are classed among the cultic commandments "which are the essence of divinity [שהם עיקר האלהות]."⁶ The fourteenth-century homilist alludes to the kabbalistic view that the ram's horn is rooted in the divine world of the *sefirot*.

---

⁵ Recanati, Sefer Ta'amei ha-Mitsvot, 3a. See Scholem, *On the Kabbalah*, 124.

⁶ Joshua ibn Shu'eib, *Sermons on the Torah* (Cracow, 1575), 89d. See Carmi Horowitz, *The Jewish Sermon in 14th-Century Spain: The Derashot of R. Joshua ibn Shu'eib* (Cambridge, MA: Harvard University Press, 1989), 99.

In a classic lecture on kabbalistic ritual, Gershom Scholem singles out the shofar as a prime example of his theme. In that lecture, the scholar delineates four main expectations that kabbalists bring to the performance of the traditional precepts.

> The attitude of the Kabbalah toward ritual is governed by certain fundamental conceptions which recur in innumerable variants. In its role of representation and *excitation*, ritual is expected, above all, to accomplish the following:
> 1. Harmony between the rigid powers of judgment and the flowing powers of mercy.
> 2. The sacred marriage, or *conjunctio* of the masculine and feminine.
> 3. Redemption of the *Shekhinah* from its entanglement in the "other side."
> 4. Defense against, or mastery over, the powers of the "other side."
>
> Over and over again we meet with these conceptions emphasizing different elements in the doctrine of the sefiroth, sometimes singly and sometimes in combination.[7]

---

[7] My emphasis. Scholem, *On the Kabbalah,* 130. Compare this general typology with the specific one outlined for de León's rationales in Elliot Wolfson, "Mystical Rationalization of the Commandments in *Sefer ha-Rimmon*," *Hebrew Union College Annual* 59 (1988): 217–51.

To exemplify this typology, Scholem adds "[t]he blowing of the shofar on New Year's Day [...] is explicitly associated with the first and fourth purposes."[8] In what follows, I demonstrate that the kabbalists expect the performance of the commandment to accomplish *all four* of these goals, and especially the second goal delineated above, namely, the hierogamy of masculine and feminine divine attributes.

This study aims to recover something of the concrete character of kabbalistic ritual performance. Therefore, its object lies beyond simply reprising the kabbalists' express declarations of ritual purpose. Rather, I focus on the medieval rabbis' "excitations," to quote Scholem, highlighting modalities of sensory experience represented within their emic discourses on ritual. I consider the kabbalistic accounts of the ram's horn in a phenomenological vein, prompted by the scholarly recovery of a "hermeneutics of visionary experience" in medieval Judaism.[9] For the kabbalists,

---

[8] Scholem, *On the Kabbalah*, 130. Also see the discussion of the shofar rites in Isaiah Tishby, *Wisdom of the Zohar: An Anthology of Texts* (tr. David Goldstein; Oxford: Littman Library of Jewish Civilization, 2002), III.1245–46, 1298–1302.

[9] I have in mind the tremendous contribution of Elliot Wolfson. For representative studies, see Elliot Wolfson, "Circumcision, Vision of God, and Textual Interpretation: From Midrashic Trope to Mystical Symbol," *HR* 27 (1987): 189–215; "The Hermeneutics of Visionary Experience: Revelation and

the shofar rites facilitate the manifestation of God as a *body of sound*, such that the experience of audition intersects with the visualization of divinity.[10] I highlight intersense modalities of experience represented in the texts, and in particular, the synesthetic intermingling of sound and vision.[11] The study draws on a rich archive of literature from Catalonia and Castile, dating from the thirteenth century. I have chosen this time and these places to

---

Interpretation in the Zohar," *Religion* 18 (1988): 311–45; and *Through a Speculum that Shines: Vision and Imagination in Medieval Jewish Mysticism* (Princeton: Princeton University Press, 1994).

[10] Thus, this exercise broadens the phenomenology of synesthesia in Jewish mysticism to include the category of instrumental sound. For earlier discussions of synesthesia, see Wolfson, *Through a Speculum*, 160, 347-51; *Language, Eros, Being: Kabbalistic Hermeneutics and Poetic Imagination* (New York: Fordham University Press, 2005), sub voce "synesthesia." Also see Eitan Fishbane, "The Speech of Being, the Voice of God: Phonetic Mysticism in the Kabbalah of Asher ben David and his Contemporaries," *JQR* 98.4 (2008): 485-521. For a survey of kabbalistic approaches to biblical cantillation, see Elliot Wolfson, "Biblical Accentuation in a Mystical Key: Kabbalistic Interpretations of the *Te'amim*," *JJML* 11 (1988-89): 1-16 and *JJML* 12 (1989-90): 1-13. On kabbalah and music generally, see Moshe Idel, "Conceptualizations of Music in Jewish Mysticism," *Enchanting Powers: Music in the World's Religions* (ed. Lawrence Sullivan; Cambridge, MA: Harvard University Press, 1997), 159-88 and *The Mystical Experience in Abraham Abulafia* (tr. Jonathan Chipman; Albany: State University of New York Press, 1988), 55-72.

[11] For a classic perspective on synesthesia from the field of ethnomusicology, see Alan Merriam, *The Anthropology of Music* (Evanston: Northwestern University Press, 1964), 85-102.

circumscribe a pivotal period of kabbalistic literary creativity. However, I limit the study to a representative selection of texts, and make no claims of offering a comprehensive treatment.

Catalonian Accounts

I will begin my analysis with R. Ezra, whose teachings provide a contemplative basis for visualizing the shofar blasts as reverberating divine attributes.[12] R. Ezra indicates that the *teru'ah* and *shevarim* patterns both correspond to divine attributes of judgment, whereas *teqi'ah* corresponds to the attribute of compassion. The association between the attributes refers to the character of the blasts, as sounds linked to judgment are discontinuous and broken, corresponding to the situation of separation. The *teqi'ah* blast, on the other hand, is sustained and steady. It is united, by contrast, corresponding to the mode of integration, reconciliation, and clemency. Moreover, *teru'ah* and *shevarim*—ciphers for *gevurah* and *malkhut*—are feminine, whereas *teqi'ah* is masculine, corresponding to *tiferet*. The proper liturgical sequence of these blasts arouses a union of contrasexual divine attributes. But this union gives rise to the appropriation

---

[12] Yakov M. Travis, "Kabbalistic Foundations of Jewish Spiritual Practice: Rabbi Ezra of Gerona—On the Kabbalistic Meaning of the Mitzvot" (Ph.D. diss., Brandeis University, 2002), 44 [Hebrew].

of the feminine voices by the masculine. With the sonic eruption of the final *teqi'ah* blast, the androgynous polyphony resolves to a male monotony. The pleroma reverberates with a single masculine voice of compassion.[13]

In Nahmanides' discussions of the shofar the sound of *teru'ah* also alludes to the feminine attribute of judgment.[14] But it is the instrument itself which alludes to the masculine power of compassion, also characterized as the male attribute of remembrance, זיכרון, alluding to זכר.[15] Moreover, Nahmanides

---

[13] For a helpful survey of perspectives on gender in kabbalah scholarship, see Hava Tirosh-Samuelson, "Gender in Jewish Mysticism," *Jewish Mysticism and Kabbalah: New Insights and Scholarship* (ed. Frederick Greenspahn; New York: New York University Press, 2011), 191–230.

[14] Here, I refer to two places in Nahmanides' corpus which treat the kabbalistic rationale for sounding the shofar on the New Year. These are in his commentary to Lev 23:24 and his late *Sermon for Rosh ha-Shanah—Kitvei ha-Ramban* I.220. On Nahmanides's attempt to redress the shofar customs of a community of French tosafists established in thirteenth-century Palestine, see Shalem Yahalom, "Historical Background to Nahmanides' Acre *Sermon for Rosh ha-Shanah*: The Strengthening of the Catalonian Center," *Sefarad* 68.2 (2008): 315–42. On esoteric rationales for the New Year's shofar rites in the tradition of Nahmanides, see Horowitz, *The Jewish Sermon*, 91, esp. n. 26.

[15] An anonymous סוד text printed in the appendix to the 1608 Basel edition of R. Moses de León's *Sefer Nefesh ha-Hakhamah* similarly upholds Nahmanides' view that shofar alludes to *tiferet* and *teru'ah* to *'atarah*, a cognomen for *malkhut*. Also see the unpublished סודות discussed in connection with R. Azriel's commentary to the additional New Year's service in Martel Govrin,

discloses the crucial detail that the proper performance of the command involves binding oneself in a mystical union with the divine sound of *teru'ah*. The sage maintains that the Torah alludes to this secret rationale, and that its interpretation has been passed down from the patriarchs and remains בידינו קבלה — "a tradition in our possession." "And whosoever merits to become a recipient of the secrets of Torah [להיות מקובל בסתרי התורה], will discern the subject expressed in scripture, and the language of scripture will be clearer to him, for the *teru'ah* has stood beside our fathers and beside us."[16] *Teru'ah* is *malkhut*, a link Nahmanides demonstrates by citing an instance where Onqelos translates *teru'ah* into Aramaic as שכינתא, the *shekhinah*, the lower feminine attribute of judgment.

Nahmanides establishes the mystical import of Psalms 89:16: "Happy are the people that know *teru'ah* [אשרי העם יודעי תרועה]." The people that know *teru'ah* are "those who draw near to her in knowledge [שמקרבת אליה הדעת]." This is because "knowing refers to cleaving [דבקות]," just as knowing, according to Nahmanides, designates sexual intercourse (citing Adam's carnal *knowledge* of Eve, and Rebeca's virginity, a man not

---

"R. Azriel of Gerona's Commentary on Prayer (Critical Edition)." (M.A. thesis, Hebrew University of Jerusalem, 1984), 22–23, 30 [Hebrew].

[16] *Kitvei ha-Ramban* I.220.

having *known* her).¹⁷ This amorous cleaving to *teru'ah* denotes Israel's mystical bond with *malkhut* while hearing the horn, its rapt absorption in divine sound. But it also refers to *teru'ah*'s attachment to *tiferet*, the feminine tone's bond to the masculine shofar. Nahmanides underscores the scriptural injunction to sound the horn on the *day* of *teru'ah* [יום תרועה]. This diurnal element alludes to the masculine attribute of compassion [*raḥamim*], associated with sunlight.¹⁸

---

¹⁷ On earlier accounts of the shofar in an erotic vein, note Wolfson's assessment that pietistic explanations of the shofar service from Ashkenaz evince the hierogamy motif, where the rites stimulate the intercourse of the upper and lower divine glories. See Elliot Wolfson, *Along the Path: Studies in Kabbalistic Myth, Symbolism, and Hermeneutics* (Albany: State University of New York Press, 1995), 52-55. For conceptions of shofar in *hekhalot*, consider the function of the horn in heralding divine vision; the *Hekhalot Zutarti* macroform relates angels blaring the threefold sequence — *teqi'ah*, *teru'ah*, and *teqi'ah* — to announce the mystic's climactic entrance into the glorious presence of the divine King. See Peter Schäfer, *Synopse zur Hekhalot-Literatur* (Tübingen: Mohr Siebeck, 1981), § 411, and compare § 250 (*Hekhalot Rabbati*).

¹⁸ In his classic study of the ram's horn from 1919, Freud's student Theodor Reik suggests that the shofar be construed as a phallic symbol. Nahmanides's repeated allusions to the instrument's masculinity anticipate the psychoanalytic interpretation by nearly seven centuries. The psychoanalyst reveals the horn's phallic character and suggests that its sound is the voice of God — both points anticipated in Nahmanides's symbolism. But for Reik, the voice of God is that of the old totemic diety. And this animal diety corresponds to the paternal ancestor who, by Freud's theory of religion, was murdered by the primordial horde. The shofar signifies the phallus because it reproduces the father's voice, the vehicle of masculine sexual potency. At the same time, the

Aware of the provocative implications of his allusions, Nahmanides quickly withdraws into the rhetoric of secrecy: "These things are among the secrets of Torah, and it is not appropriate to speak of them with many, nor even to individuals."[19]

Castilian Accounts

We find allusions to kabbalistic secrets of shofar in an elusive text from Castile by R. Jacob ben Jacob ha-Kohen of Segovia — the *Sefer ha-Orah*. It survives in a fragmentary state, and the section of the text dedicated to the ram's horn — פירוש תקיעת שופר — has not been preserved in known recensions of the work.[20] However, in extant portions of the text, R. Jacob identifies the shofar's call with the voice of the angel Metatron, who, in turn, represents a universal intellect or logos principle.[21] Elsewhere, recounting the theophany at Sinai, R. Jacob describes the gorgeous music of the spheres descending upon Moses and

---

father's voice provokes castration anxiety and the collective guilt of the patricidal community. Insofar as its sounds — which symbolically reenact the original crime — call to mind the cries of the murder victim, the shofar, according to Reik, functions as a call to moral conscience. Theodor Reik, *Ritual: Psycho-Analytic Studies* (tr. Douglas Bryan; London: Hogarth, 1931), 279-88.

[19] *Kitvei ha-Ramban* I.220.

[20] Daniel Abrams, "*The Book of Illumination* of R. Jacob ben Jacob Ha-Kohen: A Synoptic Edition from Various Manuscripts" (Ph.D. dissertation, New York University, 1993), 156 [Hebrew].

[21] Abrams, "*The Book of Illumination*," 327.

compares it to the sound of the ram's horn.²² Consequently, Israel, he recounts, responded to the transmission of the primordial intellect to their prophet with a blaring crescendo of shofar sound.²³ In both cases, the reverberations issuing from the horn signal the dissemination of noetic substance from on high.

In a treatise attributed to R. Jacob's brother R. Isaac ben Jacob ha-Kohen, we find a kabbalistic rationale for the shofar rites focused on the symbolic import of the horn's animal source. The text justifies the rabbinic specification that on the New Year, Israel is commanded to sound the horn of a ram²⁴—and emphatically *not* that of a goat—because the former is rooted in the divine element of compassion whereas the latter is entrenched in judgment.²⁵ Here, the compassion-versus-judgment binary signifies the opposition of the right and left powers, personified as Abraham and Isaac respectively. This is based on the

---

²² See Maimonides, *Guide of the Perplexed* II.8. For Gikatilla on the acoustics of celestial motion, see Y. Tzvi Langerman, "Hebrew Astronomy: Deep Soundings from a Rich Tradition," *Astronomy across Cultures: The History of Non-Western Astronomy* (ed. Helaine Selin; Dordrecht: Springer, 2000), 560–61.

²³ Abrams, "The Book of Illumination," 226.

²⁴ On the ram's horn and the imaginative theory of Jubal as a ram-diety, who is a god of instrumental music, see Reik, *Ritual*, 276–77.

²⁵ Gershom Scholem, "The Traditions of R. Jacob and R. Isaac ha-Kohen," *Madda'ei ha-Yahadut* II (1927): 119 [Hebrew].

rabbinic view that the horn of the ram is sanctioned because it commemorates God's clemency on Mt. Moriah, when Abraham sacrificed that particular animal in Isaac's stead.[26] The treatise goes on to cite a late *midrash* on the biblical episode,[27] which describes the interventions of the pernicious angel Samael. This satanic figure tries to thwart Abraham's sacrifice. He ensnares the ram's horns "between the trees,"[28] symbolically suspending the offering between the opposing realms of sanctity and impurity. Nonetheless, sanctity prevails when the ram paws Abraham's prayer shawl, so that the patriarch's compassionate substitution of animal for human victim may take place. Samael, according to this theosophic interpretation of the late *midrash*, comes from the female power of judgment, whereas Abraham, like the ram, is linked to masculine compassion.[29] By implication, the sanctioned

---

[26] b. Rosh ha-Shanah 16a.

[27] Pirqei de R. Eliezer § 31.

[28] See Gen 22:13. For the view that the tether of the horns in the brush resembles Israel's entanglement with sin, see Joshua ibn Shu'eib, *Sermons on the Torah*, 90b.

[29] On the identification of the shofar with *raḥamim*, note that R. Isaac specifies the name שגזריאל—"that God decreed"—for the angel of the ram's horn. This name, apparently, a variation of the more typical גזריאל, is an acrostic for the phrase שופר גדול זה רחמים—"this great shofar is compassion." See Scholem, "The Traditions of R. Jacob and R. Isaac," 110. On angelological lore related to the shofar, see Yehudah Liebes, "The Angels of the

performance of the shofar rites contravenes satanic meddling, which, if unrestrained, would lead to the harsh sentencing of Israel on the day of their judgment.[30]

The writings of Toledan sage R. Todros ben Joseph ha-Levi Abulafia yield a variation on this tradition attributed to R. Isaac, also related to the echelons of sinister angelic power.[31] R. Todros bases the preference for the ram on that animal's association with Israel's advocacy. In this case, the kabbalist discusses the proscription of the bullhorn, which is prohibited due to the bull's association with Israel's prosecution.[32] Thus, the people sound the instrument of its advocacy in order to bring about a mystical union of the divine gradations encompassing the entire

---

Shofar and Jesus the Prince of the Countenance," *Early Jewish Mysticism: Proceedings of the First International Conference on the History of Jewish Mysticism* (ed. Joseph Dan; Jerusalem: Hebrew University of Jerusalem Press, 1987), 171-96 [Hebrew].

[30] On dispersing demons and confounding diabolical schemes, see *m. Rosh ha-Shanah* 3:7; *b. Rosh ha-Shanah* 16a-b; and *Zohar* I.114b, 152a; II.196b, 237b-238a; III.99b. On the use of shofar in exorcism by latter-day kabbalists, see J. H. Chajes, *Between Worlds: Dybbuks, Exorcists, and Early Modern Judaism* (Philadelphia: University of Pennsylvania Press, 2003), 82-83.

[31] On the discipleship of R. Todros to R. Isaac, see Kushnir-Oron's scholarly introduction to Todros Abulafia, *Sha'ar ha-Razim* (ed. Michal Kushnir-Oron; Jerusalem: Mosad Bialik, 1989).

[32] For the farfetched theory that a prehistoric succession from the totemic worship of the bull-god to a ram cult underlies the rabbinic prohibition against the bullhorn, see Reik, *Ritual*, 227.

nation, a union in which the masculine power of compassion will predominate: "And our entire intention [in sounding the shofar] is to unify the entities, to draw down compassion, to band together the camp, to become one."[33]

This instrument's capacity to effect such a bond is underscored by R. Todros' folk etymology of the term *teru'ah* [תרועה]. He teaches that the term connotes the cohesive principles of love and affection— אהבה וריעות.[34] The mystical bond effected by the shofar is comprehensive, encompassing the thirty tiers of supramundane reality. The Toledan sage elucidates this point through an ontologizing interpretation of the thirty-fold structure of the shofar service, where he explains why the ten-fold sequence of horn calls is thrice repeated.[35]

> Below the supernal emanation [of ten gradations], there is a second emanation of ten gradations by which the prophets prophesied,

---

[33] Todros Abulafia, *Otsar ha-Kavod*, 47a; compare 56a: "and the *teqi'ah* is [blown] to assemble the camps, in order to unify the entities, and to draw down to us the grace and the compassion."

[34] Todros Abulafia, *Otsar ha-Kavod*, 49a. As in R. Ezra, the sounds of *teqi'ah* are masculine, while those of *teru'ah* are feminine. But here, *teru'ah* also functions as an inclusive term for the shofar sounds collectively. On these sounds, see 56a. Compare *Sha'ar ha-Razim*, 123.

[35] In his commentary on the secrets of Psalm 19, the author dispatches with the rhetorical attribution of this doctrine to "some of the kabbalists"—see *Sha'ar ha-Razim*, 126.

apart from our teacher Moses, peace upon him. And those who speak in the holy spirit, each of them do so according to their rung and their gradation. And below those is a third emanation, which is the emanation of the ten [celestial] spheres.[36]

According to this esoteric teaching,[37] the hyperdimensional expanse of supramundane being spans three tenfold worlds of emanation. In character, one dimension is divine, one spiritual, and one celestial. Elsewhere, R. Todros delineates these three tenfold dimensions as contemplative, prophetic, and cosmological.[38] The annual performance of the shofar rites, which is structured according to this ontological framework, effectively coordinates and synchronizes all levels of being.[39] Moreover, it is the instrumental sound which renders these subtle realities apparent to the mind's eye.

R. Moses ben Shem Tov de León, a kabbalist associated with R. Todros's family, discusses the

---

[36] R. Todros Abulafia, *'Otsar ha-Kavod*, 49a. Here, R. Todros expounds the matter in the name of "some of the kabbalists," but not so in *Sha'ar ha-Razim*, 126.

[37] The text links this thirty-fold schema to the scribal convention of representing the Tetragrammaton with a triple *yod* insignia. For similar articulations of this secret, see Moshe Idel, "The Sefirot above the Sefirot," *Tarbiz* 51 (1982): 245–46.

[38] R. Todros Abulafia, *Sha'ar ha-Razim*, 126.

[39] Scholem and Kushnir-Oron have shown that this doctrine derives from R. Isaac ha-Kohen. See *Sha'ar ha-Razim*. 126 n. 434.

commandment of the shofar at several places in his copious Hebrew writings. For this figure, the shofar belongs to the hidden world of *binah*.[40] The link to *binah* is demonstrated by that power's correspondence to a number of sacred figures associated with the shofar, such as the Jubilee, the Day of Atonement, and repentance. In terms of divine anatomy, *binah* corresponds to the divine womb, but a womb which takes on a phallic character when it issues offspring.[41] The issue of the horn, of course, is sound. And the corporeal dimensionality of acoustical phenomena is underscored in de León's accounts. *Binah*'s emanation of the elemental attributes of *ḥesed*, *gevurah*, and *tiferet* is described in terms of water, fire, and wind issuing from the shofar. *Tiferet*, which encompasses all of these, is the sound of the ram's horn — also identified as the voice of Jacob the Patriarch. I interpret the water, fire,

---

[40] On purported tensions between R. Moses de León, see Haviva Pedaya, *Nahmanides: Cyclical Time and Holy Text* (Tel Aviv: Am Oved, 2003), 439–65 [Hebrew]; and "The Great Mother: The Struggle Between Nahmanides and the Zohar Circle," *Temps i espais de la Girona jueva; actes del Simposi Internacional celebrat a Girona* (2011): 311–28. Pedaya describes "the collapse of the conception of Great Mother as one of the main issues in the struggle between the Circle of Nahmanides and the Zohar Circle."

[41] On the phallic potentiation of the uterine *binah*, see Elliot Wolfson, *Circle in the Square: Studies in the Use of Gender in Kabbalistic Symbolism* (Albany: State University of New York Press, 1995), 99–106; and *Language, Eros Being*, 356–71.

and wind in connection with the wet embouchure, the labial friction, and directed breath of the horn player. De León describes this divine eruption of sound in strikingly physical terms: "When the aperture gives power to unfold, the shofar becomes stronger and stronger, and it releases a wind comprised of fire and water, which arises from the striking of the air against the outside [בדפיקת האויר לחוץ] which produces sound."[42] Or again: "the sound produced by the shofar, comprised of the unity of fire, water and wind, projects outwardly by the horn's perceptible striking of the air [בדפיקת האויר הנתפס]. And its outward emission makes [the elements into] a single entity, which becomes audible sound. And this is the audible sound of the shofar which emanates from the *great voice* which is *inaudible* from without, for it is the inner, subtle voice."[43] The audible gives voice to that which lies beyond audition, just as the horn sound derives from soundless breath, as *tiferet* emanates from *binah*.[44]

---

[42] Moses de León, *Sefer ha-Rimmon* (ed. Elliot Wolfson; Altanta: Scholar's Press, 1988), 96; and cf. *Sefer Sheqel ha-Qodesh* (ed. Charles Mopsik; Los Angeles: Cherub Press, 1996), 26.

[43] de León, *Sefer ha-Rimmon*, 143. This elemental manifestation of sound is similarly attested in de León, *Sefer Mishkan ha-'Edut* (ed. Avishai Bar-Asher; Los Angeles: Cherub Press, 2013), 35; and *Sefer ha-Mishqal* (Jochanan Wijnhoven, "Sefer ha-Mishkal: Text and Study" [PhD diss., Brandeis University, 1964], 118–120). Compare *Zohar* I.114a–b; II.81b and 184b.

[44] In like manner, an untitled composition by de León

De León goes on to reiterate R. Ezra's identification of *teqi'ah* with the attribute of compassion and *teru'ah* with the attribute of judgment.⁴⁵ However, he transposes the disharmony between these sounds into the register of interreligious polemic, where the two sound-types correspond to Jacob and Esau respectively. The rabbinic conventions of typological exegesis equate the younger son of Isaac with Israel and the elder with Christendom. De León links the steady and unwavering sound of *teqi'ah* to the smooth surface of Jacob's body—איש חלק—and the bleating sound of *teru'ah* to the goat-like aspect of Esau—איש שעיר. The kabbalist asserts that by performing the sanctioned rites of the ram's horn, "we bind the attributes together to arouse the secret of compassion, which encompasses all of the [attributes]. And in so doing, we encompass those with these, making everything a single secret […] and such is the

---

describes the phonation of shofar in terms of a manifestation of audible from inaudible sound. See Ms. Bayerische Staatsbibliothek München, Cod. Hebr. 47. Fol. 359a. The kabbalist refers to an earlier discussion of this topic in a portion of the text which has not been preserved. Elsewhere, de León mentions the "voice emanating from the midst of the shofar, by the mystery of the *great voice*," see Moses de León, *Sefer Shushat 'Edut*, printed in Gershom Scholem, "Two Treatises of R. Moses de León," *Kovets 'al Yad* 8 (1976): 342.

⁴⁵ Compare discussion of shofar sounds in *Sod 'Eser Sefirot Belimah*, printed in Scholem, "Two Treatises of R. Moses de León," 382; and see *Zohar* III: 231b.

secret of sounding the ram's horn [סוד תקיעת שופר]."⁴⁶ Again, the rites are *instrumental* in forging a theoerotic bond between compassionate and judgmental attributes, a bond which heralds the monotonization of discordant sound-types. The rites express the acoustical form of the divine body in sound-images.

A recently located fragment composed by de León preserves a unique rationale for the commandment. The text is a vestige of the kabbalist's lost commentary on Ecclesiastes.⁴⁷ As in the treatise attributed to R. Isaac, the text represents the horn rites as an effective means for wrangling with impure forces.⁴⁸ The fragment describes the vulnerability of Israel to satanic prosecution during the New Year's tribunal, when the nation appears before God in judgment. In this instance, Israel sounds the shofar to call Samael—who is identified both as Satan as well as

---

⁴⁶ de León, *Sefer ha-Rimmon*, 145.

⁴⁷ Avishai Bar-Asher, "Samael and his Wife: The Lost Commentary on Ecclesiastes of R. Moses de León," *Tarbiz* 80.4 (2012): 539–66 [Hebrew]. The scholar discusses this fragment in his painstaking effort to piece together the remnants of the lost commentary, also known by the title *Sha'arei Tsedeq*.

⁴⁸ For an alternate account of blowing the shofar on the New Year to overturn the rule of the sinister forces of Esau, see de León, *Sefer Mishkan ha-Edut*, 34–36. The polemically anti-Christian tone of that account is evident from the kabbalist's assertion that "the audible sound that is unified as one will drive the foreskin away from its place." The same circumcision language appears in de León, *Sefer ha-Mishqal*, 120.

Esau — off to hunt game in the field.⁴⁹ There, the accuser encounters demonic feminine powers who tempt him with illicit sex. The shofar breaks Samael's resolve to prosecute Israel, because it causes the demonic females to occupy him with their seductions.⁵⁰ The fragment identifies these female forces with idolatrous witches who weave coverings for the goddess Asherah.⁵¹ Instead of aiming at a heavenly marriage of *tiferet* and *malkhut*, this rationale explains that Israel blows the shofar to arouse the heteroerotic union of sinister elements. It is of historical relevance to observe that, here, de León imagines Israel's shofar as a *cor de chasse*, the instrument used to signal the hunt in medieval western Europe.⁵²

The writings of R. Joseph ben Abraham Gikatilla⁵³ contain several diverse accounts of the

---

⁴⁹ Based on Gen 27:5.

⁵⁰ Bar-Asher, "Samael," 554.

⁵¹ Alluding to 2 Kngs 23:7. On the representation of Asherah as the wife of Asher, see *Zohar* I.49a.

⁵² For some early descriptions of hunting-horn signals, which nonetheless postdate this fragment by approximately one century, see Kurt Taut, *Beiträge zur Geschichte der Jagdmusik* (Leipzig: Radelli & Hille, 1927), 74–106. The kabbalist may intend that, to the Christian ear, the shofar calls register as hunting signals, and thus they produce the effect of dispatching the demonic forces linked to Esau.

⁵³ On Gikatilla's reservations with respect to the enterprise of enumerating 613 commandments, see Ephraim Gottlieb, *Studies in the Kabbalah Literature* (ed. Joseph Hacker; Tel Aviv: Tel Aviv

shofar.⁵⁴ Most importantly, his *Sha'arei Tsedeq* works out a theosophic distinction between two divine ram's horns. To one gradation, he assigns the "great shofar" mentioned in Isaiah 27:13, which heralds the ingathering of the exiles. To another gradation, he assigns the shofar which resonates during the theophany at Sinai and on the New Year.⁵⁵ The former alludes to *binah*.⁵⁶ The latter alludes to *raḥamim*. Gikatilla establishes the connection to *raḥamim* in a circuitous way. Drawing on ancient lore associating the ram's horn with the binding on Mt. Moriah, the kabbalist teaches that the shofar linked to *raḥamim* is, in fact, played by Isaac. But the horn itself corresponds to his son Jacob.⁵⁷ The sound potentiates the emanation of *din* (Isaac) via *raḥamim* (Jacob) — the expression of judgment requiring compassion just as the player's articulation depends on his horn. Ultimately, the

---

University Press, 1976), 121–28 [Hebrew].

⁵⁴ For an elaborate esoteric exposition of the New Year's liturgy from an earlier phase in the development of this kabbalist's teaching, see Joseph Gikatilla, *Ginnat 'Egoz* (Hannau, 1615), 47b–50a.

⁵⁵ Joseph Gikatilla, *Sha'arei Tsedeq* (Cracow, 1881), 30a.

⁵⁶ The identification of the "great shofar" with *binah* also appears in Joseph Gikatilla, *Sha'arei Orah* (ed. Joseph Ben-Shelomo; Jerusalem: Mosad Bialik, 1981), II.68–9 and in the kabbalist's glosses on Maimonides; see Gottlieb, *Studies*, 108.

⁵⁷ Compare Joseph Gikatilla, *Sha'arei Tsedeq*, 36a, where the shofar invokes the potencies of Abraham and Jacob.

player and his horn draw their power from the "great shofar," which is *binah*.

In a subsequent work, Gikatilla suggests another connection between Isaac and the New Year's shofar rites. Psalm 81:4 instructs Israel to sound the shofar on the new moon, in the darkness of their festival day—כסה ליום חגנו. Gikatilla links the concealment of the moon at New Year to the dimming of Isaac's vision.[58] However, this dark scenario, where judgment predominates, is overcome when the shofar service restores light, which is to say, vision, and judgment is mitigated by compassion. Thus, Gikatilla cites Psalm 89:19, which instructs that those glad knowers of *teru'ah* will walk in the light of the Lord's countenance.[59] The outpouring of theophanic light and the emission of instrumental sound are bound together at the phenomenal level. In other words, vision is restored with sound.

In a rationale attributed to the enigmatic Iberian kabbalist called "R. Joseph of Hamadan,"[60] we find similar elements.[61] As in Nahmanides and Gikatilla,

---

[58] Gen 27:1.

[59] Joseph Gikatilla, *Sha'arei Orah*, I.232.

[60] For a recent discussion of the scholarship on this figure, see Leore Sachs Shmueli, "I Arouse the *Shekhinah*: A Psychoanalytic Study of the Kabbalist's Anxiety and Desire in Relation to the Object of Taboo," *Kabbalah* 35 (2015): 227–66 [Hebrew].

[61] See Menahem Meier, "A Critical Edition of the *Sefer Ta'amey ha-Mitzwoth* Attributed to Isaac ibn Farhi: Section 1.

the *shofar* refers to *tiferet*. But the occasion of Rosh Hashanah corresponds to *binah*, which R. Joseph calls "the beginning of judgment." In addition to the New Year, "the Sabbatical Years, the Jubilee Years, and the Day of Atonement all come from the attributes of *binah*, and each comes to play upon the ram's horn. [This is] because all of the [lower] powers receive overflow from the emanation of *binah*, and freedom comes into the world." The emancipation associated with these occasions, which the text personifies as horn players, proceeds through the intermingling of male and female attributes. Freedom comes when the lower attributes *suckle* [יונקים] from the supernal powers of holiness and purity. Listening is figured in terms of suckling nourishment from *binah*, the maternal potency. The lower attributes hearken to the heartbreaking strains of the horn, drinking in their emancipation, sustaining Israel with divine abundance:

> They blast the shofar in order to break the heart so that overflow will come by means of the straight path, that nourishment will come to the world of souls, to the world of angels, and to the mundane realm, and that Israel will merit the land of life, which is *shekhinah*.

The text advises the reader to intend that "one thing corresponds to another," and, specifically, that

---

Positive Commandments" (PhD diss., Brandeis University, 1974), 208–12.

the shofar service corresponds to a supernal wedding of the assembly of Israel to the King, Lord of Hosts — a hierogamy uniting *malkhut* and *tiferet*. The text specifies that the music of the horn allays the bride's reluctance to consummate the marriage. This is based on a rabbinic pun that the word שופר derives from the verb שפר, to improve.[62] Accordingly, the horn is sounded "in order to improve the bride in the eyes of her husband. Then, the King, Lord of Hosts, embraces her, and mingles compassion with judgment, and all of Israel are inscribed for life." Here, the music of the shofar sets an amorous mood. This rationale provides yet another theoerotic variation on the theme of visualizing instrumental sound by effectively inviting the participant into the intimate precinct of the divine bridal chamber.

Although *Sefer ha-Zohar* contains many relevant accounts of the shofar,[63] recent critical scholarship compels a revision of the assumption that the bulk of the vast literary anthology may be placed squarely within the historical boundaries I have established for this study, namely, the parameters of the thirteenth

---

[62] This world-play is based on *Pesiqta DeRab Kahana* 23:8. Compare Todros Abulafia, *Sha'ar ha-Kavod*, 56a.

[63] Some Sephardic versions of the liturgy integrate an influential text on the shofar from the *Ra'aya Mehemna* stratum (*Zohar* III.98b).

century.[64] Nonetheless, to conclude my analysis, I will discuss one remarkably vibrant zoharic text, without attempting to determine its precise derivation.[65] Suffice it to say that the passage reprises various motifs exhibited in the late thirteenth-century accounts of Gikatilla, de León, and R. Joseph of Hamadan.

While traveling on the road, R. Simeon bar Yohai and his friends encounter an unnamed elder, who delivers an inspired homily about the New Year. The old man teaches the rabbis that Rosh Hashanah is a time when the sinister "other side" eclipses the lunar light. He intimates that the natural phenomenon of the moon's disappearance signals the capture of *shekhinah* by the judgmental forces. The captivity is such that the "other side" deposits an impenetrable sediment upon the moon. Nothing can breach its crust, but by God's express advice (Ps 81:4), which enjoins Israel to sound the shofar on the new moon, in the *covering* of their festival.

> [Thus, Israel blow the ram's horn] in order to break that covering, by which the moon is covered and cannot shine. When Israel below

---

[64] See statement of the problem and relevant bibliography in Elliot Wolfson, "Zoharic Literature and Midrashic Temporality," *Midrash Unbound: Transformations and Innovations* (ed. Michael Fishbane and Joanna Weinberg; Oxford: Littman Library of Jewish Civilization, 2013), 321-25.

[65] *Zohar* II.184a-b. Remarkably close is de León, *Sefer ha-Mishqal*, 118-20.

> arouse the shofar, the sound issuing from it strikes the air [בטש באוירא] splitting firmaments until it rises to that mighty rock covering the moon. [...] Then that sound persists and removes judgment. Once compassion has been aroused below, so too above, another, supernal shofar is aroused, emitting a sound that is compassion; and sound meets sound, compassion meets compassion. By arousal below, there is similarly arousal above.[66]

As in de León's accounts, this text emphasizes the physical impact of the blast. The piercing call reaches *shekhinah* and shatters the rock, which isolated her from *raḥamim*, her compassionate husband.[67] The ritual performance below restores the bride to her bridegroom, and stimulates the flow of compassionate sound to *raḥamim* from God's shofar — *binah*. The elder describes a stereophonic confluence of divine and human sound, upper and lower blasts converging upon the imperiled bride. And, again, with the theophonic performance comes the return of theophanic light.[68] So illuminated, *shekhinah* is no

---

[66] With slight adaptation, I cite Daniel Matt's elegant translation from *The Zohar: Pritzker Edition* (vol. VI; Stanford: Stanford University Press, 2011).

[67] In *Sefer ha-Mishqal*, 18–20, de León visualizes the covering of the moon on the New Year, the blockage of excessive judgment, as a foreskin covering the male organ of the divine body. The shofar's incisive tone severs the foreskin, revealing an opening within the Godhead through which Israel's prayers may enter.

[68] See above for Gikatilla's parallel interpretation of Psalm

longer beleaguered by dark rock, but rather shines as a "precious stone."

> Israel hastens to arouse a sound through the shofar—mystery of compassion, comprising fire, water, and air, becoming one. Ascending, it strikes this precious stone—בהאי אבן ובטש טבא—which is imbued with the colors of that sound. Then, according to her appearance, so she draws from above. Once she is arrayed by this sound, compassion issues from above and settles upon her, and she is encompassed from below and above. Then the other side is confounded: he looks and sees the radiant face and his power weakens and he cannot accuse. And this precious stone displays radiance in every direction, radiance below and radiance above.[69]

The elemental emission of *binah* and the language of acoustical impact are obvious motifs from de León's Hebrew writings. In particular, this text captures the intersense modality of the horn's emanation by describing sound's manifestation as color.[70] When the shattering eruption of the shofar

---

81:4.

[69] Again, adapted from Matt.

[70] See Gershom Scholem, "Colors and Their Symbolism in Jewish Tradition and Mysticism," *Diogenes* 108 (1979): 84–112. For more recent studies on color, see the bibliography provided in Moshe Idel, "Visualization of Colors, 1: David ben Yehudah he-Ḥasid's Kabbalistic Diagram," *Ars Judaica* 11 (2015): 31, n. 1.

reveals the feminine *shekhinah*, she glows as a translucent gem, refracting the sonic reverberations of the male in variegated light. As in the above-cited rationale attributed to R. Joseph, the horn's music beautifies the bride in the eyes of her bridegroom, while their conjugal union beatifies Israel. Moreover, the intensity of her splendor overpowers the "other side," and the forces of prosecution abate. Thus, she is encompassed by her divine lover above, and the human celebrants below in a mystical pageant of sound and color.

Conclusion

The material collected here exhibits a range of traditional strategies for anchoring the ancient shofar rites in the symbolism of the *sefirot*. The shofar is sometimes identified with *raḥamim*, sometimes with *binah* (or both, in the case of Gikatilla). Similarly, the texts coordinate the various appurtenances of the shofar service — such as the sounds produced by the horn, the occasion of its performance, the identity of the *baal toqeah* or horn-blower, the animal from which the horn is sourced, etc. — with corresponding divine potencies and their interactions. The texts also deal with the mystical effects of the shofar rites. Most of these accounts situate the ram's horn at a junction where visual and auditory modes of apprehending divinity intersect. More than simply teaching us about kabbalistic attitudes toward archaic forms of instrumental music, the accounts bespeak an intersense dimensionality of experience. In so doing, they supply important data for augmenting the phenomenology of synesthesia in Jewish mysticism. Moreover, this exercise in reading kabbalistic rituology has implications for expanding the scholarly representation of ritual in medieval kabbalah, so as to account for the broadest spectrum of sensory and intersense phenomena.[71]

---

[71] On the intersection of taste and vision, see Joel Hecker, *Mystical Bodies, Mystical Meals: Eating and Embodiment in Medieval Kabbalah* (Detroit: Wayne State University Press, 2005), 57–59, 207–08, n. 13.

Sephardic Shofar Practices
Theology and Mysticism

Haim Ovadia

The Poetic Theological Introduction to the Shofar

When I was asked to write about the shofar practices in Sephardic communities, three Hebrew words came into my mind: עוקד והנעקד והמזבח. These words are the refrain of a poem chanted immediately preceding the blowing of the shofar by all Sephardic communities, from the Iberian Peninsula to North Africa, from Iran to Jerusalem. The meaning of these words is: He who binds; He who is bound; The Altar.

Those three Hebrew words encapsulate the tremendous theological and emotional tension of the momentous event of the Binding of Isaac. They draw the readers' attention and force them to focus on the singularity, deep pain, and desolate loneliness of the moment. At that moment, there are only two people in the whole world. Abraham and Isaac. No one else is aware of what is soon about to take place. Sarah was never told that her husband plans to slaughter her only child, the one she bore him when she was ninety years old, and the two attendants are waiting at the foot of the mountain. On top of the mountain there are only Abraham and Isaac, father and son, a devoutly religious man and a young innocent child, slaughterer and sacrifice. It is a terrifying image: a knife-wielding man looming over a small, helpless body of a child, who, with hands and feet bound together, is curled up on top of a pile of firewood, about to be slaughtered and burned. They are alone only on the human plane, though, for they are joined by the altar, which seems to be a representation of a blood-thirsty and cruel deity, one who demands human sacrifices. So the poem zooms in on the three tragic protagonists in their total isolation: He who binds, he who is bound, and the altar.

The poem was written by Rabbi Yehudah (Abu-Al-Baqqa Yahya) ben Shemuel ibn Abbas.[1] There is only fragmented information regarding his life, but it is known that he was a contemporary of the great poets of the Golden Age in Spain, Rabbi Yehudah HaLevi (1075–1141) and Rabbi Moshe ibn Ezra (1058–1138), and that he passed on, at the earliest, in 1167. It is not clear if he ever lived in Al-Andalus, and he was probably born in the Maghreb, or North Africa, and

---

[1] Jefin Schirmann, "Poets Contemporary with Mose ibn Ezra and Yehuda Hallevi (III)," *Studies of the Research Institute for Hebrew Poetry in Jerusalem* 4 (1945): 297–99.

visited Aleppo and Iraq. He is the only non-Spanish poet whom Yehudah Al-Harizzi included in his essay on the Jewish poets of Spain. As we shall see, his poem about the *Akedah* is a powerful theological debate about the balance between religious devotion and human interaction with God, and since his son Shemuel converted to Islam, there were those who suggested that the poem is a eulogy for his son. This theory is questionable because the father did not know of his son's conversion until shortly before his death, and I believe that the conversion of the son was a result of the theological struggles of the father, described in the poem.

The fact that the poem is still part of Sephardic liturgy around the world, despite the tarnished reputation of the poet as the father of a son who converted to Islam and then attacked Judaism, is a testament to the more flexible nature of the authors of Sephardic prayer books, as well as to the mesmerizing hold of the poem on the reader.

There are several tunes for that beautiful poem,[2] as well as different practices for chanting it. The following practices are all part of the diverse tapestry

---

[2] For the full text of the poem as well as for audio recordings of the different traditions, see http://old.piyut.org.il/articles/1169.html.

which is commonly referred to as Jerusalem Sephardic practice:
1. The whole poem is recited together by cantor and congregation. The cantor repeats the last stanza.
2. The cantor reads the first and last stanzas. The other stanzas are chanted by qualified members of the congregation. In most Sephardic synagogues there is no choir, but some members, vetted for their musical talent or revered status, are invited to take part in chanting. Being named to read one of these stanzas is a coveted honor, and I have personally witnessed in my first position as a cantor two men fighting over that honor.[3]
3. Only the first three and last three of the fourteen stanzas are chanted by the whole congregation, and the rest is read quietly. The cantor repeats the last stanzas.
4. The congregation and the cantor chant together the first nine stanzas in one tune. The cantor then switches to a more solemn and mournful tune and chants the tenth and eleventh stanzas solo. These are the stanzas which describe Isaac's dialogue with his

---

[3] Yefeh Nof Sephardic synagogue, Jerusalem.

father and his concern for his mother, and seeing people crying at that point is not a rare sight. The congregation then resumes with the cantor the reading of the last three stanzas, and the cantor then repeats the last stanza.

In the third stanza, the poet seems to embellish the biblical story by adding a conversation between Abraham and Sarah, probably on the night before the journey. That conversation is first imagined in the *midrash*:[4]

אמר אברהם: מה אעשה? אם אגלה לשרה, נשים דעתן קלה עליהן בדבר קטן כל שכן בדבר גדול כזה. ואם לא אגלה לה ואגנבנו ממנה בעת שלא תראה אותו תהרוג את עצמה, מה עשה ...אמר לה: "את יודעת, כשאני בן שלוש שנים הכרתי את בוראי, והנער הזה גדול ולא נחנך. יש מקום אחד רחוק ממנו מעט ששם מחנכין את הנערים, אקחנו ואחנכנו שם" אמרה לו "לך לשלום".

[When Abraham was told to sacrifice Isaac] he thought "what am I going to do? If I tell Sarah, [she will not be able to decide what to do because] women are slow to decide even when dealing with a minor issue, how much more so with such a major decision. If I do not tell her and steal the boy from her, when she will not find him she will kill herself." What did he do? ...he told her, "You know that I have come to know God when I was three years old, and this boy has already grown up and has not been educated yet

---

[4] *Midrash Tanhuma*, Warsaw edition, on Gen 22:1.

[lit. dedicated]. There is a place, not too far from here, where young boys are educated [lit. inaugurated], let me take him there." She answered, *"Go in peace."*

In the *midrashic* version, Sarah, the hidden protagonist, is revealed, but for only a brief encounter. Abraham contemplates whether he should tell his wife Sarah, the mother of the unsuspecting sacrifice, about the divine commandment, and eventually rules against it. He decides to tell Sarah that he is going to perform an act of חנכ with Isaac. This root has a double meaning of either educating the child through a rite of passage, or dedicating him to God as a sacrifice. Sarah is described in the *midrash* as unsuspecting, and she gives her curt approval.

In the poem, the author takes the conversation to a new depth by adding several words to Sarah's response. When Abraham tells her that her cherished one, Isaac, has to learn how to serve God, she answers:

לכה אדון, אבל אל תרחק
Go, master, but do not go too far.

It is as if her heart, a mother's heart, senses the ominous danger. Her plea with Abraham refers not only to physical distance, but to religious extremism as well. "When you perform the rituals in your service of God," she tells him, "do not go too far…"

Abraham answers with ambiguous words, not necessarily calming her fears:

> ענה יהי לבך באל בוטח
> *He answered: let your heart trust God.*

The answer leaves her hanging. Does he mean that Isaac will return sound and safe, as she wants? Does it mean that God will do with him as He wishes, leaving her no choice but to accept the divine verdict?

Later, as Abraham and Isaac approach the mountain alone, Isaac asks his father a seemingly innocent, but truly chilling question: "where is the sacrificial lamb?"[5] The poet rewrites this question, turning it into a piercing theological debate:

> ויקרבו שניהם לעשות במלאכה
> ויענה יצחק לאביו ככה
> אבי הנה אש ועצי מערכה
> איה אדוני שה אשר כהלכה
> האת ביום זה דתך שוכח
>
> *They both approached to do the service,*
> *When Isaac spoke to his father thus:*
> *Father, here are the fire and the wood for the altar*
> *Where, my master, is the lamb required by law?*
> *Are you, on this day, forgetting your religion?*

Whereas in the biblical story Isaac addresses his father before they reach the mountain, asking him where is the sacrificial lamb, the poet keeps Isaac silent until his engagement in the process of building the altar. In the Bible, the question is almost theoretical, but in the poem, it dawns on Isaac, as he is preparing for

---

[5] Gen 22:7.

the offering of a sacrifice, that something is terribly wrong. He addresses his father as "master" and the subliminal message of the question: "have you forgotten your religion?" is directed not at the lack of a sacrificial lamb but at Abraham's future act. Isaac is asking him: "How can you prepare yourself to offer me as a sacrifice? Wouldn't such an act violate your belief system?"

This question reflects the author's struggle with the phenomenon of voluntary martyrdom, which has become prevalent in Europe during the crusades. Not only did Jews sacrifice their lives to avoid being captured and converted to Christianity, they also took the lives of their children.

This is attested to in the *Daat Zeqenim* commentary on the Torah, anthologized from the writings of Jewish German scholars of the twelfth to thirteenth centuries:

> There was one rabbi who slaughtered many children at the time of the decrees [i.e., the Crusades] because he was worried that they will be forced to convert to Christianity. There was a rabbi there who was very upset with him and called him a murderer, but he did not pay heed. The [opposing] rabbi said, "If I am right, that rabbi will suffer a cruel and unusual death," and so it was... later the decree was nullified, and [it turned out that] had he not killed those children they would have been saved.

But the challenge to Abraham is not over yet. In the tenth and eleventh stanzas, the poet puts in Isaac's mouth a gut-wrenching farewell speech in which he forces his father to consider the consequences of the act he is about to perform. The poet skillfully weaves *midrashic* elements into a new narrative, in which Isaac reminds his father that while sacrificing his child demands one moment of devotion, it will bring in its wake a life of sorrow and contempt. In the following few lines we find a full theological treatise, one which Sephardic Jews analyzed and reflected on every Rosh Hashanah as they were preparing to blow the shofar:

שיחו לאמי כי ששונה פנה
הבן אשר ילדה לתשעים שנה
היה לאש ולמאכלת מנה
אנה אמצא לה מנחם אנה
צר לי לאם תבכה ותיפה

Tell my mother that her joy's sun has set
The son she bore after ninety years
Has been consumed by knife and fire
Where can I find consolation for her, where?
I feel for my mother, who will cry and weep.

ממאכלת יהמה מדברי
נא חדדה אבי ואת מאסרי
חזק ועת יקד יקוד בבשרי
קח עמך הנשאר מאפרי
ואמור לשרה זה ליצחק ריח

From the knife my words hum
Please sharpen it, dad, and my ropes

> *Tighten them, and as the fire consumes my flesh*
> *Take with you what is left of my ashes*
> *And tell Sarah, "This is Isaac's fragrance."*

Listening to the poetic Isaac talking to his father, we are unsure whether he has accepted the verdict and is truly preparing to die, or whether this is a last attempt to dissuade his father. Be it as it may, he addresses Abraham and an unknown audience, perhaps the witnesses of the persecutions of all generations, and asks them to inform his mother that the joy of her life has been put out. The poet expresses his disbelief that a loving God could demand such sacrifices of the Jewish people and not consider the tremendous pain caused by that demand. The poet intensifies this feeling of discord by using the word ריח—smell or fragrance—when speaking of Isaac's ashes. On one hand, the word connotes the sweet smell of a baby cuddled in his mother's lap, symbolizing the deep love and connection between the two, and on the other, it reminds the reader of the biblical concept of ריח ניחוח—the smell of burnt flesh and bones of the sacrifices, which is supposed to appease and satisfy God. Isaac reminds Abraham that upon returning to his tent he will have to reveal the truth to Sarah and then, for the rest of his life, deal with her shock, pain, and accusations. When we couple this with the third stanza, in which Abraham lies to Sarah, telling her that he is taking Isaac for a rite of passage, the full spectrum of the theological debate emerges.

The poet poses tough questions to himself and to the readers: "How do you know that your actions please God?"; "If people have to conceal their actions from their own spouses, is it not an indication that the deed is wrong?"; "Are you always aware of the full consequences of your religious actions?"; and, most importantly, "Does God want people to suffer and die for His Name's sake?"

The answers to these questions, subtly but painfully presented by the poet, suggest that God never wanted Abraham to take his son's life. He wanted him to protest and refuse. Abraham had to understand that if he has to lie to Sarah, for fear that she would not be able to handle the divine command, it means that he should not follow that command. Isaac keeps mentioning this to him, first claiming that Abraham is abandoning his religion, and then explaining to his father the life-long implications of his actions.

Abraham's dilemma is acknowledged in the ninth stanza:

הכין עצי עולה באון וחיל
ויעקוד יצחק כעקדו איל
ויהי מאור יומם בעיניו ליל
והמון דמעיו נוזלים בחיל
עין במר בוכה ולב שמח

> *[Abraham] prepared the firewood with might*
> *Then bound Isaac as one would a ram*
> *Daylight turned in his eyes into night*
> *Rivers of tears streaming from his eyes*
> *Eye bitterly crying but heart rejoicing.*

Here Isaac is already bound, in a fetal position, hands and feet tied together. Until Isaac's dialogue in the next stanza, Abraham is the only active figure. He performs his duties mechanically, as he did in the past with the many altars he erected, but this time something is different. The light of the day has turned into darkness. Is it the darkness of Abraham's eyes, the darkness of religious fanaticism, or the realization that bleak future awaits him? His heart and eyes disagree on their reaction to the whole process. The eyes, perhaps representing emotion, stream tears, while the heart, representing faith, rejoices in the fulfilment of the divine commandment.

As I have mentioned earlier, the chanting of this poem in Sephardic synagogues is awe-inspiring and almost ecstatic. The congregants identify with the dilemmas of the protagonists, Abraham and Isaac who are mentioned in the Torah, and especially Sarah who is ignored in the biblical narrative. When the cantor performs solo the two stanzas where Isaac addresses his father, many tears are shed, and when towards the end Isaac is redeemed, a sigh of relief undulates through the crowd.

The choice of this poem, from among many other liturgical pieces written about the binding of Isaac, is not coincidental and had tremendous influence on the course of Sephardic history. It is very probable, in my opinion, that Rabbi Yehudah Shemuel ibn Abbas's theological questions and his refusal to accept an image of a wrathful God who demands human sacrifices, whether from Abraham at Mount Moriah or from Jews in France and Germany during the crusades, led to the conversion of his son to Islam. However, the poem remained in the Sephardic prayer book and conveyed the message that one must take into account all factors before committing suicide in God's name.

This theological position, infused into the Sephardic psyche for centuries, was probably one of the major factors in the decision of Iberian Jews to leave Spain and Portugal, or to superficially convert, rather than remain there and become martyrs. It was a decision which was later denounced by historians and scholars as stemming from weakness, but in fact it was well informed and rooted in generations of theological debates, delivered to many by means of this poem read on Rosh Hashanah.

The reading of the poem immediately before blowing the shofar frames the experience in the context of complex relationships between God and the individual, and between that individual and other humans. It is not just the vertical line connecting heaven and earth, calling upon humans to confess and repent before God, lest they will be punished, but also the horizontal axis, reminding humans that no action is taken in a vacuum and that they have to consider the full impact of their religious and personal decisions upon others. The poem forces the readers to think of repentance not only for transgressions, but for deeds they consider acts of religious devotion. In addition, the poem elevates the congregants to a position of power, from which they can accuse God of being too cruel and demanding, and therefore ask for pardon. Indeed, the atmosphere in the synagogue between the reading of the poem and the blowing of the shofar is electrifying and emotional, making the shofar an unforgettable experience.

The Number of Sounds

In all Sephardic communities today, it is customary to sound the shofar one hundred and one times. Thirty of these sounds, or notes, are sounded before *musaf* in the format of three sets of TSRT, TST, TRT,[6] while the congregation is seated. Thirty more are sounded during the silent prayer, and another thirty

---

[6] The sounds of the Shofar will be referred to here by the traditional acronym according to which the letter T stand for *teqi'ah*, a long flat sound; S is for *shevarim*, three short bursts; and R for *teru'ah*, a vibrating sound.

during the repetition. There are different customs as to how these thirty sounds are formatted. According to one tradition, the sets are TSRT, TST, TRT, after each one of the additional Rosh Hashanah blessings. According to another tradition, mainly found in books printed in Baghdad, the order is three times TSRT after the first special blessing, three sets of TRT after the second, and three sets of TST after the third one. Ten more are added in the middle of the full *Kaddish* after the *Amidah*, in the format of TSRT, TST, TRT. Finally, at the conclusion of prayers, a long vibrating sound, known as *teru'ah gedolah*, is performed.

This practice, which is widespread today, was unknown to Sephardic communities until the 1500s, as we shall soon see. In the twentieth century, however, Rabbi Benzion Meir Hai Uziel, who was famous for his modern and liberal approach,[7] writes very emphatically against attempts to cancel some of the one hundred and one sounds of the shofar:[8]

> Regarding the cancellation of the practice to blow the shofar ten times at the end of *musaf* prayer: It is already an established practice

---

[7] Rabbi Uziel supported women's right to vote as early as 1921. On his life and theology see Marc D. Angel, *Loving Truth and Peace, the Grand Religious Worldview of Rabbi Benzion Uziel* (Northvale, NJ: Jason Aronson, 2013).

[8] Benzion Meir Hai Uziel, *Mishpete Uziel*, vol. 3 (Jerusalem: Vaad LeHotsaat Kitve Maran, 1995), 5:5.

among all Jewish communities to sound the shofar one hundred times during Rosh Hashanah. It has been supported by the verse which appears in the psalm designated for Rosh Hashanah:[9] כל העמים תקעו כף – All nations, clap hands. The word כף – hand, equals one hundred in numerical value. This is followed by the great ululation. God forbid, one should not change the practice of the Jewish people, which is regulated and transmitted by our Sages, of blessed memory. He who changes [tradition] is frowned upon by the sages.

The language Rabbi Uziel uses is emphatic, unambiguous, and even aggressive, which is atypical for him. He says that the practice is already widespread through the whole nation, he supports the practice with a biblical verse and numerical values, he adds that it is unthinkable to change the practice which originated with the sages of the Mishnah, and finally ends with a statement against those who introduce changes.

Before analyzing the sources of the practice to blow the shofar one hundred and one times, I must remark that the last statement, about changing the words of the sages, is of special interest. This is because Rabbi Uziel presents it as if it were a Mishnaic or Talmudic statement, while it is actually an amalgam of

---

[9] Psalm 47:2.

two phrases in the Talmud dealing with two completely different topics, both unrelated to shofar.[10] This clever usage of rabbinic passages, in addition to the reference to the practice as established by the sages of the Mishnah, shows that Rabbi Uziel was particularly concerned about the suggested change.

A possible explanation to his staunch opposition to this change might have to do with the two-year period in which he served as the rabbi of the community of Salonika (1921-1923), also called Jerusalem of the Balkans, which was at one point home to the largest Sephardic community in the world. Rabbi Uziel was succeeded by Rabbi Isaac Emmanuel, a graduate of the Jewish Theological Seminary in Breslau. Many of the seminary's graduates became prominent leaders of non-Orthodox Judaism, and it is possible that Rabbi Uziel, who was in close contact with Rabbi Emmanuel, was concerned that the Salonika community would follow the path of the Reform and Conservative movements. This theory could explain his unyielding approach regarding the number of times the shofar should be blown, which is

---

[10] The first half of the formula "he who changes" appears in *m. Bava Metzi'a* 6:2 and in *m. Shevu'ot* 8:6. There, it refers to one who changes the original intention of a business contract. The second half: "is not looked at favorably by the sages" appears three times in the Mishnah in a positive sense, "is looked favorably," and only once in the negative form, in *m. Bava Batra* 8:5.

incongruent with his generally flexible approach to Jewish law.[11]

As previously mentioned, the custom in the Sephardic world[12] was not always to sound the shofar one hundred and one times. In *Sheiltot* of Rav Ahai,[13] we find the following instructions:

> Before praying *musaf*,[14] the cantor should stand up while the congregation [lit. the whole world]

---

[11] On the rabbinate in Salonika in the early years of the twentieth century, see Devin E. Naar, *Jewish Salonika: Between the Ottoman Empire and Modern Greece* (Stanford: Stanford University Press, 2016), 89–137.

[12] When discussing Sephardic tradition, I include writings from the Geonic period, even though most of the activity of the Geonim took place in Babylonia. That is because the term "Sephardic" in the context of Halakhah and practice is much more than a geographic marker. It describes a theology and an ideology which have begun to take root in the Geonic era in Babylonia, were carried over to Spain, and then globally promulgated after the expulsion.

[13] Rav Ahai (680–752) was the leading scholar in the Pumbedita school of Bavel following the Talmudic period. Despite his greatness, he never held the position of Gaon, which was reserved for the head of the school. His book of *Sheiltot*, or questions, is the first systematic work of Halakhah to be written after the Talmud.

[14] The term "repetition of the *Amidah*" cannot be used here, since the *musaf* recited silently and the one recited by the cantor were not identical. The personal Amidah was written in the same formula of Shabbat and Holiday prayers, with one central blessing called קדושת היום —Sanctifying the Day, flanked by three blessings on each side. In the public recitation, led by the cantor, the prayer was performed as we know it today, with the three blessings dedicated to Rosh Hashanah in the center.

is seated, and hold the trumpet in his hand [Rav Ahai explained previously that the terms trumpet and shofar are interchangeable]. He should recite the blessings... and then blow TSRT, TST, TRT. He repeats this set three times... again when the cantor recites the *musaf* in loud voice, he blows TSRT after *Malkhuyot*, TST after *Zikhronot*, and TRT after *Shofarot*.

We learn two important things from the words of Rav Ahai:

1. The total number of sounds was forty; and
2. The shofar was not blown during the silent *Amidah*.

In *Seder Rav Amram Gaon* we find the following description:

> Where a cantor is present, they stand up for *tefilah* [i.e., *musaf*]. The individuals recite seven blessings. When the cantor recites the *tefilah*, for the first blessing they blow TSRT, for the second TST, and for the third TRT. Following the prayer they sound a long vibrating voice — *teru'ah*, without *teqi'ah* or *shevarim*.

Another *halakhic* responsum from the Geonic period provides an interesting explanation of the great *teru'ah*, which Rabbi Uziel mentions as part of an ancient tradition:[15]

---

[15] *Teshuvoth HaGeonim, Shaare Teshuvah*, Hazzan Edition, Livorno, 1869, ch. 45.

You have asked about the shofar of Rosh Hashanah [since you have heard] that the practice of the Geonim is to blow a great *teru'ah* after the prayer is over in order to confuse the Satan, and that this is the practice in both Yeshivot [Sura and Pumbedita in Babylonia]. We saw fit to answer you that we do not do this as a practice, and we have not heard that our forefathers did so, rather each individual does as he wishes. They rely on the statement of Rav Yitzhak bar Yosef:[16] "When the cantor would finish blowing the shofar in Yavneh [the spiritual center in Israel after the destruction of the Second Temple], one could not hear himself because of the many shofars which were blown. We have learned from here that in previous generations, individuals used to blow shofar after the *tefilah*. They were not obligated, because the cantor already represented them, but it is an additional measure to blow after the prayers to confuse the Satan, and if they did not do it, no harm was done. Other Geonim are of the opinion that the great *teru'ah* is mandatory.

This response indicates that there were no clear rules regarding shofar blowing after the *musaf* and that, following the last blows by the cantor, disorder would ensue, as each person would blow his shofar. Though the author mentions that some people believed that by

---

[16] b. Rosh HaShanah 30a.

doing so they would confuse Satan, the divine prosecutor, one cannot escape the feeling that the reason is much simpler, and that people wanted to take part in the *mitzvah* and blow their own shofar, as happens today in many synagogues.

From the Geonic period literature, which speaks of forty sounds during prayers and an ambiguous practice of great *teru'ah*, or great noise, after prayers, we move to the legal codex of Rabbi Yosef Karo (1488-1575), the *Shulḥan Arukh*.

In *Oraḥ Ḥayyim* 590:2, Rabbi Karo writes that because we are not sure what is the nature of *teru'ah*, we have to use different combinations, which bring the total number of shofar sounds before the *musaf* prayers to thirty. In chapter 591, which discusses the silent *musaf* prayer, Rabbi Karo does not mention a practice to blow shofar. This is reserved, according to him, to the cantor's repetition of the *musaf*. During that repetition, writes Rabbi Karo:

> The cantor repeats the prayer, and they blow the shofar following the blessings, for *Malkhuyot*[17] TSRT once, for *Zikhronot* TST, and for *Shofarot* TRT. Now the practice is to blow for

---

[17] *Malkhuyot*, *Zikhronot*, and *Shofarot* are the three special blessings added in *musaf* of Rosh Hashanah, named after their main themes, respectively: God's Sovereignty, Remembrance, and the Shofar.

Malkhuyot TSRT three times, for *Zikhronot* TST three times, and for *Shofarot* TRT three times.

Rabbi Karo presents two practices for blowing shofar during the repetition of *musaf*: One set of each of TSRT, TST, TRT, or three sets of each. These two practices would bring the total number of times the shofar is blown, together with the sounds blown before the *musaf*, either to forty or sixty, still a far cry from the one hundred and one sounds Rabbi Uziel defends so adamantly.

The question which must be asked is what has changed between the publication of the *Shulḥan Arukh*, in which ancient Geonic traditions are reflected, and the response of Rabbi Uziel in the twentieth century.

The answer, rooted in mysticism, is found in the writings of a non-Sephardic author, Rabbi Yeshayahu HaLevi Horowitz. Rabbi Horowitz, better known as the Shelah, after his book *Shene Luhot HaBerit*, was born in Poland in 1558 and migrated to the Holy Land in 1621. He came through the city of Aleppo, in Syria, and then spent some time in Jerusalem before settling in Safed. In the century before his arrival in Safed, the city had been the center of Sephardic scholarship and mystical activity. It is not a surprise, then, that the Shelah's introduction of a kabbalistic reason for blowing the shofar a hundred times, was readily accepted by the Sephardic community.

This is what Rabbi Horowitz tells us about the number of shofar sounds:

> I have found nice booklets.... Hidden until the arrival of the Arizal [R. Isaac Luria]... they establish the practice of blowing one hundred sounds: thirty sounds seated, and thirty in the silent prayer, and thirty in the repetition of the prayer by the cantor, and ten after the prayer is over.[18]

In conclusion, we see that after over a thousand years in which the Sephardic practice was to blow the shofar in only two sections of the prayer, before the silent prayer and during the repetition, the introduction of kabbalistic teachings has generated a new practice of blowing one hundred notes to which was added the traditional long *teru'ah* for a total of one hundred and one. It was a new practice, which very quickly became the main practice of Sephardic communities worldwide.

---

[18] Yeshayahu Horowitz-HaLevi, *Shene Luhot HaBerit* (Haifa: Yad Ramah, 1995), tractate *Rosh HaShanah* 68.

Each One Blowing its Own Horn
Sounding the Shofar in American Maḥzorim

Joel Gereboff

The sounding of the shofar is the most distinct element of the Rosh Hashanah liturgy. Biblical texts speak of the first day of the seventh month as a day of "sounding of horns" or "a day of remembrance through sounds of horns." Neither the specific instrument, nor the exact purpose for blowing the horns is explicit in these references. Early rabbinic texts, especially Mishnah, identify the shofar as the instrument, including the animals from which it may be produced, and begin to detail rules regarding its use in the liturgy of the day. The Babylonian Talmud and several homiletical *midrashic* documents present a number of opinions regarding the purposes for the blowing of the shofar and for whose benefit it is sounded. The most common view is that God is the primary intended audience, and when hearing the blowing of the shofar, God will arise from the throne of justice and sit upon the throne of mercy. God may also be moved to remember Isaac's dedication and willingness to serve as a sacrifice. Other sources speak of Satan, the accuser in the heavenly court, as the intended hearer, with the goal that he will be "confused" thereby. A small number of *midrashim* see human beings as those who should be moved by the shofar blowing to change their ways.[1] In the medieval era each of these notions of intended purpose and audience for the shofar blowing is elaborated upon. A particularly important development occurs through kabbalistic influences, both from the Zohar and writings of Isaac Luria and others. These texts speak of a complex set of effects upon both heavenly beings and the deity that result from the very notes of the shofar.

American Jewish liturgists from the nineteenth century onwards have drawn upon these views, and the previously formulated, more formalized liturgical

---

[1] My other essay in this volume, "The Emotional Resonance of the Shofar and the Preacher's Voice," presents a full discussion of the various views on the purposes of sounding the shofar. In commenting on the blowing of the shofar in the new Reform *mahzor, Mishkan HaNefesh,* Richard Sarason puts matters clearly: "All of this activity (the repeated shofar blasts) was clearly intended to get God's attention and to draw down God's providential favor. This surely is the primary meaning of the rite — but generations of commentators have seen less theurgic (or magical) meanings in the activity; the shofar blasts call us to accounting and repentance, reminding *us* of our duties to God and our fellow humans. Their impact is on *us* rather than on God." Richard Sarasan, "The Shofar Service: Malchiyot, Zichronot, Shofarot," *RJ.org* (April 18, 2013): http://blogs.rj.org/ blog/2013/ 04/18/the-shofar-service-malchiyot-zichronot-shofarot (accessed 12/18/16).

rites of Ashkenazim and Sephardim, and have produced many prayer books that frame in quite different ways the various soundings of the shofar over the course of the morning services. The different movements of American Judaism, or individuals identified with those groups, have published a number of *mahzorim* (prayer books specifically for holidays, including for Rosh Hashanah). In the following I analyze the diverse understandings associated with the sounding of the shofar in these liturgical texts. I focus upon Orthodox works with brief comments on those of more liberal movements. Some *mahzorim* continue to see God alone as the primary audience, while some speak of a more complex heavenly realm impacted by the performance. Other liturgies present humans as those most to be moved by hearing the shofar. Among the latter views, most accentuate a spiritual consequence, though two types of such change appear in different works. The spiritual transformation may align with more traditional understandings—people are to assess their deeds of the past year and be moved to repent and seek God's forgiveness. More recent liturgies allude to more generalized spiritual self-reflection resulting in a person's rethinking his or her relationship to others and to all that exists. By contrast, other texts emphasize human involvement in social actions as a consequence of listening to and internalizing the notes of the shofar.

Thus an examination of this portion of the liturgy for Rosh Hashanah reveals the diverse and changing religious views of American Jewish prayer books and their composers.

There has never been one Jewish prayer book. Prior to the development of the printing press, while basic liturgical rubrics followed views of Talmud and the liturgies of *Siddur Rav Amram Gaon* or *Siddur Rashi* or *Machzor Vitry*, there were a number of local variations. After the invention of the printing press, more commonly, though not uniformly shared, Ashkenazic and Sephardic liturgies emerged. But even at this point, beyond all sorts of local variations in the actual rituals, there also remained divergent prayer texts. For example, the emergence of Lurianic kabbalah in the sixteenth century resulted in a number of prayer books, Ashkenazic and Sephardic, that included prayers shaped by these mystical views. To understand American Jewish liturgical productions it is, however, possible to speak of the core elements of the shofar service and then note some commonly shared variations between earlier Ashkenazic and Sephardic prayer books.

The Talmud already calls for two distinct soundings of the shofar—the *teqi'ot meyushav*, the sounding while the congregation is seated (although today nearly all congregations actually stand at this point), which occurs after the *haftarah*, and the *teqi'ot me'umad*, the sounding while standing, which occurs after each of the central units of the *musaf* (the additional service): *Malkhiyot, Zikhronot,* and *Shofarot*. Even by the middle ages variations emerged concerning how many shofar notes are blown for each of these prayer rubrics, and we will not discuss these. With regard to the blowing of the shofar during *musaf,* the Ashkenazic and the Sephardic rites largely agree. Each section begins with an opening rabbinic prayer. A series of ten biblical verses already detailed in the Babylonian Talmud follows, and a concluding petitionary prayer ending in a specific blessing for each section concludes that unit. The shofar is then sounded, followed in both the Ashkenazic and Sephardic rites by the prayer *Hayom Harat Olam* ("This day the world was created") and in the Ashkenazic *mahzor* by *Areshet Sifatenu* ("May the utterances of our lips be pleasant before You"). Ashkenazic and Sephardic rites also share elements for the sitting shofar blowing. Both include the recitation of Psalm 47, and a unit that opens with Psalm 118:5 "From out of the straits I called unto God," which moves to seven biblical verses whose opening letters spell out the words *qera satan* (tear up Satan). The two blessings before the sounding of the shofar follow, and then the shofar is sounded in three different units consisting of different combinations of notes. The shofar service concludes with verses from Psalm 89:16–18.

The Sephardic ritual differs from the above in its inclusion of a number of other *piyyutim*, liturgical poems, and citations of biblical verses interspersed in the material preceding the blessing for sounding the shofar. The most moving of these additional elements is the *piyyut, Et Sha'arey Ratzon Lehitpateach* ("At this hour when the gates of favor will open"). Various petitionary prayers (*baqashot* or *tehinot*), some for the person who sounds the shofar, some to be recited by the congregation, have been inserted at various points into this service. Many of these are strongly kabbalistic in nature. Some European *mahzorim* included some of these prayers; others largely omitted them. As we shall see, American Orthodox *mahzorim* vary in terms of the amount and formulation of these prayers that focus the blowing of the shofar on its impact on God and on other heavenly beings.

We now turn to an analysis of these different prayer books.[2] Our comments focus upon the actual

---

[2] For general overviews of American Jewish liturgical efforts, see the essays in Sharona R. Wachs, *American Jewish Liturgies: A Bibliography of American Jewish Liturgy from the Establishment of the Press in the Colonies through 1925* (Cincinnati: Hebrew Union College Press, 1997); Lawrence A. Hoffman, "American Jewish Liturgies: A Study of Identity," *Beyond the Text: A Holistic Approach to Liturgy* (ed. Lawrence A. Hoffman; Bloomington: Indiana University Press, 1987), 60–74; Eric L. Friedland's essay "Introduction: Jewish Worship Since the Time of Its Standardization," in his book, *"Were Our Mouths Filled with Song": Studies in Liberal Jewish Liturgy* (Cincinnati: Hebrew Union

liturgical texts included in the *maḥzorim*, especially in the section for the sitting blowing of the shofar, but with some attention to changes made in the inclusion of responsive readings during the three sections of the *musaf* service. Of note will be the relationship between English translations and the original Hebrew, for at times portions of the Hebrew are left untranslated, rendered more as a paraphrase, or significantly altered. We also comment upon explanatory notes and optional prayers included in these prayer books.

Orthodox *Maḥzorim*[3]

Orthodox (traditional) *maḥzorim*[4] published in America with English translations between 1837 and the last third of the twentieth century tend to connect the blowing of the shofar with divine sovereignty over all of creation, the messianic deliverance and restoration of the people of Israel, the merit of the Patriarchs—especially Isaac's willingness to be

---

College Press, 1997), 1-16.

[3] There is very little scholarship on Orthodox liturgical products in America. Various commentators offer episodic observations on Orthodox publications in their analysis of prayer books produced by non-Orthodox writers.

[4] Lawrence Hoffman in "American Jewish Liturgies" comments on the inappropriate use of movement or denominational labels in many early American liturgical products, for it was through the interaction with alternative views that such terminology emerged.

sacrificed to God by Abraham and the contribution of these efforts—along with those of the person hearing the shofar and reciting the prayers in seeking God's forgiveness for their sins. Some prayer books invoke the early rabbinic view that it is hoped that God, when hearing the shofar, will arise from his throne of justice and sit upon that of mercy. Some *mahzorim* also speak of silencing Satan or those who may accuse Israel, though these allusions are generally left unexplained. Congregants should be moved by hearing the shofar and the recited prayers and should come to acknowledge the above and thereby see themselves as seeking and requiring divine mercy. Although the notion of repentance is mentioned explicitly only occasionally, most often through citation of Saadia Gaon's ten reasons for sounding the shofar, it is implicit in the notion of imploring God to be merciful. In most American *mahzorim* from these years, kabbalistic allusions to angels, or to the power of divine names, or to removing heavenly barriers impeding either the prayers of Israel or the notes of the shofar from reaching God, do not often appear in the Hebrew text, or if they do, they are left untranslated. Recent *mahzorim* include many of these features as well as comments on the psycho-spiritual impact of the shofar blowing.

Western Sephardic prayer books by Isaac Leeser, published in 1837, and by David de Sola Pool, published one hundred years later, and the widely used 1951 Ashkenazic *maḥzor* of Philip Birnbaum, focus the shofar blowing upon its impact on God and indirectly upon the hearers. They omit the kabbalistically oriented material. Leeser's *siddur*, *Siftey Tzadiqim* (*The Forms of Prayers According to the Custom of the Spanish and Portuguese Jews, Volume II: New-Year Service*),[5] opens the shofar service with the moving *piyyut Et Sh'arey Ratzon*, upon which he comments, "Before the blowing of the Shophar the following is sung in commemoration of the intended sacrifice of Isaac, [for] the blowing of the cornet is a time of mercy." On the centenary of the publication of Leeser's prayer book, David de Sola Pool, the rabbi of the Spanish Portuguese synagogue in New York, published his *Prayers for the New Year*, which he hoped would become the common prayer book for all Sephardic American Jews.[6] It largely adheres to

---

[5] Isaac Leeser, Siftey Tzadiqim (*The Forms of Prayers According to the Custom of the Spanish and Portuguese Jews*, Volume II: *New-Year Service*) (Philadelphia: Haswell, Barrington and Haswell, 1837). On Leeser, see Lance Sussman, *Isaac Leeser and the Making of American Judaism* (Detroit: Wayne State University Press, 1995), though Sussman says little about Leeser's liturgical productions; and Abraham Karp, "America's Pioneer Prayer Books," *Jewish Book Annual* 34 (1976-77): 15-25.

[6] David de Sola Pool, *Prayers for the New Year* (New York: Union of Sephardic Congregations, 1936). On de Sola Pool see Marc Angel, "Rabbi Dr. David de Sola Pool: Sephardic Visionary and Activist," *Ideals: Institute for Jewish Ideas and Ideals* (n.d.):

Leeser's prayer book but adds in the Preface some comments on the shofar, and in the actual service for blowing the shofar it includes a petitionary prayer that is said in some congregations by the person sounding the shofar, as well as Psalm 47. In a paragraph in the Preface de Sola Pool states, "The Call of the Shofar adds the clamant appeal to that of the human voice. The stern and weird tones of the instrument of primitive simplicity are a summons to judgment. The Shofar pleads for the merit of the patriarchs to sway the balance of judgment in favor of their children."[7] The petitionary prayer *Ribbono Shel Olam* ("Lord of the universe") also speaks of the merits of the ancestors and seeks for God to go up from his throne of judgment to the throne of mercy. It then continues with a section in which the shofar blower acknowledges his limitations, which include his lack of knowledge of the proper intention (*kavanot*) for the shofar notes: "what knowledge and understanding have I to put depths of meaning into the sounding of the shofar." Its final section asks God to have His mercy, temper His justice at the call of the shofar and to deal with us beyond the

---

https://www.jewishideas.org/article/rabbi-dr-david-de-dola-pool-sephardic-visionary-and-activist (accessed 12/18/16) and de Sola Pool's autobiographical reflection in Louis Finkelstein, ed., *Thirteen Americans: Their Spiritual Autobiographies* (New York: Institute for Religious and Social Studies, 1953), 201–17.

[7] de Sola Pool, *Prayers for the New Year*, x.

measure of our deserts. The Hebrew text seeks for God to silence the mouth of Satan so that he cannot accuse us. In the English this is translated, "Suffer no accusations to be charged against us."[8] de Sola Pool here tones down the traditional allusion to an actual heavenly accuser, and as we shall see shortly, other versions of this petitionary prayer contain additional kabbalistic references which he has omitted.

Birnbaum's *mahzor*, an effort to produce a well translated and cleanly published Ashkenazi *mahzor*, also includes a quite limited shofar service devoid of all mystical elements.[9] He includes Psalm 47 and the verses spelling out *qera satan*. In a note he indicates the acrostic spells out "cut off the accuser," but he offers no explanation of who the accuser is. In the one included *yehi ratzon*, petitionary prayer, he simply states, "May it be thy will, Lord, our God and God of our fathers, to let the sounds that come forth from our shofar ascend and plead before thy glorious throne for pardon of all of our sins. Blessed art those, O Lord of mercy." A comparison of this version of this petitionary prayer

---

[8] de Sola Pool, *Prayers for the New Year*, 224-25. This version of the prayer largely corresponds to that of the Rodelheim *Mahzor* edited in the nineteenth century by Wulf Heidenheim, though that version also adds, after the comments about not knowing the intentions for the shofar notes, words about not knowing how to combine the divine names.

[9] Philip Birnbaum, *High Holyday Prayer Book* (New York: Hebrew Publishing, 1951).

with those found in many other Ashkenazic *maḥzorim* clearly underscores the more rationalistic nature of Birnbaum's prayer book.

Traditional prayer books, both Ashkenazic and Sephardic published in Europe in the nineteenth century, are typical of works that include Lurianic kabbalistic efforts. They make evident how many American *maḥzorim* of the nineteenth and twentieth centuries have systematically omitted or left untranslated these components. The kabbalistically informed words include many references to having specifically appointed angels bring the shofar notes before God, as well as texts that speak of various divine names that also aid Israel in its quest for forgiveness. A *maḥzor* for Rosh Hashanah, according to the custom of the holy congregations in Constantinople and in Eastern and Western Lands and in Italy, printed in 1837 in Livorno, Italy, contains these sorts of elements. A petitionary *yehi ratzon* seeks that "the holy and pure divine names that come forth from the shofar shall remove the partitions that divide You from Your children." It asks that "the appointed angels for the notes bring them before Your throne and may they plead for us. May You shut up the mouth of Satan." In a petitionary *ribbono shel olam* prayer that is like the one in de Sola Pool's *maḥzor*, after noting the lack of knowledge of the shofar blower of the proper intentions for the shofar notes, it continues with comments about the lack of knowledge of "the combination of the divine names, the joining of the divine elements (*yihudim*), the joining of the higher attributes and the mitigations of strict justice that correspond to them."[10]

The frequently published Ashkenazic *Mahzor Kol Bo* from Vilna, reissued in New York in 1900, also contains many kabbalistic elements. These include references to the lack of knowledge for how to join divine names and attributes; requests that designated angels bring forward the shofar notes to vindicate the people of Israel and invoke divine mercy; invocations of various divine names alluded to in various verses; and a *yehi ratzon* seeking for specific angels to form the shofar notes into a crown for God and embroider them on the heavenly curtain, or to bring them forth to plead for goodness for Israel and for their atonement. By contrast, Birnbaum includes only the references to the notes and omits all references to angels.

Many *mahzorim* with English translations published from 1889 until the issuing of Birnbaums' *mahzor* either include references to angels but fail to translate them, or entirely omit them. These include a

---

[10] It also includes a note to the shofar blower to confess silently his sins after each shofar note, for it is a propitious moment. Anyone who is aroused to cry at this moment discloses that his soul is good and repaired, and one can thereby annul his evil inclination that leads to idolatry and the spilling of his seed (semen).

mahzor entitled *Forms of Prayers for the New Year,* published in 1889 in New York by J. Rosenbaum,[11] and an early twentieth-century *mahzor* by A. Th. Philips. The *mahzor* published by the Chief Rabbi of Britain, Herman M. Adler, which appeared in various editions in London and New York, in some editions omits the petitions after the shofar notes, or substitutes an alternative *ribbono shel olam* prayer for the Hebrew that in other versions refers to angels bringing the shofar notes and that concludes with, "Help us, O God our salvation, to subdue our stubbornness and to bend our will that it may become subservient to thee, that we may perform thy will with love.... Blessed art thou, O God of mercy."[12] The psychological terms referring to stubbornness (*orpenu*) and will (*yitzrenu*) are classic rabbinic notions; yet there appears here a more overt psychological interpretation of the purposes of blowing the shofar, even while the Hebrew speaks of angels.

Several Sephardic and Ashkenazic *mahzorim* with English translations published since the 1980s are more explicit in their references to angels and other

---

[11] This approach already appears in D. A. de Sola, *The Festival Prayers According to the Custom of German and Polish Jews* (London: Vallentine, 1860), where he leaves untranslated the *yehi ratzon* prayers following the sounding of the shofar.

[12] Arthur Davis and Herman Adler, *Service of the Synagogue: New Year* (New York: Hebrew Publishing, 1938), 127.

kabbalistic ideas, though they differ in how mystical they are, and also in terms of their more generalized spiritual messages.[13] Examples of these are the Sephardic *mahzorim* of Earl Klein and Moises Benzaquen issued in 1995, *Mahzor Ori Veyishi*,[14] Eliezer Toledano's *Mahzor Qol Yehudah*,[15] and the *ArtScroll Machzor*. Both of the Sephardic prayer books reflect eastern Sephardic practice; thus, they contain far more mystical elements along with appeals to spiritual dimensions of the human than did de Sola Pool. For example, *Ori Veyishi* cites Maimonides's notion that the shofar is meant to awaken one and to stimulate one to search one's deeds, as well as a statement by Samson Raphael Hirsch on the moral lessons of the physical form of the shofar: "The shofar must be a product of nature, not artificially made and it is given life by the breath and spirit of man. One cannot obtain to God by artificial means." In addition to a *yehi ratzon* — a meditation that seeks for the angels to lift up the shofar sounds to God's throne — and a fully translated *ribbono*

---

[13] See Gabriel A. Sivan, "Developments in the Orthodox Liturgy and New Editions of the Traditional Prayer Book," *Encyclopedia Judaica Yearbook* (1990/1991): 140–44.

[14] Earl Klein and Moises Benzaquen, *Mahzor Ori Veyishi: A Prayerbook for Rosh Hashanah According to the Oriental Sephardic Rite* (Los Angeles: Tefillah Publishing, 1995).

[15] Eliezer Toledano, *Mahzor Kol Yehudah: The Orot Sephardic Rosh Hashanah Mahzor, A New Linear Sephardic Mahzor* (Lakewood, NJ: Orot, 2013).

shel olam prayer for the shofar blower, referring to combinations of holy names, all the unifications and pairing of higher attributes, as well as to Satan, the adversary, there is an explicit *leshem yiḥud* prayer that connects the blowing of the shofar to the unification of the Holy One. All these elements are also found in the Toledano *maḥzor*, which additionally includes extensive explanatory notes, some of which identify relevant kabbalistic sources. These eastern Sephardic prayer books diverge from the far more rationalistic works by western Sephardic editors, and underscore the greater comfort with mystical aspects of Judaism in these communities.

The Ashkenazi *Complete ArtScroll Machzor: Rosh Hashanah*, first published in 1985,[16] also contains numerous explanatory notes, unapologetic references to Jewish superiority and its mission, comments highlighting the sinfulness of humans, and mystical dimensions. It opens the shofar service with two full

---

[16] Nosson Scherman and Meir Zlotowitz, *Complete ArtScroll Machzor: Rosh Hashanah* (New York: Mesorah, 1985). Jeremy Stolow, *Orthodox by Design: Judaism, Print Politics and the ArtScroll Revolution* (Berkeley: University of California Press, 2010), provides a detailed study of various aspects of the production, purchase, and use of this publisher's works. While he does speak about the general tone of the ArtScroll *siddur*, he does not comment at all on the contents of their *maḥzor*. He does include references (p. 185, n. 15) to other scholarship that has generally been critical of the scholarly merits and the ways in which these works present "Judaism."

pages of explanatory information, including a psycho-spiritual comment: "The Talmud teaches that the shofar is the instrument through which the remembrance of the Jewish people is brought before God so that He may benefit them. How is the shofar the agency for this task? The unmusical piercing blast of the shofar symbolizes the inarticulate cry from the heart of the Jew who has strayed far from God's path. It is the longing of a stained soul that begs to be cleansed but does not know how."[17] The special status of Israel is noted via a comment by Sforno on Psalm 47:3, "He shall lead nations under us and kingdoms beneath our feet." Sforno observes, "God will lead the nations from the ends of the earth to Jerusalem, to bring them under Israel's rule. This will be for the benefit of the nations themselves, for they will then be guided by Israel in sincere, intelligent service of God."[18] More liberal *mahzorim* omit comments about Jewish superiority. The mystical elements are similar to those in the other *mahzorim*, though its *yehi ratzon* prayer for the shofar blower includes the line asking God, "May You be filled with mercy upon your people and may you contemplate the ashes of Isaac, our forefather, that are heaped upon the Altar." It also offers several explanations of the idea of impeding Satan, defining

---

[17] Scherman and Zlotowitz, *ArtScroll Machzor*, 430.
[18] Scherman and Zlotowitz, *ArtScroll Machzor*, 432.

Satan as anything that impedes or hinders progress, including our internal evil inclination. Several additional notes expand these comments to refer to the deep spiritual and psychological meaning of the shofar. For example, the authors cite a remark by Shem MiShmuel that explains the symbolic meaning of the fragmented *teru'ah* note. That note

> represents a broken heart. But there are two causes for a broken heart. A person may fall into a state of depression, look at the world through lenses of hopelessness and be heartbroken as a result. This is not the broken heart sought by God. Praises are befitting the heart which is broken through one's intelligent realization of his worthlessness in comparison with the Creator. A broken, contrite heart, humbled not by melancholia but by knowledge of God and His ways, is the allusion of the *teru'ah*. Thus the verse reads, who know the *teru'ah*.[19]

Koren Publishers has put out a number of works meant to offer a modern Orthodox alternative to the Haredi works of ArtScroll. Jonathan Sacks's *The Koren Rosh Hashana Maḥzor* of 2011 includes some passages referring to angels while omitting more complex kabbalistic ideas.[20] For example, the *ribbon*

---

[19] Scherman and Zlotowitz, *ArtScroll Machzor*, 439.
[20] Jonathan Sacks, *The Koren Rosh Hashana Maḥzor*

olamim petitionary prayer for the shofar blower refers only to that person's lack of knowledge of "the correct intentions with the right holy names," but does not speak of various *yeḥudim,* unifications.[21] The *yehi ratzon* passages that follow each sounding of the shofar contain references to specific angels and their missions. These are translated, but no explanatory notes are provided. While Sacks underscores that the shofar is connected to divine judgment, the tone of his commentary is positive and speaks at times to a richer spirituality. For example, he comments on the natural state of the shofar and connects this to core Jewish values. He notes that although the Torah stipulates the blowing of both a shofar and the two metal trumpets on Rosh Hashanah, only the shofar has survived.

> In Jewish history, the simple has tended to prevail over the sophisticated, for God seeks the unadorned heart. The shofar is the wordless cry at the heart of a religion of words. Judaism is a profoundly verbal culture. Yet there is a time for emotions that lie too deep for words. The sound of the shofar breaks through the carapace of the self-justifying mind and touches us directly at the most primal level of our being.[22]

(Jerusalem: Koren, 2011).

[21] Sacks, *The Koren Rosh Hashana Mahzor*, 492.

[22] Sacks, *The Koren Rosh Hashana Mahzor*, 498. A similar

With Sacks we return to the earlier trends to minimize, but not eliminate entirely, some of the kabbalistic elements. Unlike the editors of some earlier Orthodox *maḥzorim*, Sacks also provides accurate translations of all allusions to angels. While Sacks still largely highlights the relationship between God and the human, and the need for human self-transformation, he also speaks of additional psycho-spiritual meanings of the ritual.

Reform, Reconstructionist, and Conservative *Maḥzorim* and Conclusions

All three liberal theistic movements of American Judaism have produced a large number of liturgical works, including texts for Rosh Hashanah.[23] The texts of each movement have changed over the years from the mid-1850s, when the earliest Reform *siddurim* came forward, until today. None include any of the kabbalistic elements, though some Conservative movement works do contain *yehi ratzon*, petitionary prayers that refer to the impact upon God. And while

---

comment appears on p. 606 via a citation of Moshe Amiel on the significance of the sequence of the shofar notes, which connects them to the stages of a human life.

[23] A fourth denomination, Humanistic Judaism, does not adhere to the traditional patterns of Jewish liturgy, and thus does not depend on a conventionally structured *maḥzor* for its commemoration of the High Holidays. The shofar is nevertheless central to Humanistic Jewish observances of those holidays.

most of these prayer books speak in some way of such an impact upon the deity, the overall emphasis is upon the intended changes in human consciousness and behavior. The titles and the layouts of the most recent *maḥzorim* of each of the movements, the Reconstructionist *Kol Haneshamah*,[24] the Reform *Mishkan Hanefesh*,[25] and the Conservative *Lev*

---

[24] David Teutsch, ed., *Kol Haneshamah: Prayerbook for the Days of Awe* (Elkins Park, PA: Reconstructionist Press, 1999). Eric Caplan, *From Ideology to Liturgy: Reconstructionist Worship and American Liberal Judaism* (Cincinnati: Hebrew Union College Press, 2002) is a detailed study of Reconstructionist liturgical efforts, with a few comments on their maḥzorim. Additional comments on Reconstructionist prayer books include Eric Friedland, "The Synagogue and Liturgical Developments," *Movements and Issues in American Judaism* (ed. Bernard Martin; Westport, CT: Greenwood Press, 1978), 217–29; and Arthur Green, "Reconstructionist Liturgy," *Encyclopedia Judaica Yearbook* (1990–91): 155–57.

[25] Edwin Goldberg, Janet Marder, Sheldon Marder, and Leon Morris, eds., *Mishkan HaNefesh: Machzor for the Days of Awe* (New York: CCAR Press, 2015). On reform of prayer books in Europe see, Jacob Petuchowski, *Prayerbook Reform in Europe* (New York: World Union of Progressive Judaism, 1968). On American Reform liturgy see the many essays of Eric Friedland, especially, *Were Our Mouths Filled with Song*, and "Historical Notes on American Reform High Holy Day Liturgy," *JRJ* 35 (1988): 57–74; Lawrence A. Hoffman, *Beyond the Text: A Holistic Approach to Liturgy* (Bloomington: Indiana University Press, 1987); and "The Language of Survival in American Reform Liturgy," *CCAR Journal* 24 (1977): 87–106; Michal Galas, *Rabbi Marcus Jastrow and His Vision for the Reform of Judaism* (Boston: Academic Studies Press, 2013); Lou H. Silberman, "The Union Prayer Book: A Study in Liturgical Development," *Retrospect and Prospect: Essays in Commemoration of the Seventy-Fifth Anniversary of the Founding of the Central Conference*

Shalem,[26] which refer to parts of the interior person, the soul, and the heart, make clear that the primary purpose for sounding the shofar is to transform the psycho-spiritual sense of each individual. Each work also consists of multiple parts: Hebrew text, translation, alternative prayers, and explanatory comments of various types, including spiritual-meditative ones. Collectively, these personal transformations may lead to actions oriented toward human betterment and social improvement. But these recent works offer tempered versions of such desired outcomes—the messianic age of world peace and justice, while announced by the shofar, is long in the

---

of American Rabbis 1889-1964 (ed. Bertram Wallace Korn; New York: Central Conference of American Rabbis, 1965), 46–80; Ruth Langer, "Continuity, Change and Retrieval: The New Reform *Siddur*," *Journal of Synagogue Music* 34 (2009): 208–23.

[26] Edward Feld, ed., *Mahzor Lev Shalem for Rosh Hashanah and Yom Kippur* (New York: The Rabbinical Assembly, 2012). Ruth Langer provides a review of the *mahzor* in *The Journal of Synagogue Music* 37 (2012): 205–13. Essays by different scholars in Robert E. Fierstein ed., *A Century of Commitment: One Hundred Years of the Rabbinical Assembly* (New York: The Rabbinical Assembly, 2000) contain information on the full range of liturgical efforts of the Conservative movement. Though criticized for its extreme sociological framework and an overemphasis on the role of the laity, Marshall Sklare's *Conservative Judaism: An American Religious Movement* (Glencoe, IL: Free Press, 1955), and reissued in an augmented edition (New York: Schocken, 1972), provides important insights regarding the interplay between the congregants' religious preferences and those of rabbinic leadership, including their manifestations in liturgical matters.

distance. The grandiose visions of such works as David Einhorn's *Olat Tamid*,[27] with its definition of Israel as a priestly people with a willingness to endure suffering to contribute to the realization of Israel's messianic destiny, or Mordecai Kaplan's seeking that "the sounds of the shofar arouse in us the determination to remove all oppression and to bring justice to all mankind,"[28] or Morris Silverman's imploring the congregation to "give heed to the sound of the Shofar, the sharp, piercing blasts of the Shofar. Rending the air with its message, its portent of heave'nly salvation, summoning man to his Father.... Infuse in your hearts a new spirit to build a new earth, a new heaven, urging us to work with our brothers to combat the ills that best man. Accept ye the challenge to triumph o'er forces of wrath and destruction and destruction, remove from your midst crime and warfare, all poverty, greed and contention,"[29] are no longer found with such optimistic conviction in these works. Rather, the more recent

---

[27] David Einhorn, *Olat Tamid* (New York: M. Thalmessinger, 1872).

[28] Mordecai Kaplan, Eugene Kohn, and Ira Eisenstein, eds., *High Holyday Prayer Book* (New York: Jewish Reconstructionist Foundation, 1948), 218.

[29] Morris Silverman, *High Holyday Prayer Book* (Hartford: Prayer Book Press, 1939), 119-20. Though not officially authorized by the Conservative movement, this work was used in many Conservative Congregations prior to the publication of the Harlow *Maḥzor* in 1972.

works call for personal self-reflection and intense hearing of the sounds of the shofar in the context of community. For example, *Mishkan Hanefesh* observes that one must hear the actual sounds of the shofar, not via an echo, for "the *mitzvah* requires immediacy, sound passing directly from the instrument to the ear. To hear the message of the shofar, we need to be fully present and focused. The shofar cannot penetrate an indifferent ear, or a closed mind or heart."[30] Similarly, *Kol Haneshamah* remarks, "The shofar with its narrow end through which we blow and the wide end from which the sound emerges symbolizes the process of spiritual liberation through divine inspiration." And in commenting on the prayer *Hayom Harat Olam*, it observes,

> Our ancestors did not say, 'the anniversary of the world's birth,' but literally, 'Today the world was conceived.' This means that we can connect in this moment to the precise energy present at creation. This awareness can lead us to identify with a reality that is not bounded by time.[31]

And finally, *Lev Shalem*, for example, explains the verses spelling out *qera satan* as focused on "our evil impulses, the variety of forces at work within us that impede us from personal self-transformation, and

---

[30] Goldberg, et al., *Mishkan HaNefesh*, 114.
[31] Teutsch, *Kol Haneshamah*, 589–90, 633.

instead to choose those that accord to the calling of our souls."[32] For its concluding remark on the shofar, after the blessing at the end of the *Shofarot* section, it cites the Hasidic master, Ze'ev Wolf of Zhitomir, who taught,

> On Rosh Hashanah the world is re-created, and so all of God's names are once again drawn into a single unity. On this Day of Judgment it is decided which name of God will descend on each individual this year. Listening to the shofar, we can each discover which name will descend upon us.[33]

All three movements still seek to situate the individual within a Jewish community and more broadly with a vision of a larger universal world in need of transformation. But the shofar is designed first and foremost to penetrate "The Jew Within," and by altering their psycho-spiritual sense of self, by situating the individual in relation to whatever understanding of the divine that uniquely speaks to that individual, to reorient their sense of their place in the world and to provide them with a sense of hope and responsibility for the coming year.

The haunting sounds of the shofar have the potential to occasion immense emotional responses. But the prayers, and over time the memories that individuals and communities bring to their hearing of

---

[32] Feld, *Lev Shalem*, 120.
[33] Feld, *Lev Shalem*, 166.

these sounds, ultimately shape their messages, meanings, and impact. Although the exact number of notes sounded varies, the same basic sounds have remained the same. These notes, the *teqi'ah, shevarim,* and *teru'ah,* combined with the compositions of diverse liturgists continue to call out and bring together individuals and communities and to move them to reflect upon the meanings and purposes of their lives in relationship to forces within and beyond themselves, within the collectivity of human beings, and within and beyond the universe.

Ancient Symbols, Modern Meanings

The Use of the Shofar in Twentieth- and Twenty-First-Century Music

Malcolm Miller

The shofar is known as one of the earliest biblical instruments still in regular use, performed annually in the ritual of the Jewish New Year, Rosh Hashanah. An aspect of the shofar that is less well known is its use within art musics, serious and popular, from the beginning of the twentieth century, and particularly from the 1980s to the present day. The largely unfamiliar, and growing, repertoire for shofar includes both those works which either make use of the instrument itself, and those which reference it through incorporation of its traditional calls or symbolic and sonorous characteristics. It is striking that the use of the shofar itself has increased in the last three decades, both as an addition to acoustic ensembles or extended through electronic manipulation.[1] At one level it

---

[1] Since my article "The Shofar and its Symbolism," *Historic Brass Society Journal* 14 (2002): 83–113, shofar repertoire and scholarly interest has expanded. The current chapter includes much new material as well as new light on the growing repertoire. The

reflects the postmodern interest in symbiotic fusion of traditions, world musics, and the balancing of regional and international music styles. The shofar takes its place alongside "non-western" and "natural" instruments, such as Middle Eastern oud and ney, Scottish fiddle and bagpipes, Chinese sheng and Iranian kamancheh, conch shells and Tibetan bowls. At the same time, the creation of innovative soundscapes with cutting-edge computer technologies transforms and extends the shofar's timbres and techniques. In all these contexts and novel techniques, it is the intersection of contemporary and richly historical symbolism that gives the instrument its unique character.

The shofar's functions were originally military and ceremonial, yet from the earliest sources its significance lay beyond the merely functional; rather it was a musical one, capable of evoking memory, *zikhron*, on the New Year particularly, and thus to

---

Appendix to this essay considerably expands the list given in the 2002 article. The only major scholarly study since is Kees van Hage's fascinating dissertation, "A Tool of Remembrance: The Shofar in Modern Music, Literature, and Art" (PhD diss., University of Amsterdam, 2014), which explores the shofar's significance in modernist music, visual arts, and literature. Much important information appears on the website www.hearingshofar.blogspot.com, edited by Michael T. Chusid, whose own three-volume ebook *Shofar: The Still Small Voice of the Ram's Horn* (2009) includes a wealth of information.

generate aesthetic experience and response. The shofar's varied symbolism, expressed in biblical texts, includes supernatural power, joy, freedom, victory, deliverance, national identity, moral virtue, repentance, and social justice. Since then, its symbolism has expanded to address new contexts: in the twentieth and twenty-first centuries, in addition to religious rites, the shofar has retained its public ceremonial and communal function in the installation of a new President of Israel, for Holocaust-related memorials, and on military occasions. Beyond the conventions of the shofar in a ceremonial and religious context, the instrument has appealed to twentieth- and twenty-first-century composers as a powerful symbol through which to respond to recent Jewish and world history: the Holocaust, the rise of the Israeli nation-state, and current issues of global politics. As we shall see, their works recall symbols of the past whilst also reinterpreting the broader ancient connotations of prophetic utopianism to highlight resonances in contemporary moral issues, such as multiculturalism, peaceful coexistence, and ecological responsibility.[2]

---

[2] The Old Testament "laid a foundation affecting the understanding of this symbolism all the way to the present." See Joachim Braun, *Music in Ancient Israel/Palestine: Archaeological, Writ ten, and Comparative Sources* (tr. Douglass W. Stott; Grand Rapids, MI: Eerdmans, 2002), 10.

Alongside programmatic and symbolic associations a central issue is musical: the extent to which the shofar, and its evocation or imitations, is integrated into musical structure.

The Dawn of the Twentieth Century
Elgar and the Shofar

The earliest use of the shofar in a major concert work is in Elgar's *The Apostles*, completed in 1903, in the "Dawn Scene" that follows the "Prologue."[3] Earlier works had made reference to shofar calls, as in Handel's *Saul* (1738),[4] where according to Ruth Smith, trombones are used to evoke shofar calls in the symphony for Saul at the Feast for the New Moon (Act 2, sc. 9), and strings imitate the *teqi'ah* with an eighteenth-century stylization. 1873 saw the composition of George Macfarren's oratorio *St John the Baptist*, which is framed by trumpet imitations of *teqi'ah* calls in the overture and final chorus.[5] Macfarren

---

[3] *The Apostles*, of which the "Prologue" and "Dawn Scene" were begun in 1901, was the first part of a triptych left unfinished; the second part, *The Kingdom*, completed in 1906, was to have been followed by a third part called *The Last Judgement, The Saints*, or *The Fulfilment*, also to have featured shofar. My discussion refers to rehearsal numbers in the full score of *The Apostles*, Op. 49, *Elgar Complete Edition, Series I: Choral Works* (vol. 8; London: Novello, 1983).

[4] Ruth Smith, "Early Music's Dramatic Significance in Handel's 'Saul,'" *Early Music* 35.2 (2007): 173–89.

[5] George Macfarren, *St John the Baptist*, vocal score, text by

stylizes the *teqi'ah* into a fourth fanfare, mostly used in groups of three which, whilst similar to the *shevarim*, are more likely to be associated with Christian symbolism for the Trinity.[6] Elgar was probably familiar with Macfarren's oratorio, since it was very popular and performed regularly until the 1890s, yet Elgar displays a more modern approach to authenticity, coupled with a desire for exoticism. The "Dawn Scene" introduces the shofar with two sequences of the three calls, *teqi'ah*, *shevarim*, and *teru'ah*, all precisely notated in "authentic" rhythms (rehearsal nos. 26, 34–35). The sonority of the shofar provides a sense of otherness and exoticism, whilst the accuracy gives a degree of realism. For instance, the *teru'ah* is notated as three groups of four sixteenth notes; modern sources like the *New Grove Dictionary of Music and Musicians*[7] give a pattern of nine divided into groups of three, which corresponds with the traditional requirement mentioned in the Mishna, but the 1906 edition of the *Jewish Encyclopedia*, co-authored by Elgar's consultant

---

E. G. Monk (London, Stanley Lucas, Weber & Co.). Charles Halle, its dedicatee, conducted the premiere on Oct. 23, 1873.

[6] The *teqi'ah* motif reappears in the subdominant (C – F), and in the final bars each of the three *teqi'ah* motifs are interspersed with orchestral chords. The rising fourth is integrated as a motivic element varied in the general texture.

[7] Stanley Sadie, ed., *New Grove Dictionary of Music and Musicians* (2nd ed.; London: Macmillan, 2001).

for Jewish sources, Rev Francis Cohen,[8] gives the pattern of twelve. Elgar departs from the sources in one important element: his interpretation of the *teqi'ah* as a rising major sixth, E♭1 to C2, differing from most sources, which give a rising perfect fifth. It is likely that this adaptation was artistically inspired, as it is well known that the earliest sketches for the oratorio contained a theme featuring a rising sixth, with symbolic connotations. A *teqi'ah* of a rising sixth, however, is plausible, since each individual shofar varies in pitch and intervals produced, according to its length and width of bore, and in my experience that interval is eminently playable.[9]

An important aspect of Elgar's treatment of the shofar, as well as his use of an "Ancient Hebrew Chant" for the setting of the Morning Psalm (Ps 132) (rehearsal nos. 28–32), is that of alterity. As defined by Lawrence Kramer, alterity is a process of "othering" which both alienates the other and also expresses an attraction to the other.[10] Thus Elgar's dramatic interest in the New Testament story focuses on the individual

---

[8] The article "Shofar," by Francis L. Cohen, Cyrus Adler, Abraham de Harkavy, and Judah David Eisenstein, appeared in the 12-volume *Jewish Encyclopedia* (1901–06).

[9] I performed on a resonant E♭ – C kudu shofar with the Winchester Choral Society in Winchester Cathedral in June 2006.

[10] Lawrence Kramer, *Classical Music and Postmodern Knowledge* (Berkeley: University of California Press, 1995), 33–66.

characters of Peter, Mary Magdalene, and Judas, and assigns them some of the richest Wagner-influenced chromatic textures and most colorful orchestration, influenced by his visit in 1902 to the Bayreuth *Parsifal* and *The Ring*.

By contrast, Elgar sets the "Ancient Hebrew Chant" apart, creating a stylistic dislocation through the simple, stolid nineteenth-century harmony, drawn from a contemporary arrangement.[11] At the same time, the F-minor/C-minor tonality relates to the A♭ major of the more chromatic sections into which it is embedded. According to Kramer's logic of alterity, Elgar has depicted the Jews as simple and earthbound in contrast to the higher inspiration of the Apostles. Yet the combined realism and exoticism of the shofar and the colorful percussion and rhythms of the "Ancient Hebrew Chant," set against its bare simplicity, provide realism and exoticism which is alluring, and brings the listener close into the drama.

The shofar's symbolism derives from the Old and New Testaments, as seen in its presentation both as a solo and integrated as a *leitmotif*, with multiple

---

[11] The prefatory "Note by the Composer" to the full score of Elgar's *The Apostles* reads, "The ancient Hebrew melody (Ps. xcii) commencing on page 30 is quoted, by kind permission of the publishers, Messrs Augener & Co., from the volume edited by Ernst Pauer, whose broad and appropriate harmony is retained in a few bars..."

harmonizations and transformations.[12] Thus it both recalls Jewish ceremonial/ritual functions to depict the rising dawn, and extends prophetic symbolism to the Christian imagery of messianic redemption. In many ways Elgar's innovative use of the shofar set the precedent for contemporary uses by later composers: the idea of a tuned shofar, with fixed pitches embedded in harmony, its motives integrated into a larger narrative drama.

One of the most striking instances is *Seven Angels* (2014) by the notable Scottish composer James MacMillan, who was inspired to fulfill Elgar's unrealized vision of *The Last Judgement* with a cantata setting texts from the Book of Revelation.[13] Ingeniously scored for two shofars alternating with two natural trumpets, the texts are illustrated at three main structural passages with traditional shofar calls, extensively transformed and adapted rhythmically and texturally, dovetailed with sustained choral humming on the contrasting pitches of each shofar,

---

[12] A fuller analysis appears in my article, "The Shofar and its Symbolism." The main notes are harmonized within A♭, F minor, C minor and E♭ chords at different points. The orchestra appropriates the motif and extends it in various ways.

[13] MacMillan's *Seven Angels* was premiered on January 31, 2015, in Birmingham Town Hall, where both *The Apostles* and *The Kingdom* had received their premieres. See John Quinn's review at http://seenandheard-international.com/2015/02/ex-cathedra-thrillingly-unveil-james-macmillans-visionary-new-work/.

and set in imitative counterpoint for both shofars, or for shofar and trumpet in duet. As if to reinforce the connection with Elgar, MacMillan uses the archaic twelve semiquaver pattern for the *teru'ah* rather than the modern nine triplet pattern, developing the pattern in new ways. Moreover, MacMillan uses the modern rising fifth for a *teqi'ah*, yet adds a lower appoggiatura (notated B - C - G), thus evoking Elgar's rising sixth.

Whist drawing on ancient symbols, these new musical contexts provide new musical meanings. The only caveat is that in Elgar's time, the work was seldom, if at all, performed on shofar; rather the optional "straight trumpet" was used. Shofars feature in more recent recordings and performances, thus pointing toward an aesthetic shift in performance practice.[14]

Instrumental Evocations of the Shofar's Calls and Symbolism

A different kind of structural integration of the shofar is that which quotes the shofar calls, rather than the instrument itself, then develops those in structural ways. A pianistic example is the repeated note motif with the remarkable and unusual expression mark *squillante – quasi shofar* in the piano suite *Le danze del Re*

---

[14] A real shofar is used in the recording conducted by Mark Elder, Hallé Records CDHLD 7534, CD, 2013.

David, Op. 37 (1925), subtitled *Hebrew Rhapsody on Traditional Themes* by the Italian-Jewish composer Mario Castelnuovo-Tedesco (1895–1968).[15] If at one level the motif resembles the coloristic repeated-note guitar effects of the Spanish school, Albeniz and Granados, it also evokes the shofar's swoop in its falling arpeggios, and repeated notes suggest the *teru'ah*. The allusion relates closely to King David's dance before the Ark (described in 1 Chron 15:28), where the shofar is a symbol of joy, praise, splendor, and royalty. The work symbolized the composer's rediscovery of his Jewish identity, as shown by the dedication to the memory of his maternal grandfather, whose collection of prayer melodies Castelnuovo-Tedesco discovered in 1924, and reused later in his *Six Preludes for Organ on a Theme of Bruto Senigaglia* (Prayers of My Grandfather) (1962).

King David's son Solomon is the topic of Ernest Bloch's *Schelomo*, a rhapsody for cello and orchestra (1915–16), one of several of Bloch's works to feature

---

[15] See Harriette M. Rosen, "The Influence of Judaic Liturgical Music in Selected Secular Works of Mario Castelnuovo-Tedesco and Darius Milhaud" (PhD diss., University of California, San Diego, 1991). The piece, one of three characteristic suites (one Viennese, one Italian, and one Jewish), was praised for its "brilliant pianistic writing" by Guido Maggiorino Gatti, "Some Italian Composers of Today, I: Castelnuovo-Tedesco," *Musical Times* 62 (1921): 403–05.

shofar motifs. The second subject highlights a distinctive leap of a fourth and repeated-note motif, introduced by woodwind, and only later repeated by the solo cello. The theme is extensively developed throughout the texture for the main part of the central section, the incisive connotations of "alarm" of the *teru'ah* now imbued with a new expressive musical quality that evokes the prophetic idea of the transformation of swords into ploughshares.

Echoes of *Schelomo* may be found in the Cello Concerto (1992-94) by the British composer Ronald Stevenson (1928-2015),[16] dedicated to the memory of Jacqueline du Pre. At the start of the scherzo movement, the brass present shofar calls, whilst the slower Trio is a setting of the *Kol Nidrei* melody; finally, an Israeli pioneer folksong is quoted in the next movement. The references to Judaism portray an aspect of du Pre and her conversion upon her marriage to Daniel Barenboim.

A different type of variant of *teru'ah*, which retains both the original ferocity and its prophetic connotations of a challenge to the conscience, occurs in "*Din Torah*," the central movement of Leonard Bernstein's Symphony no. 3 (1963), subtitled "*Kaddish*," dedicated to the memory of President John F. Kennedy.

---

[16] Martin Anderson, "Ronald Stevenson's Cello Concerto," *Tempo* 196 (1996): 47–49.

The percussion motif is stated three times, imitated by woodwinds, with the allusion to the shofar immediately reinforced by saxophone doubling sustained choral lines. Even more striking shofar allusions are heard in two of Bernstein's most popular works. The overture to *Candide* (1956) begins with a rising brass fanfare highly suggestive of a *teqi'ah*, integrated and developed motivically. A fully orchestral *teqi'ah* occurs in the opening of *West Side Story* (1957), a conscious musical reference that is consonant with the original Jewish, rather than Puerto Rican, setting of *West Side Story*.[17]

In the introduction to the third movement of Lukas Foss's biblically-inspired work for mezzo-soprano and orchestra, *Song of Songs* (1947), shofar motifs in the woodwinds combine with more "biblical" orientalisms that contribute to a mood of Near-Eastern, archaic grandeur.

Chamber works that explore the shofar's sounds and gestures include Robert Fleisher's *Meditations* for soprano saxophone and trumpet in B♭ (1988), composed following a residency in Jerusalem.[18]

---

[17] Bernstein's allusions are the topic of articles and broadcasts by Raphael Mostel, whose works for shofar are discussed here.

[18] The piece was commissioned by the Ruttenberg Arts Foundation and the Graduate School of Northern Illinois University, inspired by a residency at the Mishkenot Sha'ananim

The duo structure symbolizes the cultural, political, and historical conflicts in the region; according to Fleisher's Preface, "The instruments... ancient and modern are evoked in the trumpet—with its Biblical connotations and the saxophone as... shofar." There are several overt references to shofar sounds: the swooping glissandi at the outset of the second piece, and *teru'ah*-like repeated-note gestures. Emmanuel Rubin's song "O die Schornsteine" ("O the Chimneys," 1955), a setting for voice and viola of a moving poem about the Holocaust by Nelly Sachs, evokes the shofar's sound and traditional call, heard in the viola's initial motif, which gives rise to much of the melodic material throughout. The Prelude to *Let the Trumpet Sound* (2013) by Samuel Adler opens with a trumpet call based on the *teqi'ah* and *shevarim*, modified to integrate into the texture. Yehezkel Braun's (1922–2014) choral *Festive Horns*, and *Teru'ah haMelech* for clarinet and orchestra by the Hungarian-Israeli André Hajdu (1932–2016), also allude to the shofar's musical role, drawing on texts and developing musical evocations of the shofar, whilst a freer meditation on the concepts associated with the shofar forms the topic of Robert Stern's oratorio *Shofar* (2006, rev. 2009) in four parts for soprano, tenor, and two bass-baritone soloists,

---

Center for Visiting Artists in Jerusalem in 1986.

chorus and orchestra, with a libretto by Catherine Madsen.

All the examples here, and many more which allude to and quote shofar motives (some listed in the Appendix), range across an emotional continuum from anguish to joy, yet all attest to continued interest in reinterpreting the shofar's ancient symbolism.

Shofar as Symbol of False Prophecy

Further examples of the quotational and integrative approach are two major stage works by the British-Jewish composer Alexander Goehr (b. 1932): *Sonata about Jerusalem*, Op. 31 (1971), and the opera *Behold the Sun* (1984). In each, the shofar as a symbol of false prophecy in medieval times acts as an allegory for contemporary social critique. *Sonata about Jerusalem*, the final music theatre piece in *Triptych*, was composed for the 1971 "Testimonium," organized by Recha Freier in Jerusalem.[19] The libretto, derived from texts by Obadiah the Proselyte and the twelfth-century Samuel ben Yahya ben al Maghribi, adapted by Recha Freier and the composer, concerns the persecuted Jews of

---

[19] "Testimonium" was organised by the writer Recha Freier in Jerusalem in 1968, 1971, and 1974, with international composers commissioned for new works on texts from Jewish, Christian, and Muslim histories of the city of Jerusalem. The 1971 theme was "The Middle Ages"; see Peter Gradenwitz, *The Music of Israel: From the Biblical Era to Modern Times* (Portland, OR: Amadeus, 1996), 399–402.

Baghdad and their belief in a false messiah, Schlomo ben Dugi, who claims they can fly to safety in Jerusalem. Five of the twelve sections are chant-like choral refrains sung in Latin: "the dust will turn to darkness and the moon to blood before the terrible coming of the Lord," each concluding with a striking *teqi'ah*, the trumpet's fourfold rising perfect fifth (C2 – G2), and the clarinet's minor sixth (C2 – A♭2), set dissonantly against the main texture to penetrating effect. In more expressionistic sections, shofar motives are integrated and transformed like leitmotifs to convey evolving action. These are assigned to trumpets and brass generally, echoed in woodwinds, and occasionally in strings and voices.

The sophistication of the structural integration is evinced in Section 5, "A crazed young boy brings news to the Jews of Bagdad of the False Messiah, Schlomo ben Dugi," with the "false prophet" conveyed through distorted, ironic shofar calls. The trumpet's rising *teqi'ah*, D1 – G1, G♯1 – E♯2 – F♯2, is followed by a powerful *teru'ah* marked *accelerando*, both repeated and extended. In between is an ironic *teqi'ah* in piccolo (C♯3 – A3) and clarinet. The trumpet's gestures are then imitated by the "crazed boy" in the angular soprano part (m. 7ff),[20] and the *teru'ah* imitated in syllabic

---

[20] My discussion refers to the measure numbers within each numbered section in the full score of Alexander Goehr's *Sonata*

repetition: "Je-ru – sa-sa-sa-sa-sa – lem" (m. 23), the *teru'ah* taken up in section 6, "The Rejoicing of the Jews," by the laughing chorus's "ha-ha-ha-ha" textures echoed by the ensemble (flute, clarinet, trumpet), with descending distortions of the earlier *teqi'ah*. The vivid characterization thus offers a fascinating instance of prophetic shofar symbolism, that of the false prophet as well as messianic redemption.[21]

The challenge of a false messiah to the people's faith also forms the theme of Goehr's opera *Behold the Sun*,[22] which alludes to the shofar's symbolism and uses the sonority of a bass trumpet to symbolize prophecy, derived from the Lutheran translation of biblical horns as *"posaune."* The trombone allusion invites comparison with Schoenberg's *Moses und Aron* in which the "Dance Round the Golden Calf" uses trombone and other low-brass textures. Yet the *posaune* idea is more explicit in *Behold the Sun*, based on historical events in the city of Munster in Germany during the reign of the Anabaptists under their spiritual leader, Melchior Hoffman. The medieval power has contemporary resonances as a critique of

---

about Jerusalem (London: Schott, 1976).

[21] A fuller analysis the work appears in my 2002 article, "The Shofar and its Symbolism," *Historic Brass Society Journal* 14 (2002): 83–113.

[22] Alexander Goehr, *Behold the Sun*, libretto by John McGrath and the composer (London: Schott, 1985).

religious fundamentalism. Messianic shofar symbolism colors the bass trumpet, played on stage in Act III, scene 1, "Entry of a Limping Prophet." Yet what is particularly significant is the irony of trombone and brass motifs distorted to the point of ridicule to characterize the Limping Prophet as false. Further references include rising horn fanfares and penetrating falling seconds in the trumpets in the "Trump of the Lord," and later a fanfare, three rising perfect fifths, in the orchestra and then in trombones. Within the post-serial modernist idiom, the allusions to the shofar thus provide potent expression of prophetic symbolism that reaches into biblical sources.[23]

The Shofar in Contemporary Opera

Two recent operas make vivid use of the shofar itself in un-tuned, ensemble contexts. The first is Shulamit Ran's *Between Two Worlds* (*The Dybbuk*), composed in 1997. In an interview with the composer I asked about her motivation for including shofar.[24] Ran commented on her use in the famous exorcism scene,

---

[23] Goehr's oratorio *Death of Moses* (1992) also evokes shofar through the saxophone's lyrical lines in "Jochebed's Search for Her Son," the poetic conclusion of this neo-Monteverdian setting. See Appendix.

[24] The opera was premiered on June 20–22, 1997. The interview appears in Malcolm Miller, "Between Two Cultures: A Conversation with Shulamit Ran," *Tempo* 58.227 (2004): 15–32.

where the sage Reb Azriel attempts to exorcise the defiant soul of the dead would-be lover Khonnon, the dybbuk, which had possessed Leya just as she was about to be wed, against her will, to a groom of her father's choosing. Ran reworks the three traditional shofar calls, in dialogue with the brass, into an intense, "almost violent section of the opera, building to a huge climax." Whilst it would be possible to perform it live with a minimum of three shofar players, Ran chose to pre-record the shofar music and have it come in, amplified, on cue. As she observed, "pitch was not a concern — I planned the music so that precise tuning is not at all of paramount importance.... The final result, I think, is quite realistic in its effect."

A more recent opera, *Babylon* (2012), by the German composer Jörg Widmann, features a group of seven shofar players on stage for a tableau near the start.[25] The symbolism of the number seven, associated with Babylonian culture, permeates the plot and the work's structure. The shofar group appears in the powerful prologue, in which a Scorpion Man grieves in an unaccompanied, beguiling wail for the destroyed urban utopia depicted in the ruins around him, the fallen city of Babylon, a metaphor for a modern-day

---

[25] I attended the world premiere on Oct. 27, 2012. See my review, Malcolm Miller, "Munich, Bayerische Staatsoper: Jörg Widmann's 'Babylon,'" *Tempo* 67.228 (2013): 71–72.

metropolis. Seven shofars are introduced near the start, producing a chaotic sonority that recalls the biblical Jericho story as an allegory of destruction.

Though brief, the shofar scene displays a taut structure with a combination of tuned and un-tuned playing. The shofar players begin with sustained tones, then the ensemble splits into low and high sounds, evolving into dissonant clusters. The texture changes as the low instruments intensify, then the entire group plays together in a blaring siren-like effect on closely matched, but not identical, pitches. Then one shofar produces a high note, which the rest strive for. Eventually the clashing calls reduce again to a single shofar on the high note. At this point the percussion section enters with the chorus on the same pitch, and what ensues is a pastiche of a Bachian chorus. To some extent the shofars are structurally integrated into the harmonic fabric of the score, and their ability to play recognizable pitch quality is exploited. According to the published synopsis: "If the decayed civilization of Babylon is the topic; the shofars here stand for the ancient, but also the primitive, the beast, the uncivilised?" In a sense, as in the Elgar, the shofar (as a Jewish instrument) is being "othered," contrasted with Bach, the zenith of German culture, though filtered through a distorted mist of parody and subversion. In contrast to the mainly colorful score and spectacular production, which is akin to a fantasy on civilization, and the connotation of Babylon as both fertile and corrupt, the Jewish characters, Ezra and the people, are tinted in dull serious tones.[26]

The Shofar, and its Evocations, as Symbol for Holocaust Memorialization

In the context of the tragedy and triumph that characterized Jewish experience in the first half of the twentieth century, it is to be expected that the shofar has provided contemporary composers in Israel, America, and Europe an effective and affective medium for the expression of profound musical responses to and commemorations of the Holocaust. Frequently encountered in commemorative works are techniques of collage and layering, highlighting stylistic confrontations and combinations, resulting from allusions and quotations. Thus one finds the shofar set alongside different emblems of Jewish life, for example cantorial music, Yiddish and Hebrew folksong, and poetry. Such postmodern aesthetics, with the potential to convey both rupture and continuity, are especially suited to the genre.

An instance of such a collage effect occurs in the oratorio *Mechaye Hametim* (1987) by Israeli composer Noam Sheriff (b. 1935), a moving large-scale Holocaust

---

[26] Those ideas are developed in my review of the premiere. See note 25.

Memorial piece that premiered in Amsterdam in 1987. Sheriff is among the foremost of the so-called second generation of Israeli composers, who extended the Mediterranean style of the pioneers of the 1930 and 40s with influences from the European and American avant-garde. Sheriff's music combines Jewish traditional musics, cantillation modes, and Arabic and Yemenite song, in a compelling postmodern symbiosis. One of several oratorios on major Jewish topics, *Mechaye Hametim* intermingles shofar calls performed by horns and modified into air-raid sirens, leading to climactic textures depicting destruction, following which a gentle Yiddish song, all that remains, is heard in the distance. Here the connotation of sirens adds a new layer of meaning and symbolism: the shofar/horn calls express the urgent message of the need to survive.

Another instance in a different genre is the Symphony no. 4 (1984) by the American-Jewish composer Benjamin Lees (1924–2010). Composed as a Holocaust Memorial work for the fortieth anniversary of the end of WWII, and premiered in 1985, the symphony features settings of three poems by Nelly Sachs (1891–1970), the first of which, "Someone Blew a Shofar," evokes shofar calls extensively in the vocal line and also in fierce brass textures, within an intense, chromatic style redolent of Shostakovich, whose music is also quoted.

The shofar itself features in *Kaddish for Terezin* by British composer Ronald Senator (1926–2015). Dedicated to the million and a half children who perished in the Holocaust, the work sets Psalms and children's poetry from Terezin, the showcase city which had a remarkably flourishing musical life, and from where many composers and musicians, who produced operas, performed recitals, and composed music, were deported to Auschwitz. In one movement, shofar calls are intermingled poignantly with children's voices reciting poetry. The work was premiered in 1986 in Canterbury Cathedral, and has since been performed all over the world, including in Terezin itself in 1995, on the occasion of the fiftieth anniversary of the liberation. A fanfare of shofars over a powerful bass pedal features at the climax of *Vanished Voices*, a Holocaust commemoration compiled by Neil Levin, based on research into pre-WWII German-Jewish music.[27] Its narrative for speaker, chorus, and soloists leads from destruction to hope with a Lewandowski choral setting of the *Kaddish* at its climax, featuring the shofars that fade to a single sustained *teqi'ah gedolah*. Here the ancient symbolism of

---

[27] *Vanished Voices* was performed under Levin's baton in 1996 at London's Barbican Centre, as well as in Los Angeles and New York.

redemption is reinforced by the contemporaneity of the ritual, leading to a joyous concluding flourish.

A more performative Holocaust commemoration that features shofar in recorded, sampled guise is *Crystal Psalms* (1988) by Alvin Curran, a prolific electro-acoustic composer and professor of composition at Mills College from 1991–2006, whose oeuvre over a fifty-year period since 1965 spans a vast array of genres, especially sound installations with numerous experimental works involving shofar (see Appendix). *Crystal Psalms* was his earliest work involving shofar and synthesized shofar, an avant-garde sonic tapestry which combines pre-recorded traditional shofar sounds with multifarious sound objects drawn from Jewish history. One of its innovative aspects was the cross-cultural cooperation of the work, with ensembles in six nations mixed together and broadcast live in stereo to listeners across Europe and Scandinavia on October 20, 1988.[28] Later remixed in 1991 by the composer, it was released as a recording of a unique event.[29]

---

[28] See Appendix for recording catalogue details. The original broadcast was remixed in 1991 by the composer; see composer's notes at http://www.alvincurran.com/writings/CrystalPsalmsnotes.html.

[29] Alvin Curran, *Crystal Psalms*, New Albion NA067, CD, 1994.

Related to Holocaust memorialization is Curran's virtuoso concerto *Shofar for Instruments and Electronic Sounds*, premiered as part of the WDR-Cologne Diaspora-Israel concert week in 1990. The work comprises a collage of Curran on large solo shofar triggering samples, a shofar ensemble, and various taped sounds based on chants of Yemenite Jews recorded at Jerusalem's Wailing Wall on Tisha B'Av, the day of mourning for the destruction of the Holy Temple.[30]

More recently, Raphael Mostel, who has composed numerous works involving shofars, composed *Night and Dawn* (*Nacht En Dageraad*) (2005) for the Royal Concertgebouw Orchestra Brass Ensemble, in commemoration of the sixtieth anniversary of the liberation of the Netherlands. The world premiere was given on May 3, 2005, in Chicago's Orchestra Hall, by the combined brass of the RCO and Chicago Symphony Orchestra, conducted by Jay Friedman, with the RCO horn players playing the optional shofars in the climax of the first part.

Perhaps the most high-profiled Holocaust memorial piece with shofars is *Tekyah* by Osvaldo Golijov (b. 1960), which makes use of non-tuned and tuned shofar sounds, as well as motivic allusions to the

---

[30] See Peter Gradenwitz, *The Music of Israel*, Chapter twelve, "Twentieth Century Hebrew Music," 299ff.

calls in different instruments. The five-minute miniature was composed for the BBC film *Music Memorial from Auschwitz*, made for the sixtieth anniversary of the Liberation of Auschwitz, and broadcast by the EBU across Europe.[31] In this first-ever film to feature music performed at the Auschwitz site, the soloist was renowned klezmer clarinettist David Krakauer, whose rhapsodic cantorial fervor, with the unusual marking *"davenen"* (praying), was accompanied with shofar motifs in accordion and brass, leading to textures involving twelve shofars, eight of them doubled by brass players, intoning the three calls, ending in a rapid *teru'ah*. In the final section the clarinet leads a solo shofar in each call pattern (*teqi'ah, teqi'ah, shevarim, teru'ah*), and is then joined by the three shofar groups in alternation, who play together for the final sequence, culminating in a powerful *teqi'ah gedolah*. Part of the effect of the work is the tension between the shofars' quasi-ritualized style (the patterns are close variants to the Rosh Hashanah sequence), and the freer, anguished melodic contours of the clarinet. The piece was later incorporated as the fifth and final movement of *Rose of the Winds* (2007), one of Golijov's works which draw on different traditions, and features an array of non-Western instruments in a

---

[31] *Tekyah* was broadcast on January 27, 2005, by the EBU, commissioned by the BBC.

multi-ethnic symbiosis. Thus in its afterlife, the Holocaust memorial was transformed into a celebration of intercultural harmony and coexistence.

Within the canon of commemorative works to memorialize the Holocaust and WWII, the shofar has thus played a significant role. Its contemporary resonances of Jewish faith, memory, and survival are extensions of ancient symbols, ranging from warfare, national calamity, destruction, and repentance, to freedom, redemption, and national identity.

Shofar, Israel and Visions of Utopia

Extending the ideas of national survival are works that commemorate the experiences and ideals of modern Israel, as well as celebrating harmony and cooperation between nations, both in the Middle East and globally. Several composers have used the shofar and its calls as potent symbols for a vision of political and spiritual utopia. Noam Sheriff's orchestral tone poem *Akedah* (1997) (The Sacrifice of Isaac) is one of several works by Israeli composers commemorating the 1995 assassination of the Israeli Prime Minister Yizhak Rabin, who, echoing the biblical tale of its title, was a sacrificial offering "on the altar of peace." The narrative of the passacaglia-structured music moves through darkness and anguish to culminate in a powerful vision of hope. Passages of neo-Mahlerian intensity give way to moments of limpid intimacy, as in a delicate duet of Middle Eastern modality between harp and trombone, suggestive of the Arabic oud and Jewish shofar. At the dreamlike climax the word "pacem" is whispered, a reconciliatory synthesis of East and West, envisioning the dream of peace.

Middle Eastern politics are evoked in several shofar-related works, an early small-scale example being the American composer Ezra Laderman's *A Single Voice* for oboe and string quartet (1967), composed at the time of the Six-Day War. The oboe, having participated in atonal expressionistic textures with strings, performs traditional shofar calls. The adaptation of ancient symbolism here has particular political meaning, since shofar playing at the Western Wall had been prohibited during the British Mandate period, and the shofar had remained silent there until the reunification of Jerusalem on June 7, 1967, where it was blown symbolically by General Rabbi Shlomo Goren, chief chaplain of the IDF. A more polemical political stance is taken in *The Tree of Knowledge Still Bears Fruit* by Rajmil Fischman, an Israeli electro-acoustic composer based in the UK, and currently a professor at Keele University. The piece is a contemporary reinterpretation of the story of the Garden of Eden, which highlights the social value of "knowledge." The climax (mm. 251–52) quotes the prophet Amos, one of the fiercest social critics in the

Bible, signaled by a distortion of the shofar call through clarinet and bassoon multiphonics.

Pitch-specific shofar (often tuned to A or B♭) is used in several biblically inspired choral-instrumental cantatas by the Israeli composer Max Stern. Stern's *Prophet or King* (2007), an incisive critique of power politics based on 1 Samuel, and *Prophecy for the End of Days* (2009), inspired by the messianic vision of the brotherhood of humankind, aim for a coexistence of European and Middle Eastern sonorities to bridge divisions in Israeli society.

A similar visionary utopianism, yet on a global scale, is evident in *Weltethos* (2009–2011) one of the last choral-orchestral works by the noted British composer Jonathan Harvey (1939–2012). The epic work for speaker, large chorus, children's choir, and large orchestra sets texts by theologian Hans Küng, exploring humanity's shared spiritual heritage based on six of the world's great religions: Confucianism, Judaism, Islam, Hinduism, Buddhism, and Christianity. In the second movement, about Judaism, "Moses on the Golden Rule," the sustained trumpets represent the shofar, whilst the woodwinds evoke klezmer.

Shared beliefs of the three monotheistic faiths form the topic of British composer Roxana Panufnik's *Three Paths to Peace* (2008), a reworking of her 2008 violin concerto *Abraham*. The evocative tone poem draws on Muslim, Christian, and Jewish musical traditions in a postmodern symbiosis, as in the *muezzin*-inspired violin soliloquy based on eastern melismatic microtonal portamenti, superimposed by peals of Anglican Church bells and, later, delicate oboe evocations of a shofar call.

Shofar and the Environment
Meira Warshauer's *Tekeeya (A Call)* for Trombone, Shofar and Orchestra (2009)

As a step on the path to utopia, the Jewish notion of *tikkun olam*, mending the world, emanates from the prophetic idea of a call to the conscience, reinterpreted in contemporary ethical and moral contexts. The themes of human responsibility for the environment, the earth's ecology, and of reconnecting the self to its source, form the focus of the most radical additions to the repertoire for tuned shofar: *Tekeeyah (A Call)* (2009) by Meira Warshauer.[32] Apart from being the first concerto ever for trombone and shofar with orchestra, its innovative aspect is that the shofar and trombone are brought into a symbiotic relationship: playing melodic pitches in various patterns, the shofar

---

[32] *Tekeeyah (A Call)*, the first concerto ever written for shofar, trombone, and orchestra, began its premiere season performances in 2009 with soloist Haim Avitsur and commissioning orchestras Wilmington Symphony (NC), Brevard Philharmonic (NC), and University of South Carolina Symphony.

takes on aspects of the trombone's identity, whilst the trombone, in turn, shares material given to the shofar. The shofar's melodic ideas are related to, yet different from, the traditional calls; more remarkably, the pitch range of the shofar, based on its possibility of playing the main E (above middle C) and higher C, is extended to an additional selection of pitches stretching up the scale, and neighboring notes attained by breath control and lip pressure, and musical effects of glissandi and note-bending. In a context of blurred textures and pitches, the shofar is accepted as an integral part of the sound source rather than as an exotic "outsider."

Tekeeyah was begun in 2008 whilst Warshauer was a fellow at the MacDowell Colony in New Hampshire, and continued in dialogue with the outstanding trombonist and shofarist Haim Avitsur, the soloist in the first performance and recording. Warshauer's liner notes to the CD highlight her ecological message and her Jewish heritage, observing that, "In this concerto, the shofar calls to all of humanity… the shofar calls us… calls us to return." The composer describes the shofar's role in three sections which "mark… shifts in the process of awakening." The first evokes "the mystery of time before we were born… here the shofar sounds in quiet embodied tones which become more intense…"; in the second "the orchestra serves as a wakeup call… shofar blasts contributing to the alarm"; the last is a "joyful dance" and culminates "in a climax of traditional shofar blasts."[33]

The rhetoric recalls Maimonides's explanation of the purpose of the shofar as a call to the conscience: "Awake, ye who slumber." Certainly it is a highly spiritual work, yet full of colorful orchestration, dramatic rhythmic energy, and poetic interludes. The harmonic idiom is sometimes redolent of a post-Coplandesque, eclectic American style and nature-film scores, with slow moving harmonies and shimmery, percussion-rich orchestration.

A scene of natural habitats, calm yet restless and mysterious, launches the concerto. Textures like high string glissandi in contrary motion, resonating exotic percussion such as Tibetan bowls, and players whispering vowels into their silent instruments, including the shofar, create the intended "otherworldly" ambience. Ingeniously, the composer thereby enables the shofar, an instrument renowned for pitch uncertainty, to flourish fully as a member of the orchestra rather than an exotic outsider. Alongside an element of unfamiliarity, the quality of shofar tone, intended to be performed on a large shofar such as a kudu horn, is suggestive at times of the human voice.

---

[33] Meira Warshauer, liner notes for *Living Breathing Earth*, Navona Records NV5842, CD, 2011.

A recurrent three-chord theme in the strings forms part of the generally rich, multilayered harmonic texture. The shofar's first gesture is a rising second, B – C♯, in a "slow glissando" (mm. 43-44), thus transforming the brash fanfare *teqi'ah* into a tender, even pleading sigh, set against a delicate string backdrop with flickering woodwind snippets. The shofar repeats and expands the interval to a third, B – D, then rising a fourth to E, one of the shofar's most stable and clearest pitches (m. 50). The shofar, ever engaged in imitative dialogue against strings, then introduces a *teru'ah* pattern, echoed in strings in luminescent harmony (m. 62), then develops to further *teqi'ah*-like sustained Es, preceded by rising swoops from D, as well as slower repeated-note patterns reminiscent of the *shevarim* (m. 71). Any sense of stasis resulting from the focus on E is countered by variations of texture, as with shimmery percussion and harp, and further transformations such as an inversion of the rising motif in a section marked "Alive, ensouled." Here the shofar intones a falling swooping semitone, a plaintive cry, from E to D♯, coming to rest on E. Similar falling sighs continue until an unexpected return to a rising second E – F♯ (m. 127), the shofar again is echoed by pulsing strings. The climax is orchestral, based on the rising motive, with a picturesque ocarina solo adding to the outdoor flavor; then the whispered mystery of the opening returns.

The second movement, "Breaking Walls," begins seamlessly, stridently emphatic with the trombone as soloist. Remarkably, the trombone takes on certain shofar characteristics, playing the sighing swoops and shofar motifs, underlining a sense of commonality between the two instruments. When the shofar starts, it is centered on the E to C rising motif, focusing mainly on E, and always supported by richly rhythmic homophonic orchestral textures. Yet as in the first section, the shofar is assigned a wider range of pitches, with swoops from E – A – E and E – G – A – E (mm. 313–20). A further focus on E and the rising sixth motif leads to the final movement, "Dance of Truth," a stark contrast that explodes into an energetic syncopated jazzy dance rhythm, again with the trombone as soloist, and again taking shofar gestures such as rising *teqi'ah* type swoops (mm. 386–95). The orchestra's quaver in a 9/8 syncopation (6+3) pattern is strongly reminiscent of the *teru'ah*. The shofar introduces the trombone's theme on the low E, then rises to the high C, dovetailed by trumpet and brass section in the orchestra. The music builds to a climax and cuts off, as if for a cadenza in a classical concerto. Set into relief, the solo shofar intones, for the first time in the work, the traditional call sequence: *teqi'ah, shevarim, teru'ah, teqi'ah*, which signals the approaching conclusion. Here the orchestra's exciting rising sequences are crowned by the shofar's sustained *teqi'ah gedolah* on C, which, in the final bars, is unexpectedly harmonized by an unambiguous C-major chord, a symbol perhaps of the shift from half-lights to clarity.

From Tuned Shofar to Melodic Shofar

Technical issues of performing tunes on a shofar are related both to the performer and availability of shofars that are flexible and easy to use. Most concert works employ the Yemenite kudu shofar, from an African antelope; the notes are loud and fulsome, yet it is difficult to obtain pitch variety; glissandi and note bending are possible, and even though the higher overtones produce closer intervals, "tuned" works like Warshauer's *Tekeeya* deliberately avoid too wide a melodic range. Smaller ram's or goat's horns, mainly used for the Rosh Hashanah ritual, offer a suppler ability to perform scales. On such instruments I can obtain chromatic scales, often of up to two octaves, ideal for performing shofar versions of classic melodies, and it is also relatively easy to find more than one instrument with the same fundamental, and thus "in tune," ideal for ensembles, or witty multi-shofar solo performance.[34]

---

[34] I used a ram's horn to perform "Land of Hope and Glory" (Elgar) and *Hatikvah* at "Simcha on the Square," at London's

Examples of works utilizing both short and long shofars in melodic and tuned contexts are, however, few and far between, though one suspects they will increase. My own *350th Anniversary Fanfare Concertino* for solo shofar, shofar chorus, and instrumental ensemble (2006) makes use of both pitched and unpitched characteristics of the shofar, and both long and short instruments.[35] It seemed appropriate to mark the 350th Anniversary of Jews in Britain (the community was officially allowed to settle by Oliver Cromwell in 1656) with the shofar's powerful, distinctive sound. The work reflects both the lyrical as well as signaling aspects of this instrument. The framing fanfares for a shofar ensemble are drawn from the traditional calls: *teqi'ah, shevarim,* and *teru'ah,* the final section ending with a *teqi'ah gedolah.* The seven titled phases attempt to characterize aspects of Anglo-Jewish history to mark its sevenfold fifty-year Jubilee: Prologue – Fanfare; I – Persecution; II – Immigration; III – Struggle; IV – Tradition; V – Emancipation; VI – Assimilation – Cadenza; VII – Celebration; Epilogue – Fanfare. Each section varies in mood evoked through the shofar's lyrical capability and the transformation of

---

Trafalgar Square on September 17, 2006, with a massed shofar chorus.

[35] The work was premiered at the Purcell Room as part of the Jewish Music Institute's "Borsht to Blighty: Jewish Culture Day at the South Bank Centre—350 years of Jewish Music in Britain."

the traditional motifs in a variety of contemporary idioms, chromatic (I and V), and atonal-textural (III). There are allusions to Ladino (II) and Klezmer (VII) styles, as well as to some familiar British themes (VI – Cadenza). The central section, IV, is a tuneful fantasy on contemporary Anglo-Jewish cantillation motifs derived from an ancient source.

I based my chamber work *Mi Yodea* for shofar, viola, and piano (2007)[36] on a Yemenite Passover melody *Ehad Mi Yodea* (Who Knows One?), listed as number 25 in volume 2 of A. Z. Idelsohn's monumental *Thesaurus of Hebrew Melodies*. The zestful tune appears complete towards the end, introduced by viola then repeated by shofar, while all the thematic material, including a rhapsodic viola solo near the start, are transformations which evoke the mode of the original. There are some improvisatory sections, such as a dialogue for shofar and viola, which exploits the piano's resonances and explores unusual contemporary shofar effects, whilst the conclusion alludes to the three traditional calls, yet in the harmonious pitched key of the work.

---

[36] *Mi Yodea* was composed for two outstanding artists to whom the work is dedicated, Rivka Golani and Eldad Neumark, premiered with myself on shofar in London in aid of a charity (CHECCH) to promote friendship amongst Muslim, Christian, and Jewish families in Israel; reviewed in *The Jewish Chronicle*, April 20, 2007.

Melodic Shofar in Jazz and Rock, and Shofar World Music

There are examples of similar pioneering of "melodic shofar" in popular music, including jazz, as a browse of the Internet can show. The growing roster of specialists includes the late Rabbi Joel Goor of the Metropolitan Synagogue, New York; and jazz saxophonists Steve Cohn (USA), Arik Livnat (Israel), and Jeremiah Lockwood of The Sway Machinery, who plays blues shofar on the track "I Heard Somebody."[37] In addition, klezmer clarinettist David Krakauer recently released a recording in which he reinterprets a Naftule Brandwein recorded melody, adding shofar calls.[38] New music for shofar in a broader world music context features in *Ceremonial for the Equinox*, performed by the group Tibetan Singing Bowl Ensemble led by their founder Raphael Mostel, who has written much about and composed several works for shofar. The climax of an extended pageant for exotic

---

[37] See www.swaymachinery.com. The Sway Machinery has a strong connection to Jewish music through the guitarist/singer Jeremiah Lockwood, who performed with and was educated by his grandfather, Cantor Jacob Konigsberg.

[38] See Randall Goldberg, "David Krakauer from Klezmer Madness! to Abraham Inc.: A Topical Narrative of Musical Identities," *Musica Judaica* 21 (2015–16): 65–112. I am grateful to Jeff Nussbaum, President of the Historical Brass Society, for this information.

gongs, Mayan rain-sticks, Celtic drums, and Tibetan singing bowls is a "Ram's horn Tocsin" for seven *shofars* with drums, which resonate eerily, especially effective in the cavernous Cathedral of St. John the Divine, New York, where it was premiered in 1995.[39]

Religious Inspiration and the Tuned Shofar

Two contrasting responses to the traditional New Year liturgy using tuned shofar may be found in compositions for synagogue and concert hall. The *Shofar Service* (1964) by Herman Berlinski (1910–2001) is one of several liturgical works composed after the composer settled in New York during WWII, having escaped both from Paris in the 1940s and his native Leipzig in 1933. Based on the Rosh Hashanah *Amidah* in the Reform movement's *Union Prayer Book*, it features solo shofar with two trumpets and organ. As Neil Levin has observed, Berlinski's innovation was to reintroduce the authentic shofar to Reform congregations, many of which had rejected it as primitive and archaic, replacing it with a trumpet.[40] The combination of both shofar and a pair of trumpets ingeniously fuses past and present, whilst adhering to the symbolism of Temple practice. Here the thirty calls

---

[39] See the *HBS Newsletter* 5 (1993): 53 regarding Scarlet Records Infinity Series IS 88801-2.

[40] Neil Levin, CD liner notes for *Herman Berlinski: From the World of My Father*, Naxos American Classics 8.559446, CD, 2006.

usual to Orthodox Judaism are reduced to ten, presented at the start of each of the three movements, introduced by a baritone in a stylized calling of the note name. Throughout, the organ pedal is tuned to low E♭, whilst the shofar's main note is B♭; there is thus a sense of tuned harmony, with the shofar rising a fifth to F (major ninth) over the organ pedal. The first two sections feature the traditional sequence (*teqi'ah, shevarim, teru'ah, teqi'ah*), with the solo and choral music accompanied by two trumpets mainly based on shofar motives. The final sequence is slightly adjusted: *teqi'ah, teru'ah, teqi'ah gedolah*. For the last tone the baritone's rising call is answered by the shofar's extended sustained B♭ – F, again clashing as a major ninth over the organ E♭ pedal. The choral and brass conclusion is brighter than before, an affirmative tonic resolution.

Berlinski's style is chromatic yet tonally rooted; that of Hugo Weisgall is grippingly contemporary, with a variety of post-tonal techniques creating rich, elusive harmonies and textures. Weisgall's symphonic poem *T'kiatot* (1987) is a profound and dramatic response to the rich content of the New Year *Amidah*, to the point of reworking the central *Aleinu* prayer theme alongside shofar motives. The shofar itself concludes each movement as if in a liturgical context, and there is a relationship of the tuning (A – E in the Milken recording) with the main harmony; in the first movement, the fifth stands apart; in the second, it resolves the triton A – E♭ to a perfect fifth; in the final movement the pattern is altered to *teru'ah, teqi'ah, teqi'ah, teqi'ah gedolah*, with the orchestral harmony a semitone away, clashing until the final rise of a further fifth, combined with percussion, offers resolution.

At the Cutting Edge: Electro-Acoustics with Shofar

Perhaps the most exciting developments in the compositional use of shofar concern avant-garde and experimental uses, which extend the potential of the natural, acoustic shofar sounds though computer programming and electronic synthesis. Alvin Curran, mentioned earlier, is one of the most prolific explorers of electro-acoustic shofar, both in composition and multimedia sound installations. He has worked on complex computer music for nearly three decades, and it was through a growing awareness of his Jewish identity that the shofar became a part of his experimental resources—what he has described as an instrument which is "a perfect fit for my 'natural sound' aesthetic" and which was also "contemporary and captivating."[41]

---

[41] Alvin Curran, liner notes to *Shofar Rags*, Tzadik TZ8176, CD, 2013.

Techniques evolved from his earliest shofar work *For Julian* (1988), through numerous installations such as *Shin Far Shofar I* (2008) for the San Francisco Jewish Museum, with a recent CD, *Shofar Rags*, presenting seven works that develop the shofar in a myriad of guises. For instance, whilst "Shofar Puro Alap" builds a rich texture from multi-tracked variety of sustained pitches, "Shofar x 17" transforms a canonic phasing of shofar in seventeen voices into a jungle soundtrack of wild animal sounds, exploring the shofar's origins, concluding with a collage of mechanical and human objects and music. "Alef Bet Gimel Shofar," by contrast, maps the sampled shofar sounds onto the Hebrew alphabet.

In Curran's autobiographical liner notes, he traces his gradual development through different instruments and software; tackling the issue of religious attitudes to shofar in secular contexts, he writes, tellingly, "For me the very act of music making is sacred, in that it transforms any sound into a metalanguage available to all people anywhere for their spiritual or secular illumination, ecstasy and delight."[42] Curran's works, which use distortions, multitracking, feedback, and more complex transformations to either project the shofar solo or to enmesh it within a collage

---

[42] Curran, liner notes to *Shofar Rags*.

of disparate sounds, are engaging essays in the realm of the experimental.

Shofar as merely "sampled" sound also occurs in the post-modern collage fusion work *Kaddish*, a CD by the British group Towering Inferno (Island Records), presented in live multimedia performances across Europe, including the 1995 Vienna Jewish Music Week. It was acclaimed in the rock and world music press for its innovative mix of multi-ethnic musics such as Hungarian folk poems and songs, African rhythms, and cantorial and shofar music within an electro-acoustic tableau.[43]

A live interactive relationship between electronic shofar and acoustic instruments forms the innovative aspect of the American composer Judith Shatin's *Elijah's Violin* (1996) for pre-recorded pitch-specific shofar and string quartet. Here the shofar's motifs are electronically manipulated and imitated by the string quartet.[44] Some of the shofar's pitches are harmonized, whilst the quotation of a well-known

---

[43] Another example is "Kaddish and Shofar" by Bela Farago, a Hungarian-born, German-based composer and artist, with shofar calls harmonized by new-age synthesised harmonies in sustained strands. The recording is *Floatation – ElektroAcoustic Research*, Hungaroton Records B002TL24SY, CD, 2009.

[44] For an interview with Shatin, see Lana Gersten, "Playing the Shofar: An Ancient Sound Finds a New Voice," *The Forward* (Sep. 18, 2008): http://forward.com/articles/14206/playing-the-shofar-02527/ (accessed 2/1/17).

para-liturgical song, *Eliyahu Hanavi*, dovetails with the shofar's pitches, later hummed by the quartet. Shatin has observed that "the electronic portion represents Heaven's call to Elijah, includes the sound of the shofar associated with Elijah, and intimates the ascent to heaven."[45] At the climax, stark electronic distortions of the shofar, anguished *teqi'ah* calls, are set dissonantly over string chords until, at the poignant final cadence, they all harmonize.

Shatin subsequently composed *Teruah* (2006) for Shofar (Yemenite style, in E♭) and *Brass Band*, a celebratory work which also makes use of the acoustic shofar's pitch specificity. After the traditional calls and dialogues with brass, a Hasidic-sounding Rosh Hashanah melody (by Shatin's grandfather-in-law, Avraham Tzvi Kubowitzki) appears in brass counterpoint, leading to an exciting galloping section with drums. The shofar calls reappear, with the brass imitating and developing the *teqi'ah*, using the rising fifth and rising octave, which is less usual. The work concludes climactically with a long *teqi'ah gedolah*.

Following Curran's lead are the radical electronic and midi sound installations and compositions of Bob Gluck, a Reconstructionist rabbi and Director of the Electronic Studio at SUNY Albany,

---

[45] See composer's note at http://judithshatin.com/elijahs-chariot/.

who has developed an "eShofar," an electronically expanded version of the ancient ram's horn, itself a thought-provokingly paradoxical clash of ancient and avant-garde. The system allows various degrees of control in sound-settings and random processes, with stirring semi-improvisational results. His *Shofar* (2005) radically transforms the sound of the shofar using processing and a specially developed spatial sensor glove, by which the way the shofar is held activates a computer program. Amongst the sounds reworked are a cantor and orchestra, and the various imaginative transformations of shofar sounds include a flock of doves and bird song. In Gluck's *Ssshofar* (2005) a sensor glove controls an eleven-track layering of real-time recorded shofar sounds and pre-recorded samples, including cantorial chant. The piece itself develops from the transformed properties and controlling effects of long notes (*teqi'ah*) and short staccato patterns (*teru'ah*) played live and filtered, enmeshed with ever-changing colors of bubbly metallic electronic sounds resulting from the live processing. Gluck's eShofar II system (2005; eShofar III followed in 2007) offered a more sophisticated interactive relationship in *Bitches Brew* (1969)/*Shofarrr* (2005), a fizzing arrangement of this classic of Davis's "electric" period.[46] Here the

---

[46] *Bitches Brew* (1969)/*Shofarrr* (2005) was later transformed into the various track listings on the *Electric Brew*

timbral nuances of the shofar are picked up and transformed in semi-predictable ways by digital filters, harmonizers, and multi-tape delays, with a resulting high level of spontaneity and surprise within an overall controlled shape. For the listener, recognisable jazz harmonies and bass patterns are subsumed into a feverish fabric of wildly evolving electronic sonorities with exhilarating effect. As Bob Gluck has observed, "When expanded with electronics, the shofar becomes a new instrument, a hybrid standing between the traditional and the modern. The shofar is not a museum piece, nor is it an object that cannot be used respectfully in new ways."[47]

Conclusion

As we have seen in the selection of disparate examples, the wide variety of uses of the shofar in art musics reaches both far back to the past and toward the cutting edge of musical developments, underlining both continuity and progress, seeking to connect structural and expressive elements with a world of spirituality. We have surveyed Holocaust memorial works, music theatre pieces, operas, oratorios, and

---

recording, given in the Appendix.

[47] "The Electronic Shofar: AE interviews Composer/Improviser Bob Gluck," *Arts Electric* (Dec. 29, 2006): www.emf.org/artselectric/stories/2006/061229_gluck.html (accessed 2/1/2017).

chamber music which use the shofar calls, or incorporate the shofar both in untuned and tuned forms, or electronically manipulate and extend the shofar's sounds and gestures, occasionally with melodic effects. Whether in the concert hall or synagogue, the shofar retains its power to remind one of the constancy of the natural world in the context of ever-changing technology. The shofar appears as both exotic and separate from traditional instruments, yet also as a long-standing insider member of the aerophones. There is still much work to be done in explicating and analyzing the imaginative ways in which the shofar has been used within a growing repertoire, a selection of which I have compiled as a separate list in the Appendix. As I hope to have shown here, the shofar's expressive meaning derives from the range of symbols emanating from its richly documented history from the Bible onwards: prophecy in Old and New Testaments, faith, survival from destruction, Jewish identity, messianism, utopianism, *tikkun olam*, and the possibility of joyful praise. It is this nexus of symbols that forms the basis for the shofar's use in twentieth- and twenty-first century art musics in many genres and styles. For whilst the liturgical context affirms the shofar's natural voice as a symbol for eternal values, constancy amidst change, so too does the shofar in art music act as a symbol bridging tradition and modernity. Whether in its original form or radically transformed, we are invited to hear and interpret the shofar anew, to discover fresh modern meanings for ancient symbols.

Appendix
List of Shofar Works by
Twentieth- and Twenty-First-Century Composers[48]

1. Works Based on the Traditional Motifs Associated with Shofar

Ben-Amots, Ofer (b. 1955): *Psalm 81* for double choir (1989); *The Odessa Trio* (in memory of J. Dorfman) for violin, cello, piano (2008).

Berio, Luciano (1925–2003): *Shofar* for choir and orchestra (1995).

Bernstein, Leonard (1920–1990): *Candide* (1956 rev 1989); *West Side Story* (1957); "Kaddish," Symphony no. 3 (1963).

Beveridge, Thomas (b. 1938): *Yizkor Requiem: A Quest for Spiritual Roots* (1959).

Bloch, Ernest (1880–1957): *Schelomo* (1915–16); (and other works).

Braun, Yehezkel (1922–2014): *Festive Horns* for mixed choir and brass octet (settings of the Mishna) (1977).

---

[48] This list is necessarily selective; I am drawing on most works I am aware of, yet the repertoire continues to expand. In contrast to twenty-four works in 2002, the current list features over sixty. I am grateful to Michael Chusid at www.hearingshofar.blogspot.com for sharing useful information.

Castelnuovo-Tedesco, Mario (1895-1968): *Le danze del Re David*, rapsodia ebraica su temi tradizionali (1925).

Dorfman, Joseph (1922-2007): *Reminiscence* for flute solo, nigun, game, dance, and shofar (2001).

Elkana, Amos (b. 1967): *Tru'a*, Concerto for Clarinet and Orchestra (1994).

Fleisher, Robert (b. 1953): *Meditations* for soprano saxophone and trumpet (1988).

Foss, Lukas (1922-2009): *Song of Songs* for mezzo-soprano and orchestra (1947).

Galtieri, Giancarlo: *Suono di shofar a Auschwitz*: cantata per coro e orchestra (2000).

Goehr, Alexander (b. 1932): *Sonata about Jerusalem*, Op. 30 (1970); *Behold the Sun (Die Wiedertaufer)*, Op. 44 (1985); *The Death of Moses*, Op. 53 (1992).

Golijov, Osvaldo (b. 1960): *Rocketekya* for klezmer clarinet and fiddle, electronic viola, double bass (1998).

Hajdu, André (1932-2016): *Teruath HaMelech (Jewish Rhapsody)* for clarinet and string orchestra (1974).

Harvey, Jonathan (1939-2012): *Weltethos* for speaker, large chorus, children's Choir, and large orchestra, text Hans Küng (2009-11).

Laderman, Ezra (1924-2015): *A Single Voice* for oboe and string quartet (1967).

Lees, Benjamin (1924–2010): Symphony no. 4, *Memorial Candles*, for mezzo-soprano, violin, and orchestra, texts by Nelly Sachs (1985).

Minsky, Aaron (b. 1958): "Sound the Shofar" from *Judaic Concert Suite* (2003).

Mishori, Yaacov (b. 1937): *Prolonged Shofar Variations* for horn solo (1981).

Panufnik, Roxana (b. 1968): *Three Paths to Peace* (2008).

Penderecki, Krzysztof (b. 1933): Symphony no. 7, Seven Gates of Jerusalem (1996).

Rubin, Emmanuel (1935–2008): *O die Schornsyeine*, (O the Chimneys) for viola and voice, setting of a Holocaust poem by Nelly Sachs (1995).

Sargon, Simon (b. 1938): *B'Kol Shofar* (With the Voice of the Shofar), three psalms for soprano, choir, brass quintet, organ (1992); *The Weeping Shofar* for cello and piano (1998).

Schachter, Michael (b. 1987): *The Ten Plagues* for jazz septet (2009).

Sheriff, Noam (b. 1935): *Mechye Hametim* (Revival of the Dead), Innovative Music Productions, Pickwick Group, MCD 21 (1987).

Stern, Robert (b. 1934): *Shofar*, oratorio (2009); *Recitative (Yom Teruah)* for solo cello (2001), version for solo viola (2006); *Tekiah G'dolah, reflections on Shofar* for cello and piano (2007).

Stevenson, Ronald (1928–2015): Cello Concerto (2nd movement) (1992–94).

Stock, David (1939–2015): *Tekiah* for trumpet and chamber orchestra (1987).

Wyner, Yehudi (b. 1929): *Passover Offering* for clarinet, bass trombone, cello, and flute (1959).

2. *Works Using Shofar or Shofar Ensemble in Non-Pitch-Specific Ways*

Anghel, Irinel (b. 1969): *Labyrinthe II* for horns, shofar, accordion, Tibetan conch, harmonic singing, trumpet, guzheng, Zen singing bowl (2004); *Images flottantes* for flute, shofar, khene, daf, accordion (n.d.).

Bakshi, Alexander (b. 1952): *The Polyphony of the World*, music theatre, for voices, dancers, multi-ethnic instruments including shofar, and orchestra (2001).

Barnes, Milton (1931–2001): *Arc of the Covenant* for oboe/shofar, harp, and percussion (1996).

Fleischer, Tsippi (b. 1946): Symphony No. 5, *Israeli-Jewish Collage*, includes pre-recorded shofar ensemble (2003).

Golijov, Osvaldo (b. 1960): *Tekeeya* (2005, rev. 2007 in *Rose of the Winds*).

Gluck, Srul Irving (1934–2002): *Heritage Dance Symphony* (1967).

Levin, Neil: *Vanished Voices* (1996).

MacMillan, James (b. 1959): *Seven Angels* for mixed chorus, soloists and small instrumental ensemble (natural trumpets, shofars, percussion, harp, cello), texts from The Book of Revelation (2014).

Miller, Malcolm (b. 1958): *Tekia Textures* for massed shofars and string trio (1984); *Trio* for shofar and strings (1995); *Israel Jubilee Fanfare* for solo and massed shofars (1998).

Mostel, Raphael (b. 1948): *Ceremonial for the Equinox*, Scarlet Records Infinity Series IS 88801-2 (1996); *Night and Dawn (Nacht en Dageraad)* for brass ensemble (2005).

Ran, Shulamit (b. 1949): *Between Two Worlds* (The Dybbuk), opera (1997).

Senator, Ronald (1926–2015): *Kaddish for Terezin*, Delos International, DE 1032 (1994).

Wayne, Hayden (b. 1949): *In Memoriam: A Celebration* for orchestra and choir with shofar (1993).

3. Works Using Tuned Shofar Within Pitch-Specific Contexts

Berlinksi, Herman (1910–2001): *Shofar Service* (1964).

Elgar, Edward (1857–1934): *The Apostles*, Op. 49 (1903).

Miller, Malcolm (b. 1958): *Concertino for Shofar and Ensemble* (2006); *Mi Yodea* for viola, shofar, and piano (2008).

Shatin, Judith (b. 1949): *Teruah* for shofar (Yemenite style, E♭ pitch), 3 horns, 2 trumpets, 2 trombones, and timpani (2006).

Stern, Max (b. 1947): *With Voices, Trumpets, and Shofars* (2012); *Jubilations Voice* (shofar tuned B♭) for choir and string quintet (2012); *Aryegh Shaag* (untuned shofars) for choir, string quintet, and shofars (2011); *Prophecy for the End of Days*, cantata for narrator, choir, children's choir, string orchestra, and shofar (2009); *Prophet or King* (text: I Sam 8), biblical episode for baritone, two narrators (soprano and alto), chorus, soloists, instrumental ensemble, and shofar (tuned A) (2009).

Warshauer, Meira (b. 1949): *Tekeeyah (A Call)* for shofar/trombone and orchestra (2009).

Weisgall, Hugo (1912–1997): *T'kiatot: Rituals for Rosh Hashana* (1986).

4. Works Using Shofar with Electronics and/or Electronic Sampling

Beck, David (b. 1959): *Concerto Grosso* for shofar, conch, and 4 laptops (2011).

Curran, Alvin (1938): *Oh Man Oh Mankind Oh Yeah*, short version, for large chorus SATB, 7 instruments, bass drum, and optional shofar (2013); *Shofar Puro Alap* for shofar and electronics (2013); *Shofar X 17* for shofar and electronics (2013); *Shofar T Tam* for shofar, tam-tam, and electronics (2013); *Alef Bet Gimel Shofar* for shofar and electronics (2013); *Shofar Der Zeit* for shofar, clarinet, broken accordion, and electronics (2013); *Oh Man, Oh Mankind, Oh Yeah* for large chorus SATB, improvising children's chorus, 7 instruments, 4 bass drums, and optional shofar with live electronics (2009); *Shofar III* for shofar, keyboard, electronics, bullroarer, corrugated tube, and percussion (2009); *Shin Far Shofar 1*, sound installation, and natural sounds with electronics (2008); *Shofar 3* for shofar and live electronics, with 1–5 acoustic instruments optional (2007); *Shofar 2* for shofar and electronics (2006); *Beams*, performance for 35 mobile musicians, including chamber ensemble, 2 brass ensembles, mixed chamber chorus, and A.C. soloist (on shofar, chair, tin can, live electronics, and sampling keyboard) (2005); *Maritime Rites Artship* for conch shell, shofar, and ship's trimmings (2002; first version 1990); *Walls of Jericho*, solo performance for shofar and computer (1993; now titled Shofar); *Call To Prayer* for chorus, church bells, synthesizers, and shofar (1990); *Shofar*, first version, for ram's horns, computer live electronics, accordion, and soprano clarinet

(1990); *Crystal Psalms*, radio concert for six choruses, six sextets each including a quartet (violas, cellos, bass clarinets, bass flutes, trombones, tenor sax/tuba), plus accordion and percussion (1988); *For Julian* for shofar, saxophone, voice, and choir (1988).

Dori, Gil: *"by my death..."* for chamber ensemble and laptop ensemble (2016).

Faragó, Béla (b. 1958): *Kaddis és sófár* (Kaddish and Shofar) (2004).

Fischman, Rajmil (b. 1956): *The Tree of Knowledge Still Bears Fruit* (2013).

Gluck, Bob (b. 1955): *Shofarot* for two ram's horns and electronics, software live performance system (2007); *Bitches Brew* (1969)/*Shofarrr* (2005), reworked into four compositions for piano, shofar, and electronics, on *Electric Brew*, EMF Media, CD069 (2007), as follows: *Electric Brew Prelude* (2005), *Electric Brew* (2005), "Pharoah's Interlude" (2006), *Pharoah's Spring* (2005); *Ssshofar*, live electronic performance for Max/MSP processed ram's horn, I-cube sensor glove controller, EMF Media, CD051 (2002); *Shofar*, live electronic performance for Max/MSP processed ram's horn, I-cube sensor glove controller, EMF Media, CD051 (2002); *Shofaralong*, live electronic performance for Max/MSP, processed ram's horn, I-Cube sensor glove controller (2001); *Jonah Under the Sea* (1997).

Kaufman, Frederick (b. 1936): *Yom Kippur War Piece* for shofar, bass drum, and electronic tape (1974).

Shatin, Judith (b. 1949): *Elijah's Violin* for pre-recorded pitch-specific shofar and string quartet (1996).

5. Shofar in rock and popular music

Cohn, Steve: *Iro Iro*, Red Toucan Records, RT 9334 (2008); *The Blair Recordings*, Leo Records, LR 335 (2002); *Bridge over the X-Stream*, Leo Records, LR288 (2000).

Lockwood, Jeremiah: "I heard somebody" from *The Sway Machinery*, CD (2000).

Kastaris, Demetrios (b. 1959): "Trombón con Sazón" from *Trombón con Sazón* for trombone, conch shell, and shofar, LJC Records (Latin Jazz Coalition), CD (2000).

Thurlow, Deborah: *Sacred Postlude (Archangel Sandalphon)* for horn, shofar, tingsha, and Tibetan bowls (2000).

Towering Inferno, *Kaddish*, Island Records, CID 8039 (1995).

6. Shofar in dance

Alonzo King Lines Ballet: *Resin*, additional arrangements by Jordi Savall (2011).

Same Signals, Different Meanings
The Shofar in Compositions by Elgar and Berio

Kees van Hage

This chapter discusses two compositions inspired by the shofar: "The Calling of the Apostles" from the oratorio *The Apostles* (1903) by Edward Elgar, and *Hör* by Luciano Berio, his Prologue to the *Requiem of Reconciliation* (1995), to which fourteen composers contributed. Whereas "The Calling" and *Hör* have many similarities, they show fundamental differences as well, and one of the causes is likely to be the turbulent history of the twentieth century.

Edward Elgar, "The Calling of the Apostles" from the oratorio *The Apostles* (1903)

In 1903, the shofar made its debut on the concert stage in the oratorio *The Apostles* by the British composer Edward Elgar (1857–1934). This work was commissioned by the prestigious Birmingham Festival, just as Mendelssohn's biblical oratorio *Elijah* was in 1846. *The Apostles* is about the beginning of Christianity. The oratorio consists of a prologue and two parts. Part I, "The Calling of the Apostles," deals with Jesus's nightly prayer on the mountain and the calling of the apostles, the Sermon on the Mount, the miracle of the walking on the water, and the conversion of Mary Magdalene. Part II deals with Judas's betrayal, the arrest of Jesus, his crucifixion, the scene at the tomb, and the resurrection. "The plan of the oratorio and the selection of words are my own,"[1] stated Elgar.

Part I is based on Luke 6:12-13, in which Jesus spends the night on a mountain to pray and to prepare himself for the calling of his apostles. After this tranquil episode in the oratorio, the shofar appears on the scene to announce the sunrise. At rehearsal mark 25, mm. 1-2, it blows a *teqi'ah*, which resounds in the clarinet and the French horns. The shofar's rising major sixth E♭4 - C5 at rehearsal mark 25, m. 5, is inverted to the minor third C4 - E♭4; on this third, the Watchers on the Temple roof sing the words, "It shines! The face of all the East is now ablaze with light, Dawn reacheth even unto Hebron!" This is a quotation from *b. Yoma* 28b: "R. Ishmael said: The morning [star] shines…. R. Judah b. Bathyra said: The whole east even unto Hebron is alight and all the people have gone forth, each to his work. If that were the case, it would be [too much of the day] too late! — Rather: each to hire working men."

---

[1] Edward Elgar, *The Apostles: An Oratorio*, Op. 49 (London: Novello, 1904), note.

Elgar may have thought of the apostles as Jesus's working men.

Already from its entry, the shofar is associated with light. The combination of the shofar blast and the light recalls Psalm 89:16: "Happy is the people who know the joyful shout;[2] / O LORD, they walk in the light of Your presence." After rehearsal mark 26, the shofar blows the three traditional blasts: the *teqi'ah* in mm. 1-3, the *shevarim* in mm. 3-4 and the *teru'ah* in mm. 4-6, the last with two trumpets added, perhaps alluding to the two *hatzotzerot*, the silver trumpets blown in the Temple service together with the shofar. At rehearsal mark 27, there is a short passage as an introduction to the psalm after mark 28; the Watchers praise the rising sun with the words, "The face of all the East is now ablaze with light, the Dawn reacheth even unto Hebron!" This city, King David's first residence, is mentioned here to confirm the claim of Jesus's descent from David.

After rehearsal mark 28, the choir in the Temple sings Psalm 92:2-5, 10, and 13. These verses proclaim God's praise, and thank him for his lovingkindness in the morning and for his divine protection: "For, lo, Thine enemies, O Lord, shall perish: all the workers

---

[2] *Teru'ah* means not only "shofar blast" but also "(joyful) shout."

of iniquity shall be scattered." Verse 11,³ "But my horn shalt Thou exalt like the horn of a unicorn," omitted by Elgar, contains the Hebrew word *qeren*, which denotes not only an animal horn as a symbol of power, divine help, victory over evil, and the Messiah's power, but also an animal horn as a signal instrument. Verse 11 is not sung, but is indicated by two *teqi'ot* of the shofar, while the choir sings verse 13: "he [the righteous] shall grow like a cedar in Lebanon." Out of the rising sixth of the *teqi'ah* grows a long crescendo, a musical picture of the sunrise, which Elgar's friend and publisher August Jaeger, in his analysis of *The Apostles*, renders as follows: "Anon the full orchestra is employed upon a crescendo of surpassing grandeur, the shofar, reinforced by trumpets, shining like a ray of dazzling brightness through the maze of orchestral sound."⁴

The *teqi'ah* of the shofar serves as a leitmotif to announce the Messiah: it returns in the scene "At the Sepulchre" in Part II of *The Apostles*; after an alto recitative, the Watchers repeat their sunrise motifs from Part I and at the words "The dawn reacheth even unto Hebron!" the shofar sounds again, this time to proclaim Jesus's resurrection. The shofar remains connected to Jerusalem, a holy place for both Jews and

---

³ Psalm 92:10 in the King James Bible, used by Elgar.

⁴ August Jaeger, *The Apostles by Edward Elgar (Op. 49): Book of Words with Analytical and Descriptive Notes by A.J. Jaeger* (London: Novello, 1905), 15.

Christians; in Elgar's oratorio, the Temple is a stage for the shofar blower, who proclaims the coming of Jesus and thereby marks holy time in the holy place.

An unusual aspect is the combined Christian and Jewish background of the shofar blasts in *The Apostles*. In 1901, Elgar spent his summer holiday on Ynys Lochtyn, a small island off the coast of Wales. Inspired by the Christian hymns sung by the local people, he wrote a number of fragments and themes for *The Apostles*. The first theme began with the interval E♭3 – C4 on half notes, followed by a melody line inspired by the falling minor thirds of many Ynys Lochtyn hymns. Elgar thought of using this theme "to invoke the great sunrise"[5] at the beginning of his oratorio. To prepare himself further for this passage about the dawn in Jerusalem and the morning service in the Temple, Elgar studied not only the Bible, but also the Talmud; in addition, he asked the advice of Francis Cohen (1862–1934), rabbi, musicologist, and musical editor of the *Jewish Encyclopedia*. In January 1903, Cohen sent Elgar the required information and suggested that he could use words from Psalm 92, which "could be prefaced with a flourish blown on the ancient Shofar, or ram's horn."[6] Elgar's biographer,

---

[5] Jerrold Northrop Moore, *Edward Elgar: A Creative Life* (Oxford: Oxford University Press, 1984), 381.

[6] Moore, *Elgar*, 384.

Jerrold Northrop Moore, concludes rightly, "Thus the first *Apostles* music had been called forth not in response to any words or themes of the Apostles' story, but in circumstances quite unconnected."[7]

After the successful introduction of the shofar in the score, the practical integration of the archaic animal horn in the modern, standardized symphony orchestra went less smoothly. Under "Shofar" in the *Jewish Encyclopedia*, Cohen had written: "The manipulation is of a very rough and empiric character."[8] He had given Elgar the pitches of his best shofar: F♯ and D♯,[9] and the composer transposed this major sixth to E♭ – C. The orchestra searched for a ram's horn with these pitches and discovered that all shofarot are different, that most horns produce a fifth instead of a sixth, and that many instruments are "out of tune." In his letter of August 28, 1903, to Hans Richter, who would conduct the first performance, Elgar suggested a stopgap solution. Elgar was exploring the technical possibilities of both his first shofar and his first typewriter:

---

[7] Moore, *Elgar*, 381.

[8] Francis L. Cohen, Cyrus Adler, Abraham de Harkavy, and Judah David Eisenstein, "Shofar," *Jewish Encyclopedia* (ed. Isidore Singer; New York: Funk and Wagnalls, 1906): http://www.jewishencyclopedia.com (accessed 11/1/16).

[9] Jaeger, *The Apostles*, 13, note.

> There is a part for the "Shofar", (the Hebrew Ram's horn) — of course the real instrument, which I am told is treacherous and next to impossible to use m u s i c a l l y, cannot be used: for the sake of effect and contrast I should like the short passage which stands out, to be played on the long trumpet; in the list of trumpet players I see Mr. Morrow is included; . . . Mr. Morrow would, always with your permission, bring his l o n g e s t and S H I N I E S T T_R_U_M_M_M_M_M_P_E_T!!!! Capable of producing the Shofar "Call". That is what I want.[10]

The "long trumpet" is the by-then already obsolete valveless trumpet, which was harder to play than the valve trumpet, but sounded more sonorous and looked spectacular because of its greater length. Elgar's comments in the letter demonstrate the obscurity of the shofar outside the synagogue. In 1873, the British composer George MacFarren wrote the oratorio *St. John the Baptist*, which opens with three upward fourths of an unaccompanied trumpet, which, according to the Introduction to the score, are blasts of "the ram's horn, or silver trumpet [sic]." And still in 1917, *The Musical Quarterly*, the premier scholarly musical journal in the United States, mentioned *The Apostles* in an article about "Exoticism in Music in Retrospect," calling the ram's horn "the shofar of the

---

[10] Moore, *Elgar*, 133.

Mohammedan [sic] world."[11] Though the shofar was being played in many synagogues throughout the Western world, it was apparently still considered by many to be an exotic instrument from a non-Western culture.

Elgar polishes the rough shofar by doubling it with modern trumpets and horns, thereby integrating the ram's horn into a modern orchestral sound. The shofar blasts are also modernized harmonically; their sixths fit in different inversions of seventh chords, making the shofar passages harmonically more dynamic than would have been possible with shofar fifths in fundamental positions of triads.

Elgar's shofar blasts proclaim the rising of the sun, which conquers darkness and proclaims the Messiah; in the words of John 1:9, "The true light, which enlightens everyone" (NRSV). In his analysis, Jaeger formulates both the Jewish and the Christian aspects of this dawn: "the watchers on the Temple roof greeted the earthly beginning of day" and "The Angel [at Jesus's nocturnal prayer on the mountain] announced the spiritual Dawn breaking for mankind."[12]

---

[11] Douglas Charles Parker, "Exoticism in Music in Retrospect," *The Musical Quarterly* 3.1 (1917): 157.

[12] Jaeger, *The Apostles*, 15.

Despite the Christian spirit of his oratorio, Elgar approached Jewish tradition with openness of mind; he called in the help of an authority like Francis Cohen and documented himself well. The oratorio was received with great acclaim, not only by publisher August Jaeger, who wrote, "That opening! & 'that there' Temple stuff with Shofar, antique cymbals, color most gorgeous & new, effects most astounding & bewildering, organ! &c&c,"[13] but also by the general public and the royal court. The London premiere of *The Apostles* in 1904 was part of a great Elgar Festival, culminating in the composer's elevation to the peerage by King Edward VII. It should not go unmentioned that the festival was created by the efforts of Elgar's patron Leo Schuster, a Jewish banker with relations at court.[14]

Though Elgar originally intended to write a trilogy about the dawn of Christianity, he only composed *The Apostles* (1903) and *The Kingdom* (1906). "What a tragedy," wrote his friend William Reed after Elgar's death, "that he never could be induced to write Part III of the Trilogy, where, as he many times told me, this same shofar was to sound the Last Trumpet."[15]

---

[13] Moore, *Elgar*, 412.

[14] Meirion Hughes, "'The Duc d'Elgar': Making a Composer Gentleman," *Music and the Politics of Culture* (ed. Christopher Norris; New York: St. Martin's, 1989), 60.

[15] William Henry Reed, *Elgar as I Knew Him* (London:

Had Elgar composed this third oratorio, the Trilogy would have been a unique work of art, connecting the first books of the New Testament, the Gospels, with the last book, Revelation, by means of the shofar. Although Elgar outlived *The Apostles* for 31 years, he possibly refrained from composing the last oratorio because times were changing after the Great War and the public was becoming less receptive to Elgar's romantic, Edwardian music. Only at the end of the century, after another World War and a genocide on Jews, would the Italian composer Luciano Berio (1925-2003) write a monumental composition with shofar blasts as numinous as the Last Trumpet.

Luciano Berio, *Hör* from *Requiem of Reconciliation* (1995)

For his composition Luciano Berio did not choose verses from the Bible, but from the German poem *Die Posaunenstelle* ("The Shofar Place"), by the Jewish poet Paul Celan (1920-1970), which will be discussed first.

In the Six-Day War of June 1967, Israel conquered the Old City of Jerusalem. As a result, the direct neighborhood of the Temple Mount became accessible to archeologists. In 1969, a team led by

---

Victor Gollancz, 1936), 145.

Benjamin Mazar found a piece of limestone measuring 1 x 2.5 meters near the southwest corner of the Mount. Judging from its form, it was a cornerstone from the wall of the Temple Mount, which could have come down at the destruction of the Temple in 70 CE. The most interesting point was the Hebrew inscription *l'veit ha-teqi'ah*, "to the house of the *teqi'ah*" or, in other words, "to the place of the shofar blowing." Most researchers interpreted the inscription as a signpost for the shofar blower, who had to announce the beginning and the end of Sabbaths, rituals, and festivals. The most important source for this assumption was the first-century historian Flavius Josephus—possibly also studied by Elgar in his preparatory work for *The Apostles*. In Book 4 of *The Jewish War* Flavius Josephus mentions the priest on one of the four towers on the Temple Mount, who "gave a signal beforehand, with a trumpet at the beginning of every seventh day, in the evening twilight, as also at the evening when that day was finished, as giving notice to the people when they were to leave off work, and when they were to go to work again."[16]

In October 1969, the Romanian Paris-based poet Paul Celan visited Israel. His poem *Die*

---

[16] Flavius Josephus, "The Jewish War," *The New Completed Works of Josephus* (tr. William Whiston; Grand Rapids: Kregel, 1999), 836.

Posaunenstelle, written in November, was inspired by the archeological find of the stone with the inscription.

> Die Posaunenstelle
> tief im glühenden
> Leertext,
> in Fackelhöhe,
> im Zeitloch:
>
> hör dich ein
> mit dem Mund.

The translation by John Felstiner reads: "The shofar place / deep in the glowing / empty-text, / at torch height, / in the timehole: // hear deep in / with your mouth."[17] The hermetic character of this concise poem has led to many different interpretations. Celan himself wrote to a reader who had difficulty understanding his poems: "For the time being, don't bother to understand, read and read again and again, immerse yourself in it, the understanding comes as a matter of course."[18] Many critics have, naturally, ignored Celan's first advice of not bothering to

---

[17] In his first translation of Celan's poem (1995), Felstiner translated *Die Posaunenstelle* as "The Trumpet Place." In *Selected Poems and Prose of Paul Celan* (2001), however, he changed the first line to "The Shofar Place," in order to avoid New Testament connotations. John Felstiner, email to the author, May 6, 2013. See Paul Celan, "The Shofar Place," *Selected Poems and Prose of Paul Celan* (tr. John Felstiner; New York: Norton, 2001), 360.

[18] Paul Celan and Ilana Shmueli, *Briefwechsel. Herausgegeben von Ilana Shmueli und Thomas Sparr* (Frankfurt am Main: Suhrkamp, 2004), 150. Translation mine.

understand, following his second advice of reading again and again, and waiting for the fulfillment of his prediction that "the understanding comes as a matter of course." The composer Luciano Berio, however, who set *Die Posaunenstelle* to music, followed Celan's advice by immersing the hearer in overwhelming and complicated music, which does not explain any details, but instead reveals the numinous character of the poem.

The German word *Stelle* can be a place in a territory or a passage in a book, while the word *Posaune* — in almost all Jewish and Christian Bible translations — denotes the Hebrew *shofar*. Aside from the Hebrew preposition *l'* ("to"), Celan's first verse corresponds to the inscription on the stone from the Temple Mount, *l'veit hateqi'ah*, "to the place of the shofar blowing."

The shofar blast, in combination with the *glühenden / Leertext* ("glowing / empty-text") seems an allusion to God's great shofar in Exodus 19:16 and particularly in Deuteronomy 4:12: "The Lord spoke to you out of the fire; you heard the sound of words but perceived no shape — nothing but a voice." The fire corresponds to *glühenden* in the poem, and the qualification "the sound of words but... no shape — nothing but a voice" to *Leertext*. [I]n *Fackelhöhe* ("at torch height") could pertain to the same biblical event of the theophany in Exodus 20:15, when after the giving of the Ten Commandments, "All the people witnessed the thunder and lightning, the blare of the horn and the mountain smoking." The Hebrew *halapidim*, "the lightning," can also mean "the torches," while *qol hashofar*, "the blare of the horn," can also be translated as "the sound of the shofar." The literary historians Stéphane Moses[19] and John Felstiner correlate Moses's ascent of Mount Sinai in Exodus 19:3, 20, and 20:18 and his descent in Exodus 19:14, 25, and 24:3, with the vertical dimension in Celan's "*Die Posaunenstelle*, and this dimension finally does seat itself in time as well as space, thereby grounding the poem in originative events from Genesis and Exodus."

Given the mystic elements in many of Celan's poems, the first stanza of *Die Posaunenstelle* could express the kabbalistic concept of *tzimtzum*, the process whereby God contracts himself temporarily, "so as to leave a kind of primordial space or nondivine vacuum within which creation can take place.... Yet even the space vacated by God during the act of *tzimtzum* is not devoid of the divine light."[20] In that case, the *Leertext*

---

[19] Stéphane Moses, "Patterns of Negativity in Paul Celan's 'The Trumpet Place,'" *Languages of the Unsayable: The Play of Negativity in Literature and Literary Theory* (ed. Sanford Budick and Wolfgang Iser; tr. Ken Frieden; New York: Columbia University Press, 1987), 214.

[20] R. J. Zwi Werblowsky and Geoffrey Wigoder, eds., *The Oxford Dictionary of the Jewish Religion* (New York: Oxford University Press, 1997), 707.

("empty text") and *Zeitloch* ("timehole") would concern this nondivine vacuum, while the glowing of the *Leertext* would express the remaining divine light.

The blank line after the first stanza of *Die Posaunenstelle* could be a typographical representation of the "timehole" and the "empty-text," while the colon at the end of the first stanza could mean that the second stanza is the conclusion from the first. John Felstiner's interpretation of the second stanza seems plausible as an imperative related to the first stanza;[21] Felstiner points to the similarity in both rhythm and speech sounds between *hör dich ein* ("hear deep in") and the shofar blast "te-qi-ah," and moreover, to the meaning of the imperative *Her dikh ayn* in Yiddish, a language Celan was familiar with: "Attention please!" or "Listen!" Building on this interpretation, it would be possible to read the sentence "hör dich ein / mit dem Mund" as related to the *mitzvah* of shofar hearing and blowing, which are considered each other's complements.

Just as Elgar's *The Apostles*, Berio's *Hör* was commissioned by a festival. The *Europäisches Musikfest Stuttgart* was founded in Germany in 1985 as an international summer festival with concerts, lectures, and master classes. The initiators, the Bach Akademie

---

[21] John Felstiner, "'Deep in the glowing text-void': Translating Late Celan," *Representations* 32 (1990): 183.

Stuttgart and their conductor Helmuth Rilling, decided to commemorate the fiftieth anniversary of the end of World War II in the festival of 1995. Fourteen composers from countries which had been involved in the war were each asked to write a part of a Latin *Requiem of Reconciliation*, which would be performed by the *Gächinger Kantorei* from Germany, the Chamber Choir of Kraków, Poland, and the Israel Philharmonic Orchestra. Thirteen composers accepted the commission. Berio, however, had objections: as a nonbeliever, he did not feel like contributing to a Catholic requiem and, moreover, he expected it to become a musical "one-pan meal." Eventually, he made a contribution entitled *Hör*, and his wife, the Israeli musicologist Talia Pecker, told how it came about:

> As far as I remember, Berio accepted to participate in the Requiem project only on the condition that *Hör* is performed as a prologue to the unique performance in Stuttgart. Once this condition was accepted by Helmut Rilling, Berio composed the piece specifically for that event, which we both attended. He then used the material of *Hör* in *Outis* and renamed *Hör* as *Shofar* so it could be performed as an independent piece.[22]

---

[22] Talia Pecker Berio, email to the author, March 17, 2011. *Outis* (1996) is a music theater piece.

Hör has nothing to do with the Latin requiem, as its character is Jewish and the text consists of the above-mentioned German poem *Die Posaunenstelle* by Paul Celan. *Hör*, in English "hear" and in Hebrew "*shema*," is the first word of the most important Jewish prayer, *Shema Yisrael*, a call to listen.

Though *Hör* lasts only five minutes, it requires just as large an ensemble as Elgar's *The Apostles*: a mixed chorus and a symphony orchestra (extended with saxophones, marimbaphone, celesta, piano, accordion, and electronic organ). It is not the composition of an intact poem, but instead, the musical expression of its essence: the attitude toward the divine mystery. With its combination of loud voices and brass instruments it resembles the *teru'ah* as a shofar blowing and shouting ritual in praise of God's kingship, as in Psalm 47:6: "God ascends midst acclamation [*teru'ah*]; / the LORD, to blasts of the horn [*shofar*]," and Psalm 89:16: "Happy is the people who know the joyful shout [*teru'ah*]; / O LORD, they walk in the light of Your presence."

Berio does not aim at an understanding of Celan's poem; instead, he makes it even more hermetic and fragmented by breaking up sentences into words, words into syllables, and syllables into speech sounds. Physical manifestations of religious emotions appear in a stylized form: the chattering of teeth before the awesome God becomes a "very fast dental tremolo *come gli stromenti*" ("just as the instruments") on long notes; and holding one's breath in awe for the mystery assumes the form of a medieval *hoquetus* (musical "hiccup") with the sopranos and altos alternately singing one syllable ("Po-sau-nen-stel-le"). Below is an example of the disintegration of the poem's first three lines; long notes have a dash added and the syllables sung with "dental tremolo" are italicized:

>Die Die Die— Die Po*sau*—*ne*— Die Posaunen*stel*—le *Die*— Die Posaunenste*lle*— Tief— Tief—Tief— Tief— Tief— Im Im Im Tief— Tief *im*— glühenden tief im *glü* im glühenden glühenden glühenden— Leertext Leer—text— Die— Posaunenstelle tief im glühenden Leer*text*—

In some passages, Berio's language is even more hermetic than Celan's and there he uses phonetic symbols instead of letters. Before Celan's poem begins, the choir sings the following sounds: "[i]—[ɔ] [a] Die [u] [ɔ]—[a]." The square brackets, sometimes used to mark phonetic symbols, are in the score and the long dashes indicate glissandos. It could be that these sounds have no semantic meaning and are meant to bridge the gap between voices and instruments. However, in Berio's native language, Italian, they provide the following sentence: "*Io a Diu o a...*" *Diu* (*Dio* in standard Italian) is the word for "God" in a number of Italian dialects, and the meaning of the unfinished sentence would then be "I to God or to...," thus expressing religious or existential doubt.

The musical core of *Hör* consists of free variants of the traditional shofar blasts in the trombone — called *Posaune* in German, just like the shofar — and Berio marks these blasts with "[SHOFAR]." At the beginning of the composition, the first trombone plays a *teqi'ah* with an upward glissando over a second instead of a fifth; a *shevarim* with tone repetition instead of three upward fifths; a *teru'ah* with the characteristic tone repetition; and again a *teqi'ah*. Due to the doubling in other wind and string instruments, this passage sounds extraordinarily powerful. These blasts constitute one of the four layers of which *Hör* is made up:

    1. the above-mentioned shofar blasts in free variants, with a powerful and energetic sound;
    2. a sound field defined by tremolo. There are different rhythms in different speeds and, as a result, the sound field lacks a clear pulse. The instruments enter in sequence, playing a free canon. In detail, this layer is highly differentiated and agile, while the whole makes a static impression. The tone repetitions are diminutions of the trombone's *teru'ah*, while they also fit in with the "dental tremolo" of the singers;

3. a sound field consisting of chord figurations, giving a harmonically diffuse overall impression;

4. polyphonic choral passages, showing a certain similarity with Renaissance polyphony by their restricted range, imitation technique, hoquetus technique, and slow harmonic cadences. These passages are notable for their passionate character.

Both apart and together, these different layers express the *mysterium tremendum*, analyzed by the theologian Rudolf Otto in *Das Heilige* (*The Idea of the Holy*) from 1917. Otto describes the effect of the *mysterium tremendum* or "awe-inspiring mystery" as follows:

> It may burst in sudden eruption up from the depths of the soul with spasms and convulsions, or lead to the strangest excitements, to intoxicated frenzy, to transport, and to ecstasy.... It has its crude, barbaric antecedents and early manifestations, and again it may be developed into something beautiful and pure and glorious. It may become the hushed, trembling, and speechless humility of the creature in the presence of — whom or what? In the presence of that which is a *mystery* inexpressible and above all creatures.[23]

---

[23] Rudolf Otto, *The Idea of the Holy: An Inquiry into the Non-Rational Factor in the Idea of the Divine and Its Relation to the*

In the numinous, defined by the *mysterium tremendum*, Otto distinguishes four elements:[24]

1. the element of awefulness (*tremendum*);
2. the element of "overpoweringness" (*majestas*), before which man feels weak and helpless;
3. the element of "energy" or urgency, related to God's deeds of love or wrath;
4. the "Wholly Other" (*mysterium*), surpassing human understanding.

These are also essential elements of the liturgy of Yom Kippur, one of the Days of "Awe": the *tremendum* is expressed in "angels rush forward, / and are held by trembling, shaking;"[25] the *majestas* in "Praise Him for His mighty deeds; praise Him for His surpassing greatness;"[26] the energy in "the upright will exult, and the pious revel in joy, … and all wickedness will fade away like smoke;"[27] and the *mysterium* in "Just as I leap toward you but cannot touch you."[28] The meaning of the Hebrew word *kippur* ("atonement" or "reconciliation") is even in line with the title *Requiem of*

Rational (tr. John W. Harvey; Oxford University Press, 1958), 12–13.

[24] Otto, *The Idea of the Holy*, 12–30.

[25] Jonathan Sacks, tr. and comm., *The Koren Yom Kippur Maḥzor* (Jerusalem: Koren, 2012), 842.

[26] Sacks, *The Yom Kippur Maḥzor*, 542, and Psalm 150.

[27] Sacks, *The Yom Kippur Maḥzor*, 864.

[28] Sacks, *The Yom Kippur Maḥzor*, 1248.

Reconciliation. Moreover, the four religious elements exactly fit the four musical layers of Berio's "Shofar": the *tremendum*, the "tremolo" passages; the *majestas*, the sound fields with their chord figurations; the "energy," the shofar blasts; and the *mysterium*, the polyphonic choral passages.

Paradoxically, the effect of the *mysterium tremendum* in *Hör* depends largely on an alienating use of clichés from distant, secular musical spheres. The trumpet with the wah-wah mute does not sound like a nightclub singer, but like a voice choked by religious shuddering; the trombone glissando is not a Dixieland effect, but an expression of divine power; and the usually cheerful and superficial accordion is transformed into an organ of intimate devotion. The falling second, the cliché *par excellence* of the *seufzer* from the Baroque lamento, is inverted into an upward second and an expression of desire for higher things.

Another paradox in this highly expressive music is the practical impossibility of performing the parts with romantic, Elgarian expression; to an either very soft or very loud tremolo, an instrumentalist can hardly add any expression, while the performance of a singer with chattering teeth is limited. This nonsubjective way of playing resembles the character of shofar blowing in the synagogue: "If its sound is thin, thick or dry, it is valid, since all sounds emitted by a shofar can pass muster," as the authors of the Talmud put it in tractate *Rosh HaShanah* 27b.

With regard to dynamics, *Hör* has an overpowering beginning followed by a long anticlimax. At three quarters of the total duration, the shuddering comes abruptly to an end, to make way for a quiet passage of the accordion with a restrained accompaniment. What the accordion plays here very softly is the rising second D – E♭, a transposition of the augmented unison C – C♯, the interval of the energetic trombone *teqi'ah* from the beginning. Of all instruments, the cheerful, secular accordion creates the moment of repentance, the *teshuvah* of the Days of Awe. By bringing the highly dynamic music to a complete halt, Berio changes the listener's experience of time, and perhaps this is his interpretation of the "negative" *Zeitloch* ("timehole") in Celan's poem. The powerful, shofar-like trombone with its "sudden eruption up from the depths of the soul" (Otto) and the subdued accordion with its "tranquil mood of deepest worship" (Otto) give voice to two sides of the same *mysterium tremendum*.

Conclusions

Elgar's "The Calling of the Apostles" from his oratorio *The Apostles* and Berio's *Hör* from the *Requiem of Reconciliation* have many points in common. Both compositions were commissioned by a festival and both are religious music for the concert hall. The composers were inspired by the shofar, though neither was Jewish. However, they knew what it meant to belong to a minority: Edward Elgar was a Roman Catholic—a drawback for his career in Protestant Britain—whereas Luciano Berio was a secular composer in Roman Catholic Italy. Both shofar episodes are parts of monumental Christian works for choir and orchestra centered around the life and death of Jesus; and both evoke the Temple in Jerusalem, a glorious building in Elgar's oratorio but a ruin in Berio's cantata. The titles, "The Calling" and *Hör*, invite a dialogue. Both composers avoid the easy way of quoting the traditional shofar blasts to a simple accompaniment: Elgar focuses on the timbre of the shofar by doubling the ram's horn with modern instruments and integrating it into a colorful orchestration, whereas Berio focuses on the rhythm of the blasts, which he varies in many ways.

The differences between the two compositions are still more striking. In contrast to Elgar, Berio prevents listeners from being carried away by the music and he states elsewhere: "I will not concern myself here with music as an emotional and reassuring commodity for the listener."[29] Elgar's shofar blasts are

---

[29] Luciano Berio, *Remembering the Future* (Charles Eliot

completely traditional, whereas Berio's blasts are distorted. Elgar's singers sing understandable words, whereas Berio's singers shudder and chatter their teeth in unintelligible syllables. Both compositions center around the light, but Elgar depicts a sunrise — "The face of all the East is now ablaze with light, the Dawn reacheth even unto Hebron!" — whereas Berio evokes a "glowing empty-text," which is a concept rather than an image. Elgar's shofar blasts proclaim a bright future; Berio's blasts, in contrast, celebrate the victims of a dark past. Even the images of God are different: in 1903, at the beginning of the century, Elgar's God is understandable, though he transcends the human scale; in 1995, at the end of the century, Berio's God is a *mysterium tremendum*.

Norton Lectures; Cambridge, MA: Harvard University Press, 2006), 2.

Sounding the Shofar in Hollywood Film Scores

Aaron Fruchtman

At the conclusion of the nativity scene in William Wyler's *Ben-Hur* (1959), a young shepherd, who remains outside the stable while the three Magi visit Mary and the baby Jesus, turns toward Bethlehem and sounds two long blasts on a ram's horn, or shofar. The first call turns the heads of the onlookers, while the second burst sounds as the camera cuts to the Christmas Star glistening above the manger. These tones echo, then segue into a three-trumpet fanfare figure that begins the main title "Prelude" of the film. Although the blasts signal the birth of Jesus, the shofar is not notated in composer Miklós Rózsa's score, as it is source music.[1]

The shofar, usually but not invariably a ram's horn, has figured prominently in Jewish narratives since biblical times. The ritual instrument is now most familiar to Jews for its liturgical use in the synagogue, specifically when the horn is played approximately a

---

[1] "Source music" is a Hollywood term meaning music from an on-screen source, as opposed to underscoring or "background music."

hundred times on Rosh Hashanah (the Jewish New Year) and once at the conclusion of Yom Kippur (Day of Atonement), with the final blast marking the end of the Days of Awe.[2] As Jewish music scholar Marsha Bryan Edelman observes, "Only the shofar, with a signaling, rather than a musical function, would retain its unique role in Jewish ritual. The shofar is thus the only instrument to remain in continuous use among all communities throughout Jewish history, to this day."[3]

After the destruction of the Second Temple in Jerusalem, musical instruments were banned, but the shofar remained a crucial sonority for the world of Judaism, serving a ritual function in the synagogue during the High Holy Days but also possessing numerous other roles.[4] In his detailed study of the biblical aerophone, Jeremy Montagu addresses the various noncultic signaling functions of the shofar, such as communal announcements and alarms, war signals, calls to assembly, judicial pronouncements,

---

[2] To emphasize the importance of the shofar to Rosh Hashanah, it is worth noting that the Torah refers to this holy day (the first of Tishri) as *yom teru'ah* (literally "the day of blowing" the shofar).

[3] Marsha Bryan Edelman, *Discovering Jewish Music* (Philadelphia: Jewish Publication Society, 2003), 282, n. 2.

[4] Jeremy Montagu explains that the shofar's dual use in religious and noncultic contexts has allowed it to survive to the present day. Jeremy Montagu, *The Shofar: Its History and Use* (Lanham: Rowman & Littlefield, 2015), 3.

celebrations, and lamentations.⁵ The instrument's most noted noncultic use was as a battle trumpet. In the book of Joshua (6:1-27), the Israelites sought to capture Jericho from the Canaanites. However, the Jewish army was unprepared to scale the city's walls, and so God commanded Joshua to have his priests circle the city seven times while sounding shofars: "And when a long blast is sounded on the horn—as soon as you hear that sound of the horn—all the people shall give a mighty shout. Thereupon the city wall will collapse, and the people shall advance, every man straight ahead" (Josh 6:5). The shofar blast, accompanied by the voices of the Israelites, shattered their enemy's fortification.⁶ This remarkable acoustic event adds a numinous quality to the shofar's sonority that some twentieth and twenty-first-century composers have drawn upon for varying dramatic goals.

A few Hollywood composers have used the shofar in their film scores. Due to the narrative content, stereotypical shofar blasts occur in the scores to the

---

⁵ Montagu, *The Shofar*, 49-59. The father of Jewish musicology, Abraham Z. Idelsohn, adds that a "Shofar of Redemption" would be blown by the prophet Elijah to announce the coming of the Messiah, similar to the treatment of the ram's horn in signaling Jesus's birth in the opening scene of *Ben-Hur* as described above. Abraham Z. Idelsohn, *Jewish Music in Its Historical Development* (New York: Dover, 1992), 9.

⁶ This famous episode is remembered in song with the African-American spiritual "Joshua Fit the Battle of Jericho."

biblical epics of the post-war era, such as *The Ten Commandments* (1956), *The Story of Ruth* (1960), and the aforementioned *Ben-Hur*, composed by Elmer Bernstein, Franz Waxman, and Miklós Rózsa, respectively. These films share stories derived from the Bible that gain musical verisimilitude—"local color"— by including conspicuous evocations of the shofar as a biblical instrument. As in *Ben-Hur*, the shofar is used exclusively as a source sound in Cecil B. DeMille's *The Ten Commandments*, in which Joshua sounds a shofar to alert Moses and the Israelites to the imminent approach of Pharaoh and his army. It is blasted again later in the film to signal Moses's furious return from Mount Sinai, after he discovers the Israelites worshipping the golden calf.[7] None of Bernstein's own themes are based on shofar calls, not even the militaristic one associated with Joshua. Waxman, on the other hand, infuses his score to *The Story of Ruth* with both statements of the shofar and brass imitations of the ritual instrument. The film begins with "The Prophet" cue, which starts with a forte statement of the main theme. This forceful tune opens with a unison ascending perfect fifth in the brass, which could be interpreted as recalling a *teqi'ah* (long) call.[8] More explicit in nature is the *shevarim*

---

[7] Arnold Schoenberg alludes to a *teqi'ah* call at this same narrative moment in his opera *Moses und Aron* (1932).

[8] Musicologist Stephen C. Meyer describes a similar type of "reference to the blast of the shofar" in Samson's theme in Victor

(three short notes) call stated by a trumpet directly before the narrator's introduction, and a modern imitation that foreshadows an actual *shevarim* call by a shofar in the upcoming "Main Title."[9] Unlike the shofar blasts in *Ben-Hur* and *The Ten Commandments*, Waxman's use of the instrument does not have a signaling function, but rather uses sonority as signifier—musical symbolism. Here, the shofar acts as an instrument of Jewish remembrance, a musical emblem of Old Testament Judaism, as it is entirely associated with Jewish characters and dramatically spiritual moments in the film.[10] The ram's horn is thus a crucial part of Waxman's remarkable score. As with *Ben-Hur*, several later musical works based on the Christian scriptures use the Jewish biblical instrument, much like Edward Elgar did in his oratorio, *The Apostles*, Op. 49 (1903). Stephen Schwartz starts his *Godspell* song "Prepare Ye, The Way of The Lord" with John the Baptist blowing *teru'ah* (a repeated call) and *teqi'ah*. Similarly, in the score to *The Gospel of John* (2003)

Young's score to *Samson and Delilah* (1949). Stephen C. Meyer, *Epic Sound: Music in Postwar Hollywood Biblical Films* (Bloomington: Indiana University Press, 2015), 23.

[9] The film's opening credits roll over a Torah scroll with a prominently displayed shofar resting beneath it.

[10] In a similar moment of reminiscence, Alfred Newman has a shofar play a *shevarim* call during a flashback scene to King Saul's death in his score for *David and Bathsheba* (1951). That is the only shofar blast in this "sword-and-sandal" epic.

by Jeff Danna, the cues "Here Comes Your King" and "Jesus at the Temple" begin with multiple *teqi'ah* calls. The latter score is filled with Middle Eastern percussion and woodwinds augmenting the traditional Hollywood orchestra. However, as in *Ben-Hur*, the shofar is not integrated into the thematic material.

Less conventional appearances of the venerable instrument occur in the film scores of Jerrald "Jerry" Goldsmith. The Academy Award-winning composer, known for his modernist compositional techniques and avant-garde orchestration choices, used the shofar outside of the more traditional biblical narratives, incorporating its use into science fiction films such as Franklin J. Schaffner's *Planet of the Apes* (1968) and Robert Wise's *Star Trek: The Motion Picture* (1979). Scholars of film music revere Goldsmith's work on *Planet of the Apes* as a landmark avant-garde score. The use of the shofar is intriguing, given that the film does not contain a biblical narrative and does not have any characters who are identified in any way, covertly or overtly, as Jewish. The closest we get to a Jewish character in the film is the Episcopalian Charlton Heston, the same lead actor who played Moses in *The Ten Commandments* twelve years earlier, and who now portrays astronaut Taylor on this "alien" planet. Nevertheless, the shofar performs a key role introducing the militaristic primates in the cue "The

Hunt."¹¹ At the first medium close-up shot of a gorilla soldier, the shofar sounds for the first time (in measure 52) as the hunting of humans commences. The ape shofar motive is an eighth note G (1) that leaps up to an eighth note tied to a half note D (5) before returning to the original pitch. The ape motive is related closely to two traditional shofar calls: *teqi'ah* (short-long-short rhythm with leaps from 1 - 5 - 8) and *shevarim* (three repeated sixteenth notes to dotted eighth notes from 1 - 5 - 1 - 5 - 1 - 5 - 5 - 8).¹² Goldsmith's musical sketch indicates the melody was to be played on a ram's horn by Carroll "Cappy" Lewis.¹³ In both shofar statements in this cue (the motive reappears in mm. 90–96), the ram's horn is acoustically prominent, with the other instruments adding color and rhythmic momentum around the calls. In an interview about Goldsmith's

---

¹¹ Goldsmith's longtime collaborator, Arthur Morton, orchestrated the cue.

¹² The melodic formulae of the calls are not *Mi-Sinai* and there are copious variations between particular synagogues and shofar blowers. However, Jeremy Montagu explains that despite the discrepancies between communities, there are certain consistent characteristics such as *teqi'ah* being a "longish call," *shevarim* being "three shortish calls," and *teru'ah* being "quavering." Montagu, *The Shofar*, 20.

¹³ Lewis was a jazz trumpeter who played in the Woody Herman band. During his time in Hollywood, he doubled on flugelhorn, harmonica, and on this occasion a shofar. For a brief bio of Lewis see: Scott Yanow, *The Trumpet Kings: The Players Who Shaped the Sound of Jazz Trumpet* (San Francisco: Backbeat Books, 2001), 232.

particular orchestration sound, recording mixer Bruce Botnick remarked, "I can always count on Jerry, always to come up with something extremely unique, that will be a character in the film."[14] Botnick astutely recognizes Goldsmith's unifying compositional approach of associating characters with instruments or sounds, which is in strong contrast to the use of Wagnerian leitmotifs as was commonly practiced in much Hollywood scoring.

Thirty-five years after composing his score, Goldsmith reflected on the shofar in "The Hunt":

> When we first see the shot of the horse, and the rider turns toward us and we see that he is a simian, the music has this organic feel which is a ram's horn actually being played, which has two notes on it, but they're effective. I think the idea is given that we're dealing with a strange race and an upside-down world; that's what we're dealing with there.[15]

Goldsmith's reminiscence is not particularly revealing. Of course the ram's horn sounds organic, while orchestral woodwinds and brass instruments sound manufactured; that is the nature of each one's

---

[14] Jerry Goldsmith, *Film Music Masters: Jerry Goldsmith*, directed by Fred Karlin (Atlanta: Karlin/Tilford Productions, 2005), DVD.

[15] Jerry Goldsmith, *The Planet of the Apes: Widescreen 35th Anniversary Edition*, directed by Franklin J. Schaffner (Beverly Hills: 20th Century Fox Home Entertainment, 2004), DVD.

construction.¹⁶ Perhaps film music writer John Takis describes the sound more aptly than the composer when he explains, "He also resurrected archaic instruments such as the ram's horn, lending a primal authenticity to cues such as 'The Hunt.'"¹⁷ "Archaic" and "primal" are closer descriptors to Goldsmith's usage of the shofar than "organic." This cue, cast in a sophisticated musical characterization of "primitivism" like that of Stravinsky's *Le Sacre du printemps*, with extreme dissonances, frenetic rhythms, and timbral oddities, parallels the scene's chaos. The ram's horn complements these musical characteristics by adding a "primal" sound with possible symbolic meanings.¹⁸

---

¹⁶ As not to seem dismissive of Goldsmith's organic comment, acclaimed musicologist Philip V. Bohlman seems to agree with Goldsmith when he explains the musical meaning of the shofar as occupying "an ontological domain between the human voice and the artifice of instrumental music." Philip V. Bohlman, "Epilogue: Beyond Jewish Modernism," *Jewish Musical Modernism, Old and New* (ed. Philip V. Bohlman; Chicago: University of Chicago Press, 2008), 154.

¹⁷ John Takis, "Good as Goldsmith: The Goldsmith Method as Revealed in Four 1960s Masterpieces," *Film Score Monthly* 9.7 (August 2004): 28–32.

¹⁸ Contemporary audiences understood the film's not-so-subtle storyline of a (white) human prisoner in a (black) simian world, and the accompanying interspecies injustices, as a thinly veiled metaphor for African Americans living in 1960s America. One wonders if Goldsmith associated the shofar, the iconic Jewish musical instrument, with the black gorillas to add a layer of musical

What separated Goldsmith from his colleagues was his distinctive timbral palette. He was not a melodist on par with his Hollywood contemporary John Williams. Instead, Goldsmith made a name for himself fashioning innovative approaches to texture and sound. Composer Irwin Bazelon describes the score for *Planet of the Apes* as partially "exciting musical sound effects."[19] Along with the shofar, Goldsmith applies the distinctive colors of stainless-steel mixing bowls, a Brazilian cuíca drum, a bass slide whistle, and brass instruments played with inverted mouthpieces.[20]

The archaic battle connotation of the shofar appears in another guise in Goldsmith's famous science fiction film score to *Star Trek: The Motion Picture*. In this, Goldsmith links the antagonist Klingons with a leitmotif reminiscent of a shofar call. Dissimilar from the modernist score he composed for *Planet of the Apes*, with *Star Trek: The Motion Picture*, Goldsmith followed the lead of John Williams and his genre-defining space opera *Star Wars* (1977), creating a

---

minority camaraderie to the film. Unfortunately, this sort of conjecturing only leads us toward fruitless armchair psychologizing, however tempting the metaphor might be.

[19] Irwin Bazelon, *Knowing the Score: Notes on Film Music* (New York: Van Nostrand Reinhold, 1975), 151.

[20] In his sketch, Goldsmith requests percussionist Emil Richards for the famous mixing bowl part. "Music Sketches: Planet of the Apes (1968)," Jerry Goldsmith Collection f.109, Margaret Herrick Library.

score that is gloriously tonal and romantic with apparent influences of Richard Strauss, Richard Wagner, and Ralph Vaughan Williams. In the opening scene, the antagonist's theme is stated in the cue "Klingon Battle." The theme is not performed by a shofar, but by two oboes, an English horn, a descant horn, three bassoons, and a tenor saxophone. However, the melodic profile is reminiscent of both the ram's horn motive from "The Hunt" and a *shevarim* shofar call. The theme opens with an upwardly leaping fifth, which is repeated four times before Goldsmith continues the motive in an altered descending major second sequence (1 – 5 – 1 – 4 – b7 – b6 – b3). This developmental process accentuates aspects of the melody's primitivism but the angular nature of the whole-step sequence creates a more melodically interesting figure than anything a shofar can produce. Film music writer Jeff Bond hears a related, yet less specifically Jewish, battle cry when he suggested that Goldsmith created a sort of "clarion call theme for the Klingons based on an open fifth."[21] The clarion, or medieval short trumpet that accompanied soldiers into combat,[22] is a descendant of the Jewish battle shofar.

---

[21] Jeff Bond, *The Music of Star Trek* (Los Angeles: Lone Eagle, 1998), 89.

[22] Reine Dahlqvist and Edward H. Tarr, "Clarino." *Grove Music Online* (January 2001): http://oxfordindex.oup.com/view/10.1093/gmo/9781561592630.article.05865 (accessed 12/18/

One can imagine either of these horns playing the primal Klingon theme. Goldsmith discussed his approach to depicting the Klingons, stating,

> The Klingon thing was instinctual, I knew that there was a barbaric quality about them, a primitive quality, and they were the aggressors.... I did want to get that into the music, and that was the sum of the intellectual rationalization. I guess they were the bad guys and they were attacking, so I figured we needed a battle cry for them.[23]

Despite Goldsmith's unambiguous statement minimizing his "intellectual rationalization," there are several reasons to believe that he was explicitly imitating shofar calls. First, and most obviously, the theme recalls Goldsmith's own shofar motive from "The Hunt," which was played on the ram's horn. Second, the theme is remarkably similar melodically to the *shevarim* shofar call. Third, there is a long history of Jewish composers imitating shofar calls with traditional orchestral instruments. These allusions or explicit imitations appear in the works of Leonard Bernstein, Aaron Copland, and Leo M. Zeitlin.[24] Due to

---

2016).

[23] Jeff Bond and Mike Matessino, liner notes for *Star Trek: The Motion Picture: Music from the Original Soundtrack*, Sony B0089G1UYC, CD, 2012.

[24] Jack Gottlieb points out that Bernstein instructs trumpeters to play "like a shofar" in a fanfare in *Candide*. Gottlieb

the shofar's tonal instability, these composers and others often chose to approximate the instrument's timbre with French horns using a brass mute. Lastly, and most persuasive, is the Klingon theme's reappearance with an altered instrumentation in *Star Trek V: The Final Frontier* (1989).[25] In this sequel, Goldsmith accompanies his now iconic Klingon theme

---

also claims that the opening three-note figure that opens Bernstein's "Symphonic Dances" from *West Side Story* is an allusion to the *teqi'ah gedolah*. Jack Gottlieb, *Funny, It Doesn't Sound Jewish: How Yiddish Songs and Synagogue Melodies Influenced Tin Pan Alley, Broadway, and Hollywood* (Albany: State University of New York Press, 2004), 179–80. Howard Pollack identifies a less obvious allusion to shofar calls in the opening motive of Aaron Copland's Piano Concerto (1926), and hopes others will investigate this connection further. Howard Pollack, *Aaron Copland: The Life and Work of an Uncommon Man* (New York: Henry Holt, 1999), 522. Paula Eisenstein Baker and Robert Nelson keenly analyze the imitative shofar calls scored for French horns (and later saxophones and trombones) found in Leo Zeitlin's *Palestina*. This overture played before the feature film at the Capitol Theatre in the weeks preceding the High Holy Days. Here the imitation is explicit and directly aimed at the Jewish movie-going audiences. Paula Eisenstein Baker and Robert Nelson, *Palestina: An Overture for the Capitol Theatre, New York* (Middleton: A-R Editions, 2014), xii. Ernest Bloch also imitates the *teru'ah* shofar figure in the second section of his *Schelomo* with a bassoon and oboe.

[25] Goldsmith did not compose the three intermediate film scores in the Star Trek franchise, between *Star Trek: The Motion Picture* and *The Final Frontier*. Hollywood newcomer James Horner scored *Star Trek II: The Wrath of Khan* (1982) and *Star Trek III: The Search for Spock* (1984), while veteran composer Leonard Rosenman wrote the score for *Star Trek IV: The Voyage Home* (1986). Neither of these Jewish composers chose to use a shofar in these scores.

in the cue "Without Help" with two blasts from a shofar, as if confirming the presumption that the theme always had this musical and symbolic association. Goldsmith identifies the shofar with primitivism in his scores to *Planet of the Apes* and the two *Star Trek* films.[26] His musical treatment of Klingons and gorillas are closely related as they both serve as archetypal antagonists.[27] Goldsmith's use of the shofar signifies primitive war and reminds the knowledgeable audience member of the instrument's role as a battle trumpet.[28]

The shofar makes brief yet significant appearances in two recent films with scores by non-Jewish composers. In the thoroughly predictable action film *End of Days* (1999), former police detective Jericho

---

[26] Goldsmith was nominated for Best Original Score Academy Awards for *Planet of the Apes* and *Star Trek: The Motion Picture*.

[27] Before Trekkers take umbrage with my broadly brushed painting of the Klingons as antagonists, let me explain. It is true Klingons are a more complicated set of characters than simply "bad guy," however Goldsmith is portraying them as such and focusing on their warrior culture.

[28] Numerous websites (including the "Shofar" Wikipedia page) incorrectly assert that Goldsmith also used the shofar in his score to the science-fiction/horror film *Alien* (1979). This false assumption likely endures due to an aural similarity between the shofar and the actual instrument used in the score—a conch shell. While both are "organic" instruments—to use the term Goldsmith preferred—the shofar does not have the larger melodic capabilities of the conch.

Cane battles Satan himself to protect a young woman from being impregnated and bearing the Antichrist. In the "Main Title" cue, composer John Debney delivers a hackneyed "spiritual" aura complete with the requisite boy soprano chanting in Latin and an orchestral quotation of the *Dies Irae* chant from the plainsong Requiem mass. Amid the cacophony of boy soloist, choir, synthesizers, orchestra, church bells, and clanging percussion, a heavily reverberating shofar blast is sounded as a single long note. The addition of the ram's horn might be construed as a mere sound effect, but the composer's usage here is an attempt to add a layer of symbolic meaning to the film. By connecting the ancient Jewish battle instrument to the film's opening cue, Debney foreshadows the spiritual battle between good and evil that concludes the movie. Regarding his choice of instrumentation in *End of Days*, Debney remarked, "There are sound environments and textural diversity that come from instruments of ancient times to the futuristic colors of electronics and techno."[29] The primal and archaic sonority conjured by the shofar attracted both Debney and Goldsmith, yet the ram horn's Jewish connotations go unmentioned by both. Instead, it is simply a musical signifier for

---

[29] Larry M. Timm, *The Soul of Cinema: An Appreciation of Film Music* (Needham Heights: Simon & Schuster Custom, 1998), 327.

"antiquity." On the subject of his later score to *The Passion of the Christ* (2004), Debney discussed traditional Jewish music, noting, "I found that it wasn't as interesting as some of the other ethnic traditional music."[30] This statement explains the hodgepodge of Indian and Arab musics that resonate through his faux-biblical score, and perhaps the shofar's inclusion in the demonic action thriller, as well.

The shofar plays a slightly more notable role in Edward Shearmur's score to Iain Softley's thriller *The Skeleton Key* (2005). Renowned blues artists such as Robert Johnson and Blind Willie Johnson occupy a significant position on the film's soundtrack along with Shearmur's accomplished, if somewhat conventional, music. The film opens with Caroline, a young caregiver, being hired to look after Ben, an immobilized stroke victim. In an early scene where Caroline discovers Ben missing from his bed, a frantic search begins. During her pursuit, Caroline becomes cognizant of supernatural forces at work in Ben's dilapidated plantation house. At this moment of realization a shofar sounds with two consecutive long tones above a pounding rhythmic pattern.[31] The shofar

---

[30] Dave Roos, "Wail Watching," *Salon* (May 2004): http://www.salon.com/2004.05/25/wails/ (accessed 12/19/2016).

[31] Multi-instrumentalist David Zasloff plays the shofar on this score.

softly appears again when Caroline stumbles on an old vinyl record titled "Papa Justify's Conjure of Sacrifice." The album contains a recording of New Orleans hoodoo rituals. Therefore, the shofar signifies primitive religion or ancient rituals and thus has no specific Jewish connotation in Shearmur's score. Additionally, Shearmur is linking the shofar's supernatural role in the Battle of Jericho to the otherworldly phenomena occurring in *The Skeleton Key*.

The intermittent practice of sounding shofars in these film scores makes for an intriguing study of the uses to which sonorities are used to suggest a plethora of different associations in the listener. Rarely do Hollywood film composers (or actors, writers, or filmmakers for that matter) overtly display their Jewishness outside of Jewish topic films such as *Exodus* (1960) or *The Chosen* (1981).[32] Therefore, it is of particular interest when a Jewish ritual instrument sounds in a Hollywood film. Most early examples of the shofar in film are straightforward attempts to add authenticity to the soundscape of a biblical film. However, some composers, such as Waxman, used the shofar quite specifically in order to represent Jewish remembrance and spirituality. While the noncultic examples, as exemplified in the scores of Jerry

---

[32] An exception to this standard occurs in the comedy genre, which often addresses American Jewishness.

Goldsmith, recall the shofar's roots as a battle trumpet. In contrast, the more recent scores by John Debney and Edward Shearmur connect the shofar to the blanket concept of "world music" and a nonspecific conjuration of generalized "ritual." These last two examples paradoxically rely on a contemporary audience's unfamiliarity with the ancient instrument, which creates a sort of sonic curiosity. It is worth noting that Shearmur and Debney are the only composers referred to in this study who are not Jewish, and their use of the shofar does not allude to its traditional function whatsoever. Instead, the sonority of the ram's horn is used by these composers to intone long-held notes for coloristic effects, unlike Goldsmith and Waxman, who create melodic material based on shofar calls. This discrepancy might imply an insider's knowledge of Jewish music (though readily available to the inquisitive composer) or simply a compositional choice for a specific score. With these last several examples by Goldsmith, Shearmur, and Debney, the shofar has been associated with negative contexts including human-oppressing apes, warlike Klingons, the eternal battle between good and evil, and witchcraft. Aside from the shofar's use in post-war biblical epics, there is a pattern of its use in relation to pejorative connotations. However, even with the instrument's technical limitations, there is not a universal consistency of the use of the shofar in

Hollywood film scores. In differing narrative contexts, the shofar is included in a score for source signaling or to symbolize biblical times, Jewishness itself, a general *religioso* feeling, paranormal activity, primitive instincts, or overt militarism.

From Stale to Silly to Sublime
The Shofar in Comic Books

Jonathan L. Friedmann

The shofar is ripe for the comic book medium. In the Hebrew Bible, the ram's horn is an ordinary object endowed with supernatural powers. It provides the theophanic soundtrack at Sinai (Exod 19:16, 19), supplies new moon ceremonies with apotropaic magic (Num 29:1),[1] announces the cultic anointment of kings (e.g., 1 Kgs 1:34; 2 Kgs 9:13), and channels divine might at Jericho (Josh 6:1-20) and Gideon's battle (Judg 7:15-23). Transformations from humdrum to extraordinary are commonplace among superheroes, many of whom begin as physically average people and receive superpowers through outside forces. A radioactive spider bite turns Peter Parker into Spider-Man, a bath of chemicals

---

[1] For the shofar's apotropaic function, see Abraham Z. Idelsohn, *Jewish Music in Its Historical Development* (New York: Henry Holt, 1929), 9; Sol B. Finesinger, "The Shofar," *HUC Annual* 8/9 (1931-32): 203; Joachim Braun, *Music in Ancient Israel/Palestine: Archaeological, Written, and Comparative Sources* (BIW; tr. Douglas W. Stott; Grand Rapids, MI: Eerdmans, 2002), 115.

makes Barry Allen the Flash, cosmic rays produce the Fantastic Four. A more proper comparison between the shofar and comic book artifacts yields further similarities. Like Thor's hammer Mjolnir and the Green Lantern's Power Ring, the shofar grants its user incredible powers. It is no coincidence that the shofar is a standard symbol in amulets unearthed in ancient Israel, just as Mjolnir figures prominently in Norse amulets.[2]

Despite lending itself to the comic book page, the shofar is an underrepresented device. It appears just once in Fredrik Strömberg's *Jewish Images in the Comics*, a compendium of graphics from 150 international comic strips, comic books, and graphic novels.[3] This chapter examines four occurrences of the shofar published over a thirty-four-year period. Two come from the Golden and early Silver Ages of comics, when the horn was confined to "young folks" Bible adaptations, such as *Picture Stories from the Bible* (1942) and *Tales from the Great Book* (1955).[4] In the 1960s, as the comic

---

[2] The shofar is typically engraved alongside other magical-ritual objects, typically the menorah and lulav. See Rachel Hachlili, *The Menorah, the Seven-Armed Candelabrum: Origin, Form and Significance* (Boston: Brill, 2001), 345–46.

[3] Fredrik Strömberg, *Jewish Images in the Comics: A Visual History* (Seattle: Fantagraphics, 2012), 90–91. Cover image from *Superman's Pal Jimmy Olsen* no. 79.

[4] For an overview of the subgenre, see Don Jolly, "Interpretative Treatments of Genesis in Comics: R. Crumb & Dave Sim," *JRPC* 25.3 (2013): 334–35.

book industry adjusted to the self-imposed Comics Code Authority, writers of superhero books turned to "safer" subject matter, including Bible-inspired whimsy. The shofar in *Superman's Pal Jimmy Olsen* no. 79 (1964) captures both the ingenuity and shortcomings of that era. A more serious example from the Bronze Age *Teen Titans* series (1976) rounds out the chapter.

Taken together, these examples chart the creative evolution of the depiction of the shofar in comics, as well as the broader maturation of the art form. It is a journey from stale to silly to sublime.

Picture Stories from the Bible

Bible comics originated with Maxwell Charles Gaines.[5] As a salesman for Eastern Color Printing, M. C. Gaines helped develop the first comic books in the early 1930s, which began as promotional giveaways and soon migrated onto newsstands.[6] He later worked for the McClure newspaper syndicate, repackaging newspaper strips into comic books with the assistance of Sheldon Mayer. Together, they recommended the

---

[5] William B. Jones, Jr., *Classics Illustrated: A Cultural History* (2nd ed.; Jefferson, NC: McFarland, 2011), 254.

[6] Gaines was instrumental in developing three of the earliest comic books—*Famous Funnies*, *Funnies on Parade*, and *A Century of Comics*—each of which collected reprinted comic strips. Dale Jacobs, *Graphic Encounters: Comics and the Sponsorship of Multimodal Literacy* (New York: Bloomsbury, 2013), 129.

Superman strip to DC Comics in 1938. Encouraged by *Superman*'s success, Gaines and DC executive Jack Leibowitz launched All American Comics the following year. The relationship between the two companies was complicated: they were separate entities in separate offices, yet they shared DC's distribution system and promoted each other's books. By 1940, DC's trademark was gracing the covers of All American books, and a formal merger was consummated in 1944. Gaines sold his share of the company to Leibowitz and went on to found EC, short for "Educational Comics."[7]

Gaines first penetrated the educational market during his later years at All American. He had always fancied himself a teacher, and dubiously claimed to have been a high school principal prior to World War I. Many believed his pedagogical aspirations had somehow been derailed, and that his notoriously nasty disposition stemmed partly from a sense of failure.[8] He created *Picture Stories from the Bible* in 1942, ostensibly to combat declining religious

---

[7] Les Daniels, *DC Comics: Sixty Years of the World's Favorite Comic Book Heroes* (New York: Bulfinch, 1995), 48.

[8] David Hajdu, *The Ten-Cent Plague: The Great Comic-Book Scare and How It Changed America* (New York: Picador, 2008), 73–74.

education in the United States.[9] In a 1943 interview in *Forbes* magazine, printed in advance of the book's fourth issue, Gaines said he got the idea for *Picture Stories* after hearing that half of American children had no religious schooling.[10] To strengthen the cause, he assembled an ecumenical advisory council to authorize the proofs.

Sales for the book were initially slow despite ambitious promotions.[11] The series got a boost when Gaines promised to donate profits accrued from the fourth issue to ten clergymen, who, in turn, advertised the book to Christian parents.[12] The Catholic Church was especially keen on Gaines's project. Nationwide, some two thousand parishes purchased books for their Sunday schools.[13] The seven-issue run, featuring highlights from selected Hebrew Bible and New Testament stories, wound up selling millions of

---

[9] Gaines retained the rights to the book after leaving All American. Jacobs, *Graphic Encounters*, 130.

[10] Jacobs, *Graphic Encounters*, 73.

[11] Promotions included a faux-academic pamphlet purporting to trace pictorial storytelling from prehistoric caves to Superman. M. C. Gaines, *Narrative Illustration, The Story of the Comics* (New York: s.n., 1942).

[12] According to David Hajdu, "Gaines followed through at a well-publicized event at the Advertising Club, where he gave ten clergymen checks of $850 apiece, drawn out of whatever he netted from the sale of a million copies of that issue." Hajdu, *The Ten-Cent Plague*, 74.

[13] Hajdu, *The Ten-Cent Plague*, 73.

copies.[14] Two of the New Testament issues were reprinted in 1945 as the 96-page *Complete Life of Christ*.[15] In 1971, Jewish publishing house KTAV reprinted the Hebrew Bible tales as *Picture Stories from the Bible: From Creation to Judah Maccabee*.[16] In 1979, Scarf Press collected the entire series as *Jimmy Swaggart Presents Picture Stories from the Bible*.[17]

The success of the series had little to do with its artwork or dialogue. As Don Jolly points out, *Picture Stories* and similar books "existed for parents to buy on behalf of their children. Materially, they were comic books, but culturally they were something else."[18] To give some context, while Gaines was pushing Church-friendly Bible books, All American was also publishing *Sensation Comics*, starring Wonder Woman as the scantily clad embodiment of female superiority.[19] The Church's National Organization for Decent

---

[14] Jones, Jr., *Classics Illustrated*, 254.

[15] Jones, Jr., *Classics Illustrated*, 254.

[16] M. C. Gaines, ed., *Picture Stories from the Bible: From Creation to Judah Maccabee* (New York: KTAV, 1971).

[17] M. C. Gaines, ed., *Jimmy Swaggart Presents Picture Stories from the Bible* (New York: Scarf, 1979).

[18] Jolly, "Interpretative Treatments of Genesis in Comics," 334.

[19] For a history of Wonder Woman and her colorful creator, William Moulton Marston, see Les Daniels and Chip Kidd, *Wonder Woman: The Golden Age* (San Francisco: Chronicle, 2001).

Literature placed *Sensation Comics* on its list of banned books. Catholics were forbidden by "debt of sin" from buying, selling, owning, lending, or reading it.[20]

Even so, Bible comics clearly borrowed their template from the superhero genre, just as superheroes had taken their cue from ancient myths.[21] Only scenes involving action, miracles, or high drama made the cut, in appropriately sterilized depictions (e.g., Creation, the Flood, the Binding of Isaac, Samson's exploits, the story of Esther). This is evidenced in the two *Picture Stories* involving the shofar.

The first is the battle of Jericho (Josh 6:1–27), complete with made-up dialogue, censored scenes, a condensed storyline, and Anglo actors reminiscent of Hollywood Bible epics.[22] At times, the language is fleshed out for good effect, as when the gates of Jericho are closed and soldiers exclaim: "The Israelites are coming!" "They shall

---

[20] Hajdu, *The Ten-Cent Plague*, 75.

[21] Many have noted the relationship between mythology and superheroes. See, for instance, Grant Morrison, *Supergods: What Masked Vigilantes, Miraculous Mutants, and a Sun God from Smallville Can Teach Us about Being Human* (New York: Spiegel and Grau, 2012); and Brian Cogan and Jeff Massey, "'Yeah? Well, MY God Has a HAMMER!' Myth-Taken Identity in the Marvel Cinematic Universe," *Marvel Comics into Film: Essays on Adaptations Since the 1940s* (ed. Matthew J. McEniry, Robert Moses Peaslee, and Robert G. Weiner; Jefferson, NC: McFarland, 2016), 10–19.

[22] Gaines, ed., *Jimmy Swaggart Presents*, 73–77.

never enter Jericho!" "We defy them and their God!" (cf. Josh 6:1). Other aspects are conspicuously left out, most glaringly the Ark of the Covenant, which is central to the biblical narrative and symbolizes the presence of God.[23] More understandable is the erasure of the brutal attack that follows the wall's collapse. In the Book of Joshua, the Israelites pilfer silver, gold, and objects of iron and copper for "the treasury of the Lord" (Josh 6:19); exterminate men, women, children, and livestock "with the sword" (Josh 6:21); and "burn down the city and everything in it" (minus the valuable metals) (Josh 6:24). In Picture Stories, the brutal episode is reduced to a single panel showing a generic and bloodless clash of soldiers (again in stereotypical Hollywood garb).

The shofar takes center stage in a four-panel sequence: (1) The priests, drawn as identical septuplets, march with the horns at their sides (they blow continuously in Josh 6:9); (2) They stop in formation to sound the horns; (3) The people join with a great shout; (4) A single priest is shown blowing the shofar as the wall crumbles in the blurry background. Oddly, after the Israelites lay waste to Jericho and spare the house of Rahab, a

---

[23] J. Gordon McConville and Stephen Nantlais Williams, *Joshua* (Grand Rapids, MI: Eerdmans, 2010), 33.

prostitute who had given aid to Israelite spies (cf. Josh 6:23-25), the comic reports: "So the city of Jericho fell and the Hebrews went to live in it." In the biblical version, there is no city left to live in, and Joshua curses anyone who might attempt to rebuild it (Josh 6:27).

The second shofar narrative is Gideon's assault on the Midianites.[24] The story spans three comic book pages, beginning with an added shofar blast to assemble Gideon's massive army. In the biblical telling, he begins with 22,000 soldiers, 12,000 of whom return home out of fear (Judg 7:3).[25] The 10,000 remaining troops are still too many for God's plan, so a "test" is devised to further trim the number. Gideon leads the men to water. Those who kneel down to drink are sent home, while those who lap up the water by hand are chosen to stay (Judg 7:4-8). The implication is that the lappers, who number just three hundred, are timid and under-skilled, whereas the seasoned warriors kneel and drink with gusto.[26] Their cowardice and small size emphasize the miracle of

---

[24] Gaines, ed., *Jimmy Swaggart Presents*, 92-96.

[25] This provision recalls the laws of war in Deut 20:8: "Is there anyone afraid and disheartened? Let him go back to his home, lest the courage of his comrades' flag like his."

[26] This is the opinion of Josephus, *Ant.*, V.vi.3. Louis H. Feldman, *Studies in Josephus' Rewritten Bible* (Boston: Brill, 1998), 172.

their pre-ordained victory. The comic inserts a very different rabbinic reading, in which the lappers were chosen because, unlike the kneelers, they do not bow down to idols.[27]

The magical battle is portrayed blandly. In Judges, each man is outfitted with a shofar for his right hand and a jar with a torch for his left, leaving no place for conventional weaponry. They line up outside of the enemy camp, out of harm's way. During the middle watch—a time of deep sleep—the three hundred men blast their shofarot, break their jars, raise their torches, and chant: "For the Lord and for Gideon!" The display sends the groggy Midianites fleeing in a confused panic (Judg 7:15-22). In the comic book, only Gideon blows the shofar; the soldiers simply shout and hold "pitchers with lighted candles." The shofar's deafening and divine-summoning effect is absent, making the wooden artwork even staler than it might have been.

Tales from the Great Book

When M. C. Gaines was killed in a motorboat accident in 1947, his son William reluctantly assumed control of EC Comics.[28]

---

[27] See Yalqut Shim'oni 2:62.

[28] See Amy Kiste Nyberg, "William Gaines and the Battle Over EC Comics," *A Comics Studies Reader* (ed. Keet Heer and Kent Worcester; Jackson: University of Mississippi Press, 2009), 58-68.

Rebranding the company "Entertaining Comics," the younger Gaines scrapped the Bible market and pioneered its opposite: horror comics. Influenced by gothic literature, noir pulps, and radio programs like *The Witch's Tale* and *Inner Sanctum Mysteries*, William Gaines, together with chief writer, artist, and editor Al Feldstein, introduced an assortment of gleefully gruesome and well-crafted books, among them *Tales from the Crypt*, *The Haunt of Fear*, *Weird Science*, and *Crime SuspenStories*. Stories of gamblers betting body parts and baseball diamonds strewn with human intestines were EC's answer to the "post-war American Dream."[29] A self-described "extreme liberal," Gaines used the gritty comics to satire McCarthy-era values and institutions, and shed a grim light on racial intolerance, police brutality, racial segregation, and other polarizing issues rarely addressed in the popular culture of the time.[30]

Shocking graphics had been a part of comics from the beginning. The Golden Age of

---

[29] Steven James Carver, "Weird Tales from the Vault of Fear: The EC Comics Controversy and Its Legacy," Paper presented at Watching the Media: Censorship, Limits, and Control in Creative Practice Symposium (Edge Hill University, Liverpool, April 2011), 2.

[30] Bradford W. Wright, *Comic Book Nation: The Transformation of Youth Culture in America* (Baltimore: Johns Hopkins University Press, 2003), 135–53.

comics (1930s to early 1950s) was an eclectic era of superheroes, detectives, funny animals, spacemen, monsters, teen romances, jungle adventures, war stories, westerns, and true crimes. Alongside the relatively tame superhero and animal books—and even tamer Bible stories— were Gus Ricca's bloody artwork for *Punch Comics*, Joe Doolin's unrestrained war stories for *Fight Comics*, and Jack Cole's diabolical drawings for *Silver Streak Comics*.[31] The target audience for such books were young men, but children also purchased them.[32]

Unsurprisingly, some parents and psychologists voiced concerns. Early research on the impact of comics on children dealt mostly with literacy, and the findings were generally positive.[33] Opinions began to shift in the 1940s. Children's author Sterling North cautioned: "Unless we want a coming generation even more ferocious than the present one, parents and teachers throughout America must band together

---

[31] See Greg Sadowski, ed., *Action! Mystery! Thrills! Comic Book Covers of the Golden Ages 1933–1945* (Seattle: Fantagraphics, 2012).

[32] Carver, "Weird Tales from the Vault of Fear," 1.

[33] For example, H. C. Lehman and P. A. Witty, "The Compensatory Function of the Sunday 'Funny Paper,'" *JAP* 11.3 (1927): 202–11 and Josette Frank, "The Role of Comic Strips and Comic Books in Child Life," *Supplementary Educational Monographs* 57 (1943): 158–62.

to break the 'comic' magazine."[34] Alarmism reached fever pitch with the 1954 publication of Frederic Wertham's *Seduction of the Innocent*.[35]

Wertham was a senior staffer at New York's Bellevue Mental Hygiene Clinic and founder of the Lafargue Clinic in Harlem, a church-basement psychiatric clinic specializing in black teenagers. Like most young people in those days, his patients were avid readers of comic books. Industry-wide sales at the time were between 70 and 150 million copies per month.[36] Speciously putting two and two together, Wertham concluded that comics were corrupting children and encouraging juvenile delinquency: "The pattern is one of stealing, gangs, addiction, comic books and violence."[37] His main concern was the popular crime genre, but he did not spare other types. He warned of the subversive influence of cartoon animals on toddlers, and argued that romance comics could lead to child prostitution.[38] He pegged Batman and Robin as homosexuals, labelled Wonder Woman as a bondage-indulging

---

[34] Sterling North, writing in the *Chicago Daily News* (1943). Quoted in Carver, "Weird Tales from the Vault of Fear," 3.

[35] Frederic Wertham, *Seduction of the Innocent: The Influence of Comic Books on Today's Youth* (New York: Reinhart, 1954).

[36] Daniels, *DC Comics*, 114.

[37] Wertham, *Seduction of the Innocent*, 26.

[38] Les Daniels, *Marvel: Five Fabulous Decades of the World's Greatest Comics* (New York: Harry N. Abrams, 1991), 71.

lesbian, and complained that Superman "undermines the authority and dignity of the ordinary man and woman in the minds of children."[39]

Hysteria bubbled up to the U.S. Senate. Wertham testified to the Senate Subcommittee to Investigate Juvenile Delinquency in April 1954, rattling off unreferenced anecdotes, fear-mongering "facts," and sensationalized statistics—all without evidence of a control group.[40] William Gaines was the principal target of the hearings. Senator Estes Kefauver of Tennessee grilled Gaines about the cover of *Crime SuspenStories* no. 22 (April/May 1954), featuring Johnny Craig's portrait of an axe-wielding man holding a woman's severed head.

Many publishers were forced out of business. EC dropped all of its titles excerpt for *MAD*, which was converted into a black-and-white magazine.[41] Companies that survived did so by creating the self-governing Comics Code Authority: a badge printed on comic book covers declaring them free of murder, gun play, horror, sex, or anything else deemed inappropriate for minors.

---

[39] Wertham, *Seduction of the Innocent*, 97–98.
[40] Carver, "Weird Tales from the Vault of Fear," 4.
[41] Daniels, *DC Comics*, 115.

Wholesome Bible comics made a comeback in this anxious atmosphere. In December 1955, Gilberton's *Classics Illustrated* released a special-edition book titled *The Story of Jesus*, scripted by former missionary Lorenz Graham. Evangelical minister Daniel A. Poling, editor of the *Christian Herald* magazine, gave a back-cover endorsement.[42] Atlas Comics, which was hanging on by a thread, published a five-issue series *Bible Tales for Young People* (1953–54), and *Classics Illustrated* and Dell Giant both published tie-ins to the 1956 film *The Ten Commandments*.

Famous Funnies entered the field in 1955 with the four-issue *Tales from the Great Book*. Like other *Silver-Age Bible* comics, the series continued the kid-friendly template of *Picture Stories*. However, the artwork and storytelling were a cut above. John Lehti, who had previously worked on *Tarzan*, *Flash Gordon*, and *Tom Corbett, Space Cadet*, infused the ancient stories with an action-adventure flair. He gave the issues exciting wraparound covers and an oversized Comics Code badge, simultaneously enticing young readers and reassuring fearful parents.

Lehti had a knack for dramatizing the typically terse biblical text. In his hands, invented dialogue, ancillary characters, and embellished

---

[42] Jones, Jr., *Classics Illustrated*, 254.

action sequences enhanced the originals. His shofar story, "Joshua Marches on Jericho," is a vibrant case in point. The story spans twelve pages in the second issue of *Tales*.[43] In anticipation of the Israelite attack, Jericho's elaborately dressed leader—identified as a "king"—commands: "Sound your trumpets... let every soldier guard the walls!" Three fancy metal trumpets are blown from the city's lavish interior, creating an effective contrast with Israel's humble horns. The Ark is restored to prominence, drawn to specifications in Exodus 25:10-22. When the Canaanite soldiers catch sight of the Israelites, one asks: "But where are their war machines? Their chariots... battering rams?" "They have none," replies another. "And that is their weakness!" But a caption retorts: "Joshua marches beside something far more powerful than a war machine—the Ark of the Covenant." Lehti has hundreds of arrows from Canaanite archers falling short of the marching Israelites. An officer yells: "It is God that protects them! The box must be captured... and their God destroyed in it."

The procession suddenly stops in front of the city gate. Joshua raises his shield and the priests give one final blow of their horns. The

---

[43] John Lehti, *Tales from the Great Book* (New York: Famous Funnies, 1955), 2: 1–12.

Israelites join with a shout, and the walls collapse violently. The devastating scene fills an entire page. A caption declares: "The rolling waves of sound break over the walls… echo through vibrating buildings… the ground trembles… the entire city shakes and… the walls come tumbling down!" (ellipses in the original). The story ends there, before the brutal invasion.

Superman's Pal Jimmy Olsen

DC Comics responded to the restrictive Comics Code Authority with an assortment of quirky comic books. DC's Silver-Age heroes were more likely to engage in competitive sports or fend off comically garish space aliens than explore society's dark side.[44] This was especially true of Superman books published under micromanaging editor Mort Weisinger. Weisinger encouraged artists and writers to take the characters in any absurd direction whatsoever, so long as they adhered to his strict rules of storytelling.[45] At the same time, he was a zealous defender of the Code,

---

[44] This section is condensed from Jonathan L. Friedmann, "When Jimmy Blew the Shofar: Midrash and Musical Invective in *Superman's Pal Jimmy Olsen,*" *JRPC* 28.1 (2016): 43–53.

[45] Les Daniels, *Superman: The Complete History* (New York: Chronicle, 1998), 107.

refusing to broach real-life subjects, like "hippies, drugs, and street people."[46]

Weisinger's formula of silly scenarios, vibrant colors, and oddball characters resonated with younger readers, but hit a snag when the first of the baby boomer generation reached their teens. Metropolis was simply not a place for graffiti, smog, ghettos, poverty, or complex societal issues.[47] While Marvel Comics introduced empathetic characters like Spider-Man (1962) and the X-Men (1963), who embodied teen angst and alienation, Superman struggled to stay hip by growing sideburns and making tin-eared Beatles references. These cringe-worthy qualities are fully displayed in *Superman's Pal Jimmy Olsen* no. 79 (1964), when the red-headed cub reporter becomes "The Red-Headed Beatle of 1,000 B.C.!"[48]

The story includes the first comic book appearance of the shofar outside of the Bible comics. Written by Leo Dorfman and penciled by Curt Swan, the zany adventure involves time travel, a whimsical take on the Samson legend,

---

[46] Jim Amash, "The Man Behind the Prez: A Brief Talk with Joe Simon, Creator of the Geek," *Comic Book Artist Collection* (ed. Jon B. Cooke; Raleigh, NC: TwoMorrows, 2002), 2: 69.

[47] John Byrne, "The Origins of Superman," *The Greatest Superman Stories Ever Told* (ed. Mike Gold and Robert Greenberger; New York: DC Comics, 1987), 10–11.

[48] Leo Dorfman and Curt Swan, *Superman's Pal Jimmy Olsen* (79; New York: DC Comics, 1964), 23–31.

and three extra-biblical uses of the horn: as a shepherd's horn, a distress signal, and a source of entertainment. Most significantly, its suggestion that Beatles' songs can be reproduced on the limitedly musical instrument—represented with unflattering sound effects "Pwaah," "Oowah," and "Phwaahh"—exposes Dorfman as an out-of-touch middle-aged grump who equates rock 'n' roll with "noise." Attempting to tap into the Beatles fad, the story winds up (intentionally?) lampooning their music and their fans.

The story begins with Jimmy dancing in his apartment to a television broadcast of the Beatles. He is wearing a mop-top Beatle wig, which is dyed red so as to preserve his signature trait. Jimmy hears the doorbell, hides the wig in his pocket, and opens the door to find Kasmir, a criminal time traveler posing as a "time policeman" from the future. Kasmir convinces Jimmy to take him to an unnamed biblical locale 3,000 years in the past, using a Legion of Super-Heroes time bubble. When they arrive, Kasmir pulls out a ray gun and fires two stray shots in Jimmy's direction. One hits the time machine and another sets fire to a pile of logs.

The logs belong to a muscular boy named Mighty Youth, who crushes Kasmir's gun with his bare hand and knocks him out with a right hook. The hero leads Jimmy to a secret lair behind a movable stone brick wall, where Jimmy dons some period clothing and sets out to get a job. He finds work with Ben-Robba the shepherd, who hands him a shofar: "Just blow the ram's horn and the sheep will come to you."

Miffed by the measly payment, Jimmy decides to collect scrap wool; buy some needles, thread, and black dye; and make Beatle wigs to sell to local youngsters. The story cuts to Jimmy's "weird performance," involving shofar blasts, a small hand drum, and awkward gyrations. Jimmy stops playing and yells: "Hold everything kids! You can't do the Beatle dance without a Beatle wig! Get 'em while they last. A silver piece each!"

Kasmir informs Ben-Robba that his wool scraps were used to make the wigs, and Jimmy is arrested. After paying Kasmir from the silver confiscated from Jimmy, Ben-Robba turns to the guards, claiming that Kasmir stole the money. Jimmy and Kasmir wind up in adjacent cells in the city jail. Jimmy blows the shofar and Mighty Youth races to the rescue, pulling the bars from the wall (cf. Judg 16:3). His turban falls off in the process, exposing a mane of long flowing hair. Jimmy recognizes him as Samson.

Jimmy and Samson, back in his Mighty Youth turban, come across Delilah, who is standing outside of her father's blacksmith shop. She professes her attraction to Mighty Youth, seductively placing her palm on his cheek. He declines her advances, showing much greater restraint than his biblical counterpart (cf. Judg 16:4-5). As this is happening, the ever-lurking Kasmir grabs some shears from Delilah's table and follows the boys to the hideout. He slips in while the boys are sleeping, and takes the stolen shears to Samson's hair—intending to zap him of his strength. But Jimmy, seeing the villain enter the cave, swiftly puts his Beatle wig on the snoozing Samson. All Kasmir gets is a bit of synthetic hair and a fist to the face.

At that moment, Superman tracks down Jimmy using the Legion's time-bubble locator. Guards suddenly burst in to arrest the escaped criminals, and Superman pushes down the supporting columns to topple the cave (cf. Judg 16:29-30). Meanwhile, Samson restrains Kasmir with one hand and hoists the time bubble over his head with the other. Jimmy follows them out of the cave. Seconds later, Superman shoots out from the collapsing rubble in his classic flying pose.
Jimmy gets one last hurrah as the Red-Headed Beatle before returning to 1964 in the repaired time machine. He strikes the familiar shofar-drum-dance pose. The youth gather around, wigs on heads, and Superman makes the cheesy remark: "You've really started a 'Beatle' fad here, Jimmy!

You seem to be as popular as Ringo, the Beatle drummer!"

The image of teens in Beatle wigs dancing ecstatically to Jimmy's shofar blasts and simple drumming is both figuratively and literally tone deaf. Their chorus of "Yeah-Yeah, Yeah-Yeah, Yeah-Yeah!" shows how the writer felt about the Fab Four's lyrics. The idea of Beatles' songs being played on the horn betrays disdain for the music. This epitomizes DC's Silver-Age references to youth culture, which, more often than not, come off as cantankerous critiques.

Teen Titans

The comic book industry matured as the 1960s turned into the 1970s. There was a growing thirst for realism, and a sense that superheroes should serve as "Captain Relevant."[49] Assassinations, riots, racism, poverty, drug addiction, environmental destruction, corporate rapacity, and the Viet Nam War were too important and ever-present to ignore. DC entered topicality with titles like *The Hawk and the Dove* (1968), centering on two super-brothers: a thoughtful pacifist and a hot-headed fighter.[50]

---

[49] Laurence Malson and Michael Kantor, *Superheroes! Capes, Cowls, and the Creation of Comic Book Culture* (New York: Crown Archetype, 2013), 175.

[50] Created by Steve Ditko and Steve Skeates. The book

That same year Mort Weisinger, who pressed on with light-hearted *Superman* books, petitioned DC to cancel the hippie-centric *Brother Power the Geek*, a cross between Frankenstein's monster and a wandering outcast philosopher.[51]

DC delved furthest into societal issues when writer Dennis O'Neil and artist Neal Adams took over the struggling *Green Lantern* title in 1970. They followed Green Lantern, the establishment "cop," and Green Arrow, the revolutionary "anarchist," on a soul-searching journey across America. The series begins with Green Lantern rescuing a businessman from a young thug, only to learn that the victim was a slumlord set on evicting elderly tenants. In a landmark sequence, an elderly black man berates the hero for helping interplanetary races of blue skins, orange skins, and purple skins, but never bothering to help the black skins on Earth.[52]

Marvel Comics entered the new era in 1971, boldly publishing *Amazing Spider-Man* nos. 96–98, a story arc dealing with drug addiction, without the Comics Code Authority seal.[53] Ties to the

---

lasted just six issues.

[51] Amash, "The Man Behind the Prez," 69.

[52] Dennis O'Neil and Neil Adams, *Green Lantern/Green Arrow* (2.76; New York: DC Comics, 1970), 6.

[53] Stan Lee and Gil Kane, *The Amazing Spider-Man* (1.96-97; New York: DC Comics, 1971).

carefree Silver Age were irreparably severed with a two-part story in *The Amazing Spider-Man* nos. 121–122 (1973).[54] Green Goblin throws Spider-Man's unconscious girlfriend, Gwen Stacy, from the Washington Bridge. Spider-Man catches her with a web strand around her legs, but when he pulls her up, he realizes her neck has been broken. The illustration suggests she died from whiplash as a result of the rescue attempt. This gray area solidified the shift from the carefree Silver Age to the grittier Bronze Age, opening the door to moral ambiguities and anti-heroes like Punisher and Wolverine (both introduced in 1974).

Teen Titans abandoned some of its zaniness in the new paradigm. Conceived as a "junior justice league," the team of sidekicks-turned-stars debuted in 1964's *The Brave and the Bold* no. 54.[55] The original Titans comprised Robin, Aqualad, and Kid Flash, with Wonder Girl added shortly thereafter. *Teen Titans* no. 1 came out in February 1966 and ran for forty-three issues before an extended hiatus in 1972. Like *Superman's Pal Jimmy*

---

[54] Gerry Conway and Gil Kane, *The Amazing Spider-Man* (1.121–22; New York: DC Comics, 1973). See Arnold Blumberg, "The Night Gwen Stacy Died: The End of Innocence and the Birth of the Bronze Age," *Reconstruction: Studies in Contemporary Culture* 3.4 (2003): http://reconstruction.eserver.org/Issues/034/blumberg.htm (accessed 12/16/16).

[55] Bob Haney and Bruno Premiani, *The Brave and the Bold* (1.54; New York: DC Comics, 1964).

Olsen, the 1960s *Teen Titans* books struggled to address the widening generation gap and the emerging youth culture. Middle-aged writers strained to deliver contemporary dialogue, and the villains they concocted were famously corny.[56] This changed somewhat in 1969, when the politically astute Hawk and Dove were added to the roster,[57] and in 1970, when the teens' missteps resulted in the fatal shooting of a peace protester.[58]

The shofar gets its fullest comic book treatment through the character of Mal Duncan, the team's first black member. In his inaugural appearance in 1970, Duncan saves the Titans from a street gang by beating its leader in a boxing match.[59] The team recruits him despite his lack of superpowers. During the second run of the series (1976–1978), Duncan discovers a strength-enhancing exoskeleton costume and acquires the power of the Guardian.[60] Editor Julius Schwartz,

---

[56] Charles Coletta, "Teen Titans," *Comics through Time: A History of Icons, Idols, and Ideas* (ed. M. Keith Brooker; Santa Barbara: ABD-CLIO, 2014), 817.

[57] Neal Adams, *Teen Titans* (1.21; New York: DC Comics, 1969).

[58] Robert Kalingher and Nick Cardy, *Teen Titans* (1.25; New York: DC Comics, 1970).

[59] Robert Kalingher and Nick Cardy, *Teen Titans* (1.26; New York: DC Comics, 1970).

[60] The Guardian costume first appeared in *Star-Spangled Comics* no. 7, in 1942. See Joe Simon and Jack Kirby, *The Newsboy Legion* (1; New York: DC Comics, 2010).

who took over with the second issue of the renewed title, hated Duncan as the Guardian, and writer Bob Rozakis immediately changed his identity to Hornblower, possessor of Gabriel's shofar.[61]

Hornblower's origin appears in issue no. 45. After being knocked unconscious by an explosion, Duncan awakens to the eerie voice of Azrael, the angel of death, who has come to claim his soul. Refusing to die, Duncan challenges Azrael to a fight. They are transported to a boxing ring, where they encounter the angel Gabriel acting as the "referee." Gabriel blows his horn, infusing Duncan with super-strength to defeat the angel of death. Azrael declares: "You beat me—so you live, for now! But I warn you, lose one fight—to anyone—and you die!" Gabriel gives Duncan the horn and tells him that blowing it will make him the equal of any opponent.

As Hornblower, Duncan brings together several folkloric elements. Azrael (also Azriel in Jewish mysticism), is a widely distributed name for the angel of death in the Judeo-Christian-Islamic world. Islamic angelology has four named archangels: Michael, Israfil, Gabriel, and Azrael, each with a specific function.[62] Gabriel is the most

---

[61] Bob Rozakis and Irv Novick, *Teen Titans* (1.45; New York: DC Comics, 1976).

[62] Scott B. Noegel and Brannon M. Wheeler, *The A to Z of*

significant as the bringer of revelations to the prophet. The Hebrew Bible and New Testament also give Gabriel a messenger function.⁶³ In the comic book, he reveals the shofar to Duncan in a quasi-mystical "vision."

The horn itself derives from Negro spirituals, where it signals salvation, announces divine judgment, and calls slaves to rise up. The earliest known reference to Gabriel as a horn blower is John Wycliffe's 1382 tract *De Ecclesiæ Dominio*.⁶⁴ John Milton's *Paradise Lost* (1667) describes Gabriel playing the horn on judgment day.⁶⁵ It is unclear how earlier conceptions inspired Milton or the spirituals, but some common themes persist. The seventh line of "Michael, Row the Boat Ashore" states: "Gabriel blow the trumpet horn, hallelujah. Jordan stream is wide and deep, hallelujah."⁶⁶ The Christmas

---

Prophets in Islam and Judaism (Lanham, MD: Scarecrow, 2010), 23.

⁶³ Daniel 8:16-17; 9:21-22; Luke 1:11-20, 26-38. The Bible does not define Gabriel's status as an angel, but he appears as an archangel in Enoch chapters 9, 20, and 40.

⁶⁴ Robert Vaughn, *Tracts & Treatises of John De Wycliffe* (London: Wycliffe Society, 1845), 79.

⁶⁵ Elisa Koehler, *A Dictionary for the Modern Trumpet Player* (Lanham, MD: Scarecrow, 2015), 67. See S. Vernon McCasland, "Gabriel's Trumpet," *JBR* 9.3 (1941): 159-61. The connection of the shofar with judgment day and the messianic era appears in prophetic books (e.g., Isa 27:13 and Zeph 1:16), and is expanded in rabbinic literature.

⁶⁶ William Francis Allen, Charles Pickard Ware, and Lucy

hymn "There's a Star in the East" instructs: "Don't wait for the blowing of Gabriel's horn; Rise up, sinner, and follow!"[67] "In Dat Great Gettin' Up Mornin'" has Gabriel blowing the horn to mark Jesus's return: "Oh blow your trumpet, Gabriel. Fare ye well, fare ye well."[68]

While some view Mal Duncan as a "stereotypical ghetto kid,"[69] he sensitively incorporates a variety of cultural references. As a non-superhero and non-white member of the Teen Titans, he struggles with feelings of inadequacy and alienation. His shofar is both a source of equalizing strength and a historical symbol of spiritual dignity and racial justice. He communicates with supernatural beings pulled from Western religions, and his shofar seems to channel God's energy, albeit implicitly. Gabriel and Azrael's appearance together may be a nod to the Nation of Islam, and the sound of his horn approximates a Jewish shofar call, "T-kee-yorrr!"

McKim Garrison, *Slave Songs of the United States* (New York: A. Simpson, 1867), 23.

[67] Carl P. Daw, Jr., *Glory to God: A Companion* (Louisville, KY: Westminster John Knox, 2016), 140–41.

[68] Ben Forkner, *A New Reader of the Old South: Major Stories, Tales, Slave Narratives, Diaries, Essays, Travelogues, Poetry and Songs, 1820–1920* (Atlanta: Peachtree, 1991), 622–23. Gabriel plays a similar role to Elijah in announcing the messiah (cf. Mal 3:23–24).

[69] Coletta, "Teen Titans," 818.

Summary

Although infrequently depicted in comic books, the shofar's limited appearances show a distinct artistic evolution. Its journey from Bible comics to *Jimmy Olsen's* pseudo-biblical setting to the urban streets of *Teen Titans* encapsulates the social forces that have shaped sequential art over the decades. Eventually, the shofar emerges as a magical instrument with a life of its own, indebted, but not beholden, to biblical narratives.

List of Contributors

Jeremy Phillip Brown earned his PhD in Hebrew and Judaic Studies from New York University. He teaches at the University of San Francisco in the Department of Theology and Religious Studies, and in the Swig Program in Jewish Studies and Social Justice, where he directs the USF Lecture Series in the History of Jewish/Christian Relations. He is a 2016–17 Research Fellow of the Memorial Foundation for Jewish Culture.

Jonathan L. Friedmann is Professor of Jewish Music History at the Academy for Jewish Religion, California, Extraordinary Associate Professor of Theology at North-West University (NWU), Potchefstroom, South Africa, and a Postdoctoral Fellow at NWU in Musical Arts in South Africa: Resources and Applications. He is the author or editor of over a dozen books, most recently *Music in Our Lives: Why We Listen, How it Works* (2015) and *Jews, Music, and the American West: Portraits of Pioneers* (2016).

Aaron Fruchtman is a musicologist, composer, and conductor. He is an Adjunct Faculty Member at California Lutheran University and California State University, Long Beach. Fruchtman earned his doctorate in musicology from the University of California, Riverside. His dissertation examines film scores of Jewish-themed movies and their composers' social and cultural world in the Golden Age of Hollywood.

Joel Gereboff is Associate Professor of Religious Studies at Arizona State University and Professor of Bible and Jewish History at the Academy for Jewish Religion, California. His research and publications focus on early rabbinic Judaism, American Judaism, Jewish ethics, and Judaism and the emotions.

Haim Ovadia is the Rabbi of Sephardic Congregation Magen David in Rockville, Maryland, and Professor of Talmud at the Academy for Jewish Religion, California. He has previously served as a rabbi in Sephardic communities in Israel, South America, and Los Angeles. Rabbi Ovadia was ordained by Israel's Chief Sephardic Rabbi, Rabbi Mordechai Eliyahu, and holds a BA in Talmud and an MA in Judaic studies.

Jeremy Montagu was Curator/Lecturer at the Bate Collection of Musical Instruments, Faculty of Music, University of Oxford. He has written many articles on instruments and a number of books, including *Musical Instruments of the Bible* (2002), *Origins and Development of Musical Instruments* (2007), *Horns and Trumpets of the World* (2014), and most relevantly *The Shofar: its History and Use* (2015), from which the material of his chapter was mainly drawn.

Malcolm Miller is a musicologist and pianist, and Honorary Associate in Arts and Associate Lecturer at the Open University, UK. He has published widely on Beethoven, Wagner, and contemporary music, and more recently on Jewish and Israeli music, including "Ernest Bloch, Wagner and Creativity: Refutation and Vindication" (*Ernest Bloch Studies*, CUP, 2016), "Music as Memory: Émigré Composers in Britain" (*The Impact of Nazism on Twentieth-Century Music*, Böhlau Verlag, Vienna, 2014), and "The 'Ud as a Symbol of Middle-Eastern Cultural Dialogue" (*ICONEA 2011 Proceedings*, London, 2014). In addition to his teaching and scholarly writings he has a special interest in the shofar as a composer, pedagogue, and practitioner.

Marvin A. Sweeney is Professor of Hebrew Bible at the Claremont School of Theology and Professor of Tanak at the Academy for Jewish Religion, California. He has previously taught at the University of Miami, and he has held research or teaching appointments at the Hebrew University of Jerusalem; the W. F. Albright Institute in Jerusalem; the Lilly Theological Endowment; Hebrew Union College—Jewish Institute of Religion in Los Angeles; Yonsei University in Seoul, Korea; and Chang Jung Christian University in Tainan, Taiwan. He is the author of fifteen volumes in Hebrew Bible and Jewish Studies, and is currently writing a survey of Jewish visionary and mystical experience from antiquity through modern times.

Kees van Hage studied at the Royal Conservatory of the Netherlands and worked as a trombone player, conductor, arranger, and music teacher. He studied musicology at the University of Amsterdam and obtained a PhD in Jewish Studies with his thesis *A Tool of Remembrance: The Shofar in Modern Music, Literature and Art*. As a writer, he has published a novel, short stories, essays, and translations, mainly from German and Yiddish. Much of his work can be read or heard on his website www. keesvanhage.wordpress.com.

Bibliography

Abrams, Daniel. "*The Book of Illumination* of R. Jacob ben Jacob Ha-Kohen: A Synoptic Edition from Various Manuscripts." PhD diss. New York University, 1993.

Abulafia, Todros. *Sha'ar ha-Razim*. Edited by Michal Kushnir-Oron. Jerusalem: Mosad Bialik, 1989.

Adams, Neal. *Teen Titans* 1.21. New York: DC Comics, 1969.

Adler, Cyrus. "The Shofar: Its Use and Origin." *Report of the United States National Museum for 1892* (1894): 437–50.

Allen, William Francis, Charles Pickard Ware, and Lucy McKim Garrison. *Slave Songs of the United States*. New York: A. Simpson, 1867.

Amash, Jim. "The Man Behind the Prez: A Brief Talk with Joe Simon, Creator of the Geek." *Comic Book Artist Collection* 2, 69. Edited by Jon B. Cooke. Raleigh, NC: TwoMorrows, 2002.

Anderson, Martin. "Ronald Stevenson's Cello Concerto." *Tempo* 196 (1996): 47–49.

Angel, Marc D. *Loving Truth and Peace, the Grand Religious Worldview of Rabbi Benzion Uziel*. Northvale, NJ: Jason Aronson, 2013.

———. "Rabbi Dr. David de Sola Pool: Sephardic Visionary and Activist." *Ideals: Institute for Jewish Ideas and Ideals* (n.d.): https:://www.jewishideas.org/article/rabbi-dr-david-de-dola-pool-sephardic-visionary-and-activist.

Arts Electric. "The Electronic Shofar: AE interviews Composer/Improviser Bob Gluck" (Dec. 29, 2006): www.emf.org/artselectric/stories/2006/061229_gluck.html.

Baker, Paula Eisenstein, and Robert Nelson. *Palestina: An Overture for the Capitol Theatre, New York*. Middleton: A-R Editions, 2014.

Bar-Asher, Avishai. "Samael and his Wife: The Lost Commentary on Ecclesiastes of R. Moses de León." *Tarbiz* 80.4 (2012): 539–66.

Bazelon, Irwin. *Knowing the Score: Notes on Film Music*. New York: Van Nostrand Reinhold, 1975.

Berio, Luciano. *Remembering the Future*. Charles Eliot Norton Lectures. Cambridge, MA: Harvard University Press, 2006.

Birnbaum, Philip. *High Holyday Prayer Book*. New York: Hebrew Publishing, 1951.

Blumberg, Arnold. "The Night Gwen Stacy Died: The End of Innocence and the Birth of the Bronze Age." *Reconstruction: Studies in Contemporary Culture* 3.4 (2003): http://restruction.eserver.org/Issues/034/blumberg.htm (accessed 12/16/16).

Bohlman, Philip V. "Epilogue: Beyond Jewish Modernism." *Jewish Musical Modernism, Old and New*, 153–78. Edited by Philip V. Bohlman. Chicago: University of Chicago Press, 2008.

Bond, Jeff. *The Music of Star Trek*. Los Angeles: Lone Eagle, 1998.

Bond, Jeff, and Mike Matessino. *Star Trek: The Motion Picture: Music from the Original Soundtrack*. Sony B0089G1UYC, CD, 2012.

Braun, Joachim. *Music in Ancient Israel/Palestine: Archaeological, Written, and Comparative Sources*. Translated by Douglas W. Stott. Grand Rapids, MI: Eerdmans, 2002.

Brueggemann, Walter. *Psalms*. NCBC. Cambridge and New York: Cambridge University Press, 2014.

Byrne, John. "The Origins of Superman." *The Greatest Superman Stories Ever Told*, 10–11. Edited by Mike Gold and Robert Greenberge. New York: DC Comics, 1987.

Campbell, Antony F. *1 Samuel*. FOTL 7. Grand Rapids, MI: Eerdmans, 2003.

———. *2 Samuel*. FOTL 8. Grand Rapids, MI: Eerdmans, 2005.

Caplan, Eric. *From Ideology to Liturgy: Reconstructionist Worship and American Liberal Judaism*. Cincinnati: Hebrew Union College Press, 2002.

Carver, Steven James. "Weird Tales from the Vault of Fear: The EC Comics Controversy and Its Legacy." *Watching the Media: Censorship, Limits, and Control in Creative Practice Symposium*. Edge Hill University, Liverpool, April 2011.

Celan, Paul. "The Shofar Place." *Selected Poems and Prose of Paul Celan*. Translated by John Felstiner. New York: Norton, 2001.

Celan, Paul, and Ilana Shmueli. *Briefwechsel. Herausgegeben von Ilana Shmueli und Thomas Sparr*. Frankfurt am Main: Suhrkamp, 2004.

Chajes, J. H. *Between Worlds: Dybbuks, Exorcists, and Early Modern Judaism*. Philadelphia: University of Pennsylvania Press, 2003.

Chusid, Michael T. *Shofar: The Still Small Voice of the Ram's Horn*. Self-published ebook, 2009.

Cogan, Brian, and Jeff Massey. "'Yeah? Well, MY God Has a HAMMER!': Myth-Taken Identity in the Marvel Cinematic Universe." *Marvel Comics into Film: Essays on Adaptations Since the 1940s*, 10–19. Edited by Matthew J. McEniry, Robert Moses Peaslee, and Robert G. Weiner. Jefferson, NC: McFarland, 2016.

Cohen, Francis L., Cyrus Adler, Abraham de Harkavy, and Judah David Eisenstein. "Shofar." *Jewish Encyclopedia* (1906): http://www.jewishencyclopedia.com (accessed 11/1/16).

Coletta, Charles. "Teen Titans." *Comics through Time: A History of Icons, Idols, and Ideas*, 816–18. Edited by M. Keith Brooker. Santa Barbara: ABD-CLIO, 2014.

Conway, Gerry, and Gil Kane. *The Amazing Spider-Man* 1.121–22. New York: DC Comics, 1973.

Curran, Alvin. *Crystal Psalms*. New Albion NA067, CD, 1994.

———. *Shofar Rags*. Tzadik TZ8176, CD, 2013.

Dahlqvist, Reine, and Edward H. Tarr. "Clarino." *Grove Music Online* (January 2001): http://oxfordindex.oup.com/view/10.1093/gmo/9781561592630.article.05865 (accessed 12/18/2016).

Daniels, Les. *DC Comics: Sixty Years of the World's Favorite Comic Book Heroes.* New York: Bulfinch, 1995.

———. *Marvel: Five Fabulous Decades of the World's Greatest Comics.* New York: Harry N. Abrams, 1991.

———. *Superman: The Complete History.* New York: Chronicle, 1998.

Daniels, Les, and Chip Kidd. *Wonder Woman: The Golden Age.* San Francisco: Chronicle, 2001.

Davis, Arthur, and Herman Adler. *Service of the Synagogue: New Year.* New York: Hebrew Publishing, 1938.

Daw, Jr., Carl P. *Glory to God: A Companion.* Louisville, KY: Westminster John Knox, 2016.

de León, Moses. *Sefer ha-Rimmon.* Edited by Elliot Wolfson. Altanta: Scholar's Press, 1988.

———. *Sefer Mishkan ha-'Edut.* Edited by Avishai Bar-Asher. Los Angeles: Cherub Press, 2013.

———. *Sefer Sheqel ha-Qodesh.* Edited by Charles Mopsik. Los Angeles: Cherub Press, 1996.

de Sola, D. A. *The Festival Prayers According to the Custom of German and Polish Jews.* London: Vallentine, 1860.

de Sola Pool, David. *Prayers for the New Year.* New York: Union of Sephardic Congregations, 1936.

Dorfman, Leo, and Curt Swan. *Superman's Pal Jimmy Olsen* 79. New York: DC Comics, 1964.
Dozeman, Thomas B. *Commentary on Exodus*. ECC. Grand Rapids, MI: Eerdmans, 2009.
_____. *Joshua 1–12*. YAB 6B. New Haven and London: Yale University, 2015.
Edelman, Marsha Bryan. *Discovering Jewish Music*. Philadelphia: Jewish Publication Society, 2003.
Einhorn, David. *Olat Tamid*. New York: M. Thalmessinger, 1872.
Elgar, Edward. *The Apostles: An Oratorio*, Op. 49. London: Novello, 1904.
_____. *The Apostles*, Op. 49. Hallé Records CDHLD 7534, CD, 2013.
Exler, Steven. "*Teki'ot* Transforming Texts: *Elul* Shofar Blasts in Medieval *Minhag*." *Milin Havivin* 2 (2000): 46–82.
Farago, Bela. *Floatation – ElektroAcoustic Research*. Hungaroton Records B002TL24SY, CD, 2009.
Feld, Edward, ed. *Maḥzor Lev Shalem for Rosh Hashanah and Yom Kippur*. New York: The Rabbinical Assembly, 2012.
Feldman, Louis H. *Studies in Josephus' Rewritten Bible*. SJSJ 58. Boston: Brill, 1998.
Felstiner, John. "'Deep in the glowing text-void': Translating Late Celan." *Representations* 32 (1990): 175–86.
Fierstein, Robert E., ed. *A Century of Commitment: One Hundred Years of the Rabbinical Assembly*. New York: The Rabbinical Assembly, 2000.

Finesinger, Sol B. "The Shofar." *Hebrew Union College Annual* 8–9 (1931–32): 198–228.

Finkelstein, Louis, ed. *Thirteen Americans: Their Spiritual Autobiographies*. New York: Institute for Religious and Social Studies, 1953.

Fishbane, Eitan. "The Speech of Being, the Voice of God: Phonetic Mysticism in the Kabbalah of Asher ben David and his Contemporaries." *Jewish Quarterly Review* 98.4 (2008): 485–521.

Forkner, Ben. *A New Reader of the Old South: Major Stories, Tales, Slave Narratives, Diaries, Essays, Travelogues, Poetry and Songs, 1820–1920*. Atlanta: Peachtree, 1991.

Frank, Josette. "The Role of Comic Strips and Comic Books in Child Life." *Supplementary Educational Monographs* 57 (1943): 158–62.

Freehof, Solomon. "Sound the Shofar—'Ba-Kesse' Psalm 81:4." *Jewish Quarterly Review* 64 (1974): 225–28.

Friedland, Eric. "Historical Notes on American Reform High Holy Day Liturgy." *Journal of Reform Judaism* 35 (1988): 57–74.

———. "The Synagogue and Liturgical Developments." *Movements and Issues in American Judaism*, 217–29. Edited by Bernard Martin. Westport, CT: Greenwood Press, 1978.

———. *"Were Our Mouths Filled with Song": Studies in Liberal Jewish Liturgy*. Cincinnati: Hebrew Union College Press, 1997.

Friedmann, Jonathan L. "The Shofar and Jewish Identity." *The Shekel: The Journal of Israel and Jewish History and Numismatics* 48.2 (2015): 44–47.

———. "When Jimmy Blew the Shofar: Midrash and Musical Invective in *Superman's Pal Jimmy Olsen.*" *Journal of Religion and Popular Culture* 28.1 (2016): 43–53.

Frolov, Serge. *Judges.* FOTL. Grand Rapids, MI: Eerdmans, 2013.

Gafni, Mordechai. "Shofar of Tears." *Tikkun* 15.5 (2000): 46–48.

Gaines, M. C., ed. *Jimmy Swaggart Presents Picture Stories from the Bible.* New York: Scarf, 1979.

———. *Narrative Illustration, The Story of the Comics.* New York: s.n., 1942.

———, ed. *Picture Stories from the Bible: From Creation to Judah Maccabee.* New York: KTAV, 1971.

Galas, Michal. *Rabbi Marcus Jastrow and His Vision for the Reform of Judaism.* Boston: Academic Studies Press, 2013.

Gatti, Guido Maggiorino. "Some Italian Composers of Today, I: Castelnuovo-Tedesco." *Musical Times* 62 (1921): 403–05.

Gereboff, Joel. "Judaism and the Emotions." *Handbook of Religion and the Emotions,* 95–110. Edited by John Corrigan. New York: Oxford University Press, 2009.

Gersten, Lana. "Playing the Shofar: An Ancient Sound Finds a New Voice." *The Forward* (Sep. 18, 2008): http://forward.com/articles/14206/playing-the-shofar-02527/.

Gikatilla, Joseph. *Sha'arei Orah*. Edited by Joseph Ben-Shelomo. Jerusalem: Mosad Bialik, 1981.

Goehr, Alexander. *Sonata about Jerusalem*. London: Schott, 1976.

Goehr, Alexander, and John McGrath. *Behold the Sun*. London: Schott, 1985.

Goldberg, Edwin, Janet Marder, Sheldon Marder, and Leon Morris, eds. *Mishkan HaNefesh: Machzor for the Days of Awe*. New York: CCAR Press, 2015.

Goldberg, Randall. "David Krakauer from Klezmer Madness! to Abraham Inc.: A Topical Narrative of Musical Identities." *Musica Judaica* 21 (2015-16): 65–112.

Gottlieb, Ephraim. *Studies in the Kabbalah Literature*. Edited by Joseph Hacker. Tel Aviv: Tel Aviv University Press, 1976.

Gottlieb, Jack. *Funny, It Doesn't Sound Jewish: How Yiddish Songs and Synagogue Melodies Influenced Tin Pan Alley, Broadway, and Hollywood*. Albany: State University of New York Press, 2004.

Govrin, Martel. "R. Azriel of Gerona's Commentary on Prayer (Critical Edition)." MA thesis, Hebrew University of Jerusalem, 1984.

Gradenwitz, Peter. *The Music of Israel: From the Biblical Era to Modern Times*. Portland, OR: Amadeus, 1996.

Green, Arthur. "Reconstructionist Liturgy." *Encyclopedia Judaica Yearbook* (1990-91): 155-57.

Hachlili, Rachel. *The Menorah, the Seven-Armed Candelabrum: Origin, Form and Significance.* SJSJ 68. Boston: Brill, 2001.

Hajdu, David. *The Ten-Cent Plague: The Great Comic-Book Scare and How It Changed America.* New York: Picador, 2008.

Halpern, Baruch. *The First Historians: The Hebrew Bible and History.* San Francisco: Harper and Row, 1990.

Haney, Bob, and Bruno Premiani. *The Brave and the Bold* 1.54. New York: DC Comics, 1964.

Hecker, Joel. *Mystical Bodies, Mystical Meals: Eating and Embodiment in Medieval Kabbalah.* Detroit: Wayne State University Press, 2005.

Hoffman, Lawrence A. "American Jewish Liturgies: A Study of Identity." *Beyond the Text: A Holistic Approach to Liturgy*, 60-74. Edited by Lawrence A. Hoffman. Bloomington: Indiana University Press, 1987.

———. *Beyond the Text: A Holistic Approach to Liturgy.* Bloomington: Indiana University Press, 1987.

———. "The Language of Survival in American Reform Liturgy." *CCAR Journal* 24 (1977): 87-106.

Horowitz, Carmi. *The Jewish Sermon in 14th-Century Spain: The Derashot of R. Joshua ibn Shu'eib.* Cambridge, MA: Harvard University Press, 1989.

Horowitz-HaLevi, Yeshayahu. *Shene Luhot HaBerit*. Haifa: Yad Ramah, 1995.

Hughes, Meirion. "'The Duc d'Elgar': Making a Composer Gentleman." *Music and the Politics of Culture*, 41–68. Edited by Christopher Norris. New York: St. Martin's, 1989.

Idel, Moshe. "Conceptualizations of Music in Jewish Mysticism." *Enchanting Powers: Music in the World's Religions*, 159–88. Edited by Lawrence Sullivan. Cambridge, MA: Harvard University Press, 1997.

———. *The Mystical Experience in Abraham Abulafia*. Translated by Jonathan Chipman. Albany: State University of New York Press, 1988.

———. *Old Worlds, New Mirrors: On Jewish Mysticism and Twentieth-Century Thought*. Philadelphia: University of Pennsylvania Press, 2010.

———. "The Sefirot above the Sefirot." *Tarbiz* 51 (1982): 245–46.

———. "Visualization of Colors, 1: David ben Yehudah he-Ḥasid's Kabbalistic Diagram." *Ars Judaica* 11 (2015): 31–54.

Idelsohn, Abraham Z. *Jewish Music in Its Historical Development*. New York: Henry Holt, 1929.

Jacobs, Dale. *Graphic Encounters: Comics and the Sponsorship of Multimodal Literacy*. New York: Bloomsbury, 2013.

Jaeger, August. *The Apostles by Edward Elgar (Op. 49): Book of Words with Analytical and Descriptive Notes by A.J. Jaeger*. London: Novello, 1905.

Jolly, Don. "Interpretative Treatments of Genesis in Comics: R. Crumb & Dave Sim." *Journal of Religion and Popular Culture* 25.3 (2013): 333–43.
Jones, Jr., William B. *Classics Illustrated: A Cultural History.* Second edition. Jefferson, NC: McFarland, 2011.
Josephus, Flavius. *The New Completed Works of Josephus.* Translated by William Whiston. Grand Rapids: Kregel, 1999.
Kalingher, Robert, and Nick Cardy. *Teen Titans* 1.25–26. New York: DC Comics, 1970.
Kaplan, Mordecai, Eugene Kohn, and Ira Eisenstein, eds. *High Holyday Prayer Book.* New York: Jewish Reconstructionist Foundation, 1948.
Karlin, Fred. *Film Music Masters: Jerry Goldsmith.* DVD. Atlanta: Karlin/Tilford Productions, 2005.
Karp, Abraham. "America's Pioneer Prayer Books." *Jewish Book Annual* 34 (1976–77): 15–25.
Kieval, Hayim Herman. *The High Holy Days: A Commentary on the Prayerbook of Rosh Hashanah and Yom Kippur.* Jerusalem: Schechter Institute of Jewish Studies, 2004.
Klein, Earl, and Moises Benzaquen. *Maḥzor Ori Veyishi: A Prayerbook for Rosh Hashanah According to the Oriental Sephardic Rite.* Los Angeles: Tefillah Publishing, 1995.
Koehler, Elisa. *A Dictionary for the Modern Trumpet Player.* Lanham, MD: Scarecrow, 2015.
Kramer, Lawrence. *Classical Music and Postmodern Knowledge.* Berkeley: University of California Press, 1995.

Langer, Ruth. "Continuity, Change and Retrieval: The New Reform *Siddur*." *Journal of Synagogue Music* 34 (2009): 208-23.

Langerman, Y. Tzvi. "Hebrew Astronomy: Deep Soundings from a Rich Tradition." *Astronomy across Cultures: The History of Non-Western Astronomy*. 555-84. Edited by Helaine Selin. Dordrecht: Springer, 2000.

Lee, Stan, and Gil Kane. *The Amazing Spider-Man* 1.96-97. New York: DC Comics, 1971.

Leeser, Isaac. *Siftey Tzadiqim* (*The Forms of Prayers According to the Custom of the Spanish and Portuguese Jews, Volume II: New-Year Service*). Philadelphia: Haswell, Barrington and Haswell, 1837.

Lehman, H. C., and P. A. Witty. "The Compensatory Function of the Sunday 'Funny Paper.'" *Journal of Applied Psychology* 11.3 (1927): 202-11.

Lehti, John. *Tales from the Great Book* 2. New York: Famous Funnies, 1955.

Levin, Neil. *Herman Berlinski: From the World of My Father*. Naxos American Classics 8.559446, CD, 2006.

Liebes, Yehudah. "The Angels of the Shofar and Jesus the Prince of the Countenance." *Early Jewish Mysticism: Proceedings of the First International Conference on the History of Jewish Mysticism*, 171-96. Edited by Joseph Dan. Jerusalem: Hebrew University of Jerusalem Press, 1987.

Lundbom, Jack. *Jeremiah 37-52*. AB 21C. New York: Doubleday, 2004.

Macfarren, George, and E. G. Monk. *St John the Baptist*. London: Stanley Lucas, Weber & Co., 1878.
Malson, Laurence, and Michael Kantor. *Superheroes! Capes, Cowls, and the Creation of Comic Book Culture*. New York: Crown Archetype, 2013.
Matt, Daniel. "The Mystic and the *Mizwot*." *Jewish Spirituality I: from the Bible to the Middle Ages*, 367–404. Edited by Arthur Green. New York: Crossroad, 1994.
———, tr. *The Zohar: Pritzker Edition* VI. Stanford: Stanford University Press, 2011.
McCasland, S. Vernon. "Gabriel's Trumpet." *Journal of Bible and Religion* 9.3 (1941): 159–61.
McConville, J. Gordon, and Stephen Nantlais Williams. *Joshua*. Grand Rapids: Eerdmans, 2010.
Meier, Menahem. "A Critical Edition of the *Sefer Ta'amey ha-Mitzwoth* Attributed to Isaac ibn Farhi: Section 1. Positive Commandments." PhD diss. Brandeis University, 1974.
Merriam, Alan. *The Anthropology of Music*. Evanston: Northwestern University Press, 1964.
Meyer, Stephen C. *Epic Sound: Music in Postwar Hollywood Biblical Films*. Bloomington: Indiana University Press, 2015.
Milgrom, Jacob. *Leviticus*. AB 3ABC. New York: Doubleday, 1991–2001.
Miller, Malcolm. "Between Two Cultures: A Conversation with Shulamit Ran." *Tempo* 58.227 (2004): 15–32.

———. "Munich, Bayerische Staatsoper: Jörg Widmann's 'Babylon.'" *Tempo* 67.228 (2013): 71-72.

———. "The Shofar and its Symbolism." *Historic Brass Society Journal* 14 (2002): 83-113.

Montagu, Jeremy. *The Shofar: Its History and Use.* Lanham, MD: Roman and Littlefield, 2015.

Moore, Jerrold Northrop. *Edward Elgar: A Creative Life.* Oxford: Oxford University Press, 1984.

Mopsik, Charles. *Les Grands Textes de la Cabale: Les rites qui font Dieu.* Lagrasse: Éditions Verdier, 1993.

Morrison, Grant. *Supergods: What Masked Vigilantes, Miraculous Mutants, and a Sun God from Smallville Can Teach Us About Being Human.* New York: Spiegel and Grau, 2012.

Moses, Stéphane. "Patterns of Negativity in Paul Celan's 'The Trumpet Place.'" *Languages of the Unsayable: The Play of Negativity in Literature and Literary Theory*, 209-24. Edited by Sanford Budick and Wolfgang Iser. Translated by Ken Frieden. New York: Columbia University Press, 1987.

Munk, Eliyahu. *Akedat Yitzchak: Commentary of Rabbi Yitzchak Arama on the Torah* 1. Jerusalem: Lambda, 2001.

Naar, Devin E. *Jewish Salonika: Between the Ottoman Empire and Modern Greece.* Palo Alto, CA: Stanford University Press, 2016.

Nelson, Richard. *Joshua: A Commentary.* OTL. Louisville, KY: Westminster John Knox, 1997.

Noegel, Scott B., and Brannon M. Wheeler. *The A to Z of Prophets in Islam and Judaism.* Lanham, MD: Scarecrow, 2010.

Nyberg, Amy Kiste. "William Gaines and the Battle Over EC Comics." *A Comics Studies Reader*, 58-68. Edited by Keet Heer and Kent Worcester. Jackson: University of Mississippi Press, 2009.

O'Neil, Dennis, and Neal Adams. *Green Lantern/Green Arrow* 2.76. New York: DC Comics, 1970.

Otto, Rudolf. *The Idea of the Holy: An Inquiry into the Non-Rational Factor in the Idea of the Divine and Its Relation to the Rational.* Translated by John W. Harvey. New York: Oxford University Press, 1958.

Parker, Douglas Charles. "Exoticism in Music in Retrospect." *The Musical Quarterly* 3.1 (1917): 134-61.

Pedaya, Haviva. "The Great Mother: The Struggle Between Nahmanides and the Zohar Circle." *Temps i espais de la Girona jueva; actes del Simposi Internacional celebrat a Girona* (2011): 311-28.

———. *Nahmanides: Cyclical Time and Holy Text.* Tel Aviv: Am Oved, 2003.

Petuchowski, Jacob. *Prayerbook Reform in Europe.* New York: World Union of Progressive Judaism, 1968.

Pollack, Howard. *Aaron Copland: The Life and Work of an Uncommon Man.* New York: Henry Holt, 1999.

Pope, Marvin. *Job.* AB 15. Garden City, NY: Doubleday, 1965.

Reed, William Henry. *Elgar as I Knew Him*. London: Victor Gollancz, 1936.

Reik, Theodor. *Ritual: Psycho-Analytic Studies*. Translated by Douglas Bryan. London: Hogarth, 1931.

Roos, Dave. "Wail Watching." *Salon* (May 2004): http://www.salon.com/2004.05/25/wails/.

Rosen, Harriette M. "The Influence of Judaic Liturgical Music in Selected Secular Works of Mario Castelnuovo-Tedesco and Darius Milhaud." PhD diss. University of California, San Diego, 1991.

Rosen-Zvi, Ishay. *Demonic Desires: Yetzer Hara and the Problem of Evil in Late Antiquity*. Philadelphia: University of Pennsylvania Press, 2011.

Rozakis, Bob, and Irv Novick. *Teen Titans* 1.45. New York: DC Comics, 1976.

Sacks, Jonathan. *The Koren Rosh Hashana Mahzor*. Jerusalem: Koren, 2011.

———. *The Koren Yom Kippur Mahzor*. Jerusalem: Koren, 2012.

Sadie, Stanley, ed. *New Grove Dictionary of Music and Musicians*. Second edition. London: Macmillan, 2001.

Sadowski, Greg, ed. *Action! Mystery! Thrills! Comic Book Covers of the Golden Ages 1933–1945*. Seattle: Fantagraphics, 2012.

Saperstein, Marc. *"Your Voice Like a Ram's Horn": Themes and Texts in Traditional Jewish Preaching*. Cincinnati: Hebrew Union College Press, 1996.

Sarasan, Richard. "The Shofar Service: Malchiyot, Zichronot, Shofarot." *RJ.org* (April 18, 2013): http://blogs.rj.org/blog/2013/04/18/the-shofar-service-malchiyot-zichronot-shofarot.

Sasson, Jack. *Judges 1-12*. YAB 6D. New Haven and London: Yale University Press, 2014.

Schäfer, Peter. *Synopse zur Hekhalot-Literatur*. Tübingen: Mohr Siebeck, 1981.

Schaffner, Franklin J. *The Planet of the Apes: Widescreen 35th Anniversary Edition*. DVD. Beverly Hills: 20th Century Fox Home Entertainment, 2004.

Scherman, Nosson, and Meir Zlotowitz. *Complete ArtScroll Machzor: Rosh Hashanah*. NewYork: Mesorah, 1985.

Schirmann, Jefin. "Poets Contemporary with Mose ibn Ezra and Yehuda Hallevi (III)." *Studies of the Research Institute for Hebrew Poetry in Jerusalem* 4 (1945): 297-99.

Scholem, Gershom. "Colors and Their Symbolism in Jewish Tradition and Mysticism." *Diogenes* 108 (1979): 84-112.

———. *Major Trends in Jewish Mysticism*. New York: Schocken, 1946.

———. *On the Kabbalah and its Symbolism*. Translated by Ralph Manheim. New York: Schocken, 1965.

———. "The Traditions of R. Jacob and R. Isaac ha-Kohen." *Madda'ei ha-Yahadut* II (1927).

———. "Two Treatises of R. Moses de León." *Kovets 'al Yad* 8 (1976): 325-70.

Shiloah, Amnon. *Jewish Musical Traditions*. Detroit: Wayne State University Press, 1992.

Shmueli, Leore Sachs. "I Arouse the *Shekhinah*: A Psychoanalytic Study of the Kabbalist's Anxiety and Desire in Relation to the Object of Taboo." *Kabbalah* 35 (2015): 227-66.

Silberman, Lou H. "The Union Prayer Book: A Study in Liturgical Development." *Retrospect and Prospect: Essays in Commemoration of the Seventy-Fifth Anniversary of the Founding of the Central Conference of American Rabbis 1889-1964*, 46-80. Edited by Bertram Wallace Korn. New York: Central Conference of American Rabbis, 1965.

Silverman, Morris. *High Holyday Prayer Book*. Hartford: Prayer Book Press, 1939.

Simon, Joe and Jack Kirby. *The Newsboy Legion* 1. New York: DC Comics, 2010.

Sivan, Gabriel A. "Developments in the Orthodox Liturgy and New Editions of the Traditional Prayer Book." *Encyclopedia Judaica Yearbook* (1990/1991): 140-44.

Sklare, Marshall. *Conservative Judaism: An American Religious Movement*. Glencoe, IL: Free Press, 1955.

Smith, Ruth. "Early Music's Dramatic Significance in Handel's 'Saul.'" *Early Music* 35.2 (2007): 173-89.

Sokoloff, Michael. *A Dictionary of Jewish Babylonian Aramaic of the Talmudic and Geonic Periods*. Baltimore: Johns Hopkins University Press, 2002.

Stolow, Jeremy. *Orthodox by Design: Judaism, Print Politics and the ArtScroll Revolution*. Berkeley: University of California Press, 2010.

Strack, H. L., and Gunter Stemberger. *Introduction to the Talmud and Midrash*. Minneapolis: Fortress Press, 1992.

Strömberg, Fredrik. *Jewish Images in the Comics: A Visual History*. Seattle: Fantagraphics, 2012.

Sussman, Lance. *Isaac Leeser and the Making of American Judaism*. Detroit: Wayne State University Press, 1995.

Sweeney, Marvin A. *1-2 Kings: A Commentary*. Louisville, KY: Westminster John Knox Press, 2007.

———. *Form and Intertextuality in Prophetic and Apocalyptic Literature*. FAT 45. Tübingen: Mohr Siebeck, 2005.

———. *Isaiah 1-39, with an Introduction to Prophetic Literature*. FOTL 16. Grand Rapids, MI: Eerdmans, 1996.

———. *Isaiah 40-66*. FOTL 17. Grand Rapids, MI: Eerdmans, 2006.

———. *King Josiah of Judah: The Lost Messiah of Israel*. Oxford: Oxford University Press, 2001.

———. *Reading Ezekiel: A Literary and Theological Commentary*. Macon, GA: Smyth and Helwys, 2013.

———. *The Twelve Prophets*. BO. Collegeville, MN: Liturgical Press, 2000.

Takis, John. "Good as Goldsmith: The Goldsmith Method as Revealed in Four 1960s Masterpieces." *Film Score Monthly* 9.7 (August 2004): 28–32.

Taut, Kurt. *Beiträge zur Geschichte der Jagdmusik*. Leipzig: Radelli & Hille, 1927.

Teutsch, David, ed. *Kol Haneshamah: Prayerbook for the Days of Awe*. Elkins Park, PA: Reconstructionist Press, 1999.

Timm, Larry M. *The Soul of Cinema: An Appreciation of Film Music*. Needham Heights: Simon & Schuster Custom, 1998.

Tirosh-Samuelson, Hava. "Gender in Jewish Mysticism." *Jewish Mysticism and Kabbalah: New Insights and Scholarship*, 191–230. Edited by Frederick Greenspahn. New York: New York University Press, 2011.

Tishby, Isaiah. *Wisdom of the Zohar: An Anthology of Texts*. Translated by David Goldstein. Oxford: Littman Library of Jewish Civilization, 2002.

Toledano, Eliezer. *Maḥzor Kol Yehudah: The Orot Sephardic Rosh Hashanah Mahzor, A New Linear Sephardic Mahzor*. Lakewood, NJ: Orot, 2013.

Travis, Yakov M. "Kabbalistic Foundations of Jewish Spiritual Practice: Rabbi Ezra of Gerona—On the Kabbalistic Meaning of the Mitzvot." PhD diss. Brandeis University, 2002.

Uziel, Benzion Meir Hai. *Mishpete Uziel* 3. Jerusalem: Vaad LeHotsaat Kitve Maran, 1995.

van Hage, Kees. "A Tool of Remembrance: The Shofar in Modern Music, Literature, and Art." PhD diss. University of Amsterdam, 2014.

Vaughn, Robert. *Tracts & Treatises of John De Wycliffe.* London: Wycliffe Society, 1845.

Wachs, Sharona R. *American Jewish Liturgies: A Bibliography of American Jewish Liturgy from the Establishment of the Press in the Colonies through 1925.* Cincinnati: Hebrew Union College Press, 1997.

Warshauer, Meira. *Living Breathing Earth.* Navona Records NV5842, CD, 2011.

Werblowsky, R. J. Zwi, and Geoffrey Wigoder, eds. *The Oxford Dictionary of the Jewish Religion.* New York and Oxford: Oxford University Press, 1997.

Wertham, Frederic. *Seduction of the Innocent: The Influence of Comic Books on Today's Youth.* New York: Reinhart, 1954.

Wijnhoven, Jochanan. "*Sefer ha-Mishkal*: Text and Study." PhD diss. Brandeis University, 1964.

Wolfson, Elliot. *Along the Path: Studies in Kabbalistic Myth, Symbolism, and Hermeneutics.* Albany: State University of New York Press, 1995.

———. "Biblical Accentuation in a Mystical Key: Kabbalistic Interpretations of the *Te'amim*." *Journal of Jewish Music and Liturgy* 11 (1988-89): 1-16; and 12 (1989-90): 1-13.

———. *Circle in the Square: Studies in the Use of Gender in Kabbalistic Symbolism.* Albany: State University of New York Press, 1995.

———. "Circumcision, Vision of God, and Textual Interpretation: From Midrashic Trope to Mystical Symbol." *History of Religions* 27 (1987): 189–215.

———. "The Hermeneutics of Visionary Experience: Revelation and Interpretation in the Zohar." *Religion* 18 (1988): 311–45.

———. *Language, Eros, Being: Kabbalistic Hermeneutics and Poetic Imagination*. New York: Fordham University Press, 2005.

———. "Mystical Rationalization of the Commandments in *Sefer ha-Rimmon*." *Hebrew Union College Annual* 59 (1988): 217–51.

———. *Through a Speculum that Shines: Vision and Imagination in Medieval Jewish Mysticism*. Princeton: Princeton University Press, 1994.

———. "Zoharic Literature and Midrashic Temporality." *Midrash Unbound: Transformations and Innovations*, 321–43. Edited by Michael Fishbane and Joanna Weinberg. Oxford: Littman Library of Jewish Civilization, 2013.

Wright, Bradford W. *Comic Book Nation: The Transformation of Youth Culture in America*. Baltimore: Johns Hopkins University Press, 2003.

Wulstan, David. "The Sounding of the Shofar." *The Galpin Society Journal* 26 (1973): 29–46.

Yahalom, Shalem. "Historical Background to Nahmanides' Acre Sermon for Rosh ha-Shanah: The Strengthening of the Catalonian Center." *Sefarad* 68.2 (2008): 315–42.

Yanow, Scott. *The Trumpet Kings: The Players Who Shaped the Sound of Jazz Trumpet.* San Francisco: Backbeat Books, 2001.

Qol Tamid
Author Index

Abrams, Daniel	94, 95
Abulafia, Todros	97-99, 108
Adams, Neal	289, 291
Adler, Cyrus	6, 170, 226
Adler, Herman	152
Amash, Jim	284, 289
Amots, Ofer	212
Anderson, Martin	175
Angel, Marc D.	129, 147
Anghel, Irinel	215
Baker, Paula Eisenstein	259
Bakshi, Alexander	215
Bar-Asher, Avishai	83, 101, 103-04
Barnes, Milton	215
Bazelon, Irwin	256
Beck, David	217
Benzaquen, Moises	153
Berio, Luciano	212, 244
Berlinksi, Herman	216
Bernstein, Leonard	212
Beveridge, Thomas	212
Birnbaum, Philip	147, 149
Bloch, Ernest	212, 259
Blumberg, Arnold	290
Bohlman, Philip V.	255
Bond, Jeff	257, 258
Braun, Joachim	167
Braun, Yehezkel	212
Brueggemann, Walter	50
Byrne, John	284
Campbell, Antony F.	45
Caplan, Eric	159
Cardy, Nick	291-92

Carver, Steven James	277-80
Castelnuovo-Tedesco, Mario	213
Celan, Paul	232, 234
Chajes, J. H.	97
Chusid, Michael T.	166, 212
Cogan, Brian	273
Cohen, Francis L.	170, 226
Cohn, Steve	220
Coletta, Charles	291, 294
Conway, Gerry	290
Curran, Alvin	187, 204-05, 217-18
Dahlqvist, Reine	257
Daniels, Les	270, 272, 279, 280, 284
Davis, Arthur	152
Daw, Jr., Carl P.	294
de León, Moses	101-03, 109-10
de Sola, D. A.	152
de Sola Pool, David	147-49
Dorfman, Joseph	213
Dorfman, Leo	284
Dori, Gil	219
Dozeman, Thomas B.	47, 51
Edelman, Marsha Bryan	248
Einhorn, David	27
Eisenstein, David Judah	170, 226
Eisenstein, Ira	161
Elgar, Edward	171, 216, 222
Elkana, Amos	213
Exler, Steven	71
Faragó, Béla	206, 219
Feld, Edward	160, 163
Feldman, Louis H.	275-76
Felstiner, John	232, 235
Fierstein, Robert E.	160
Finesinger, Sol B.	58, 267
Finkelstein, Louis	148
Fischman, Rajmil	219
Fishbane, Eitan	89

Fleischer, Tsippi	215
Fleisher, Robert	213
Foss, Lukas	213
Freehof, Solomon	58
Friedland, Eric	144
Friedmann, Jonathan L.	58, 283
Forkner, Ben	294
Frank, Josette	278
Frolov, Serge	41
Gafni, Mordechai	71
Gaines, M. C.	271-73
Galas, Michal	159
Galtieri, Giancarlo	213
Gatti, Guido Maggiorino	174
Gereboff, Joel	58
Gersten, Lana	206
Gikatilla, Joseph	105, 106
Gluck, Bob	209, 219
Gluck, Srul Irving	215
Goehr, Alexander	180, 213
Goldberg, Edwin	159, 162
Goldberg, Randall	201
Golijov, Osvaldo	213, 215
Gottlieb, Ephraim	104, 105
Gottlieb, Jack	258-59
Govrin, Martel	91-92
Gradenwitz, Peter	178, 188
Green, Arthur	159
Hajdu, André	213
Hajdu, David	270, 271, 273
Halpern, Baruch	50
Haney, Bob	291
Harvey, Jonathan	213
Hecker, Joel	113
Hoffman, Lawrence A.	144, 145, 159
Horowitz, Carmi	86, 91
Horowitz-HaLevi, Yeshayahu	137
Hughes, Meirion	229
Idel, Moshe	85, 89, 99, 111

Idelsohn, Abraham Z.	9, 249, 267
Jacobs, Dale	269, 271
Jaeger, August	224, 226, 228,
Jolly, Don	268, 272
Jones, Jr., William B.	269, 272, 281
Josephus, Flavius	231, 275
Kalingher, Robert	291, 292
Kane, Gil	290
Kantor, Michael	288
Kaplan, Mordecai	161
Karlin, Fred	254
Karp, Abraham	147
Kastaris, Demetrios	220
Kaufman, Frederick	219
Kidd, Chip	272-73
Kieval, Hayim Herman	58
Kirby, Jack	292
Klein, Earl	153
Koehler, Elisa	293-94
Kohn, Eugene	161
Kramer, Lawrence	170-71
Laderman, Ezra	213
Langer, Ruth	160
Langerman, Y. Tzvi	95
Lee, Stan	290
Lees, Benjamin	214
Leeser, Isaac	147
Lehman, H. C.	278
Lehti, John	282
Levin, Neil	202, 215-16
Liebes, Yehudah	96-97
Lockwood, Jeremiah	220
Lundbom, Jack	38
Macfarren, George	168-69
Malson, Laurence	288
Marder, Janet	159
Marder, Sheldon	159
Massey, Jeff	273
Matessino, Mike	258

Matt, Daniel	83, 110-11
McCasland, S. Vernon	294
McConville, J. Gordon	274
McGrath, John	180
Meier, Menahem	106
Merriam, Alan	89
Meyer, Stephen C.	251
Milgrom, Jacob	53
Miller, Malcolm	58, 181-82, 215-16
Minsky, Aaron	214
Mishori, Yaacov	214
Monk, E. G.	169
Montagu, Jeremy	58, 248-49, 253
Moore, Jerrold Northrop	225-27, 229
Mopsik, Charles	83, 101
Morris, Leon	159
Morrison, Grant	273
Moses, Stéphane	234
Mostel, Raphael	216
Munk, Eliyahu	80
Naar, Devin E.	132
Nelson, Richard	47
Nelson, Robert	259
Noegel, Scott B.	293
Novick, Irv	292
Nyberg, Amy Kiste	277
O'Neil, Dennis	289
Otto, Rudolf	240-41
Panufnik, Roxana	214
Parker, Douglas Charles	228
Pedaya, Haviva	100
Penderecki, Krzysztof	214
Petuchowski, Jacob	159
Pollack, Howard	259
Pope, Marvin	40
Premiani, Bruno	291
Ran, Sulamit	181, 216
Reed, William Henry	229
Reik, Theodor	93-95, 97

Roos, Dave	262
Rosen, Harriette M.	174
Rosen-Zvi, Ishay	79
Rozakis, Bob	292
Rubin, Emmanuel	214
Sachs, Nelly	177, 185, 214
Sacks, Jonathan	156-57, 241
Sadie, Stanley	169
Sadowski, Greg	278
Saperstein, Marc	82
Sarasan, Richard	140
Sargon, Simon	214
Sasson, Jack	41
Savall, Jordi	220
Schachter, Michael	214
Schäfer, Peter	93
Schaffner, Franklin J.	254
Scherman, Nosson	154-56
Schirmann, Jefin	116
Scholem, Gershom	85-88, 95, 96, 99, 102, 111
Senator, Ronald	216
Shatin, Judith	207, 216, 219
Sheriff, Noam	214
Shiloah, Amnon	58
Shmueli, Ilana	232
Shmueli, Leore Sachs	83, 106
Silberman, Lou H.	159
Silverman, Morris	161
Simon, Joe	292
Sivan, Gabriel A.	153
Sklare, Marshall	160
Smith, Ruth	168
Sokoloff, Michael	70, 71
Stern, Max	216-17
Stern, Robert	214
Stevenson, Ronald	214
Stock, David	215
Stolow, Jeremy	154

Strack, H. L.	72
Strömberg, Fredrik	268
Sussman, Lance	147
Swan, Curt	284
Sweeney, Marvin A.	33, 35, 39, 41, 46-47, 49, 53-54
Takis, John	255
Tarr, Edward H.	257
Taut, Kurt	104
Teutsch, David	159, 162
Thurlow, Deborah	220
Timm, Larry M.	261
Tirosh-Samuelson, Hava	91
Tishby, Isaiah	88
Toledano, Eliezer	153
Travis, Yakov M.	90
Uziel, Benzion Meir Hai	129
van Hage, Kees	166
Vaughn, Robert	293
Wachs, Sharona R.	144
Warshauer, Meira	195, 217
Wayne, Hayden	216
Weisgall, Hugo	217
Wertham, Frederic	279, 280
Wheeler, Brannon M.	293
Wijnhoven, Jochanan	101
Williams, Stephen Nantlais	274
Witty, P. A.	279
Wolfson, Elliot	87-89, 93, 100-01, 109
Wright, Bradford W.	277-78
Wulstan, David	58
Wyner, Yehudi	215
Yahalom, Shalem	91
Yanow, Scott	253
Zlotowitz, Meir	154

Qol Tamid Scripture Index

Genesis
14	12
22	22, 66
22:1	119
22:7	121
22:13	96
27:1	106
27:5	104
30:32	11
47:3	12

Exodus
19	12, 51
19:3	234
19:13	11
19:14	234
19:16	1, 11, 60, 233, 267
19:19	11, 267
19:25	234
20-23	52
20:13	52
25:10-22	282

Leviticus
10:10-11	34
23	60
23:23-24	14
23:23-25	55
23:24	1, 5, 73, 78, 91
25:8-10	61
25:9	5, 52
25:9-10	1, 15

Numbers

10	13
10:1	12
10:10	19, 64
23:24	61
25:8-10	61
29	60
29:1	1, 5, 14, 61, 69, 70, 267
29:1-6	55

Deuteronomy

4:12	233
20:8	275

Joshua

6	16, 40, 47-49, 60, 249, 267, 273
6:1	274
6:5	249
6:9	274
6:19	274
6:21	274
6:23-24	275
6:24	274
6:27	275

Judges

3:12-30	41-43
3:27	1, 17
5:28	69, 70
6-7	43
6:1-9:56	43-45
6:34	17, 44
7	44
7:3	275
7:4-8	275
7:15-22	276
7:15-23	67
16:3	286
16:4-5	287

16:29-30	287

1 Samuel
13-14	45-46
13:3	45

2 Samuel
2	46
2:28	1, 46
6:5	18
6:15	1, 18

1 Kings
1	49
1-2	35
1:34	1, 18, 49, 267
1:39	18, 49
1:41	49

2 Kings
9:13	1, 267
23	36

Isaiah
6:13	76
18:3	39
27:1	53
27:13	23, 53, 62, 64, 105, 294
58:1	39, 53, 62, 83

Jeremiah
2-6	35
2:2-4:2	36
4:3-6:30	37
4:5-8	37
6:1	37
42:14	38
51:27-28	38

Ezekiel
3:16-21	34
3:17	34
33:1-20	34
33:3-6	18, 34
33:11	75
40:1	55

Hosea
8:1	38-39

Joel
2:1	18, 53, 77
2:5	18
2:15	53

Amos
2:2	39
2:6-16	52
3:6	39, 60, 75, 77, 79, 80

Zephaniah
1:16	294

Zechariah
9-11	46
9:14	1, 46, 65

Psalms
2	50
19	98
47	143, 148, 149
47:2	130
47:3	155
47:6	54, 62, 72, 76, 237
81	18-19, 30, 74
81:4	54, 62, 74, 106, 110-111
81:4-5	19
89:16	92, 223, 237

89:19	106
92	225
92:2-5	223
92:10	223, 224
92:13	223
98	18
98:4-6	60
118:5	143
132	170
150	18, 241
150:1	60
150:3	54
150:6	60

Job
39:24-25	40

Daniel
8:16-17	293
9:21-22	293

Nehemiah
4	18
4:12	18
4:14	18

1 Chronicles
15:28	18, 174

2 Chronicles
5:12	18

Qol Tamid
Subject Index

350th Anniversary Fanfare Concertino	199
Aaron	13, 35
Abaye	69-70
Abiathar	35, 49
Abimelech	43, 45
Abner	46
Abraham	11, 12, 22, 66, 73, 95-96, 105, 115-116, 119-126, 127, 146
Abraham	192-193
Abshalom	46
Adams, Neal	289
Adler, Cyrus	5-6
Adler, Herman M.	152
Adler, Samuel	177
Adonijah	49
Akedah (composition)	190-191
Akkadian	6, 31, 41
Aleinu	203
Aleppo	117, 136
All American Comics	270, 271, 272
Amalekites	43-44
Amarna letters	41
The Amazing Spider-Man	290
Amidah	25-26, 67, 81, 129, 132, 133, 202, 203
amulets	268
Anabaptists	180
Anathoth	35
The Apostles: An Oratorio	7, 9, 168-173, 221-230, 231, 235, 237, 243-244, 251

apotropaic magic	267
Aqualad	291
Areshet Sifatenu	143
Ark of the Covenant	16, 17-18, 50-51, 174, 274, 282
ArtScroll Machzor	153, 154-156
Asch, Moses	6
Asher	44
Asherah	104
Assyria	36, 38, 52, 53, 64
Atlas Comics	281
Auschwitz	186, 189
Avitsur, Haim	193, 194
Azrael	292-293, 295
baal toqeah	112
Babylon	182-184
Babylonia (Babylon)	18, 20, 21, 28, 33, 34, 35, 36, 38, 132, 134
Babylonian Exile	18, 33-35
Bach, J.S.	183
Bach Akademie Stuttgart	235-236
Baghdad	129, 179
Balkans	131
baqashot	144
Barenboim, Daniel	175
Bath Sheba	49
Batman	280
Bazelon, Irwin	256
Beatles	284, 285, 288
Behold the Sun	178-181
Bellevue Mental Hygiene Clinic	279
Ben-Hur	247, 249, 250-251, 252
Benjaminites	35, 37, 41-42, 46
Benzaquen, Moises	153
Benzion Meir Hai Uziel	129-131, 133, 136
Berio, Luciano	9, 221, 230, 233, 235-245
Berlinski, Herman	202-203
Bernstein, Elmer	250

Bernstein, Leonard	174-175, 258
Bethlehem	247
Between Two Worlds (*The Dybbuk*)	181-182
Bible Tales for Young People	281
Binah	100, 101, 105, 106, 107, 110, 111, 112
Binding of Isaac (Akedah)	22, 65-66, 73, 80-81, 105, 115-128, 273
Birkat Kohanim	30
Birmingham Festival	221
Birnbaum, Philip	147, 149-150, 151
Bloch, Ernest	174-175
Bodleian Library of Oxford	26
Bond, Jeff	257
Botnick, Bruce	254
Brandwein, Naftule	201
Brass Band	207
Braun, Yehezkel	177
The Brave and the Bold	291
British Mandate	191
Brother Power the Geek	289
Buddhism	192
Byzantine medal	3
Cairo Geniza	26
Canaanites (Canaan)	41, 43, 47, 49, 249, 282
Candide	176
Canterbury Cathedral	186
Castel, Moshe	7
Castelnuovo-Tedesco, Mario	174
Cathedral of St. John the Divine	202
Catholicism	236, 244, 271, 273
Celan, Paul	230-238, 243
Ceremonial for the Equinox	201
Chagall, Marc	7
Chamber Choir of Kraków	236
Cherubim	51
Chicago Symphony Orchestra	188
The Chosen	263

Christian Herald	281
Christianity	103, 104, 122, 169, 172, 178, 192, 193, 200, 221, 225, 228-229, 233, 244, 251, 271
Christmas	247, 294
Classics Illustrated	281
Codex Adler	26, 27
Cohen, Francis	170, 225-226, 229
Cohn, Steve	201
Cole, Jack	278
Coleman, Ornette	83
Comics Code Authority	269, 280-281, 282, 283, 284, 290
Confucianism	192
Conservative Judaism	131, 158-160, 161
Copland, Aaron	195, 258, 259
Covenant Code	52
Craig, Johnny	280
Crime SuspenStories	277, 280
Cromwell, Oliver	199
Crusades	122, 127
Crystal Psalms	187
Curran, Alvin	7, 188, 204-206, 207
Daat Zeqenim	122
Das Heilige	240
David	17-18, 35, 46, 49-50, 174, 223
Davidic monarchy	36, 40, 42, 43, 45
DC Comics	270, 283-284, 288-289
De Ecclesiæ Dominio	293
de Sola Pool, David	146, 147-149, 150, 153
Dead Sea Basin	42
Debney, John	261-262, 264
Delilah	287
Dell Giant	281
DeMille, Cecil B.	250
Deuteronomistic History	41

Die Posaunenstelle	230-238
Dies Irae	261
Doolin, Joe	278
Dorfman, Leo	285
du Pre, Jacqueline	175
dybbuk	181-182
EC Comics	270, 277-280
Edelman, Marsha Bryan	248
Eglon	42
Egypt	11-12, 36, 38, 39, 41, 53
Ehad Mi Yodea	200
Ehud	41-42
Einhorn, David	161
Eleazar	35
Electronic Studio (SUNY Albany)	207
Elgar, Edward	7, 9, 168-173, 183, 221-230, 231, 235, 237, 242, 243-245, 251
Elgar Festival	229
Eli	35
Elijah	207
Elijah	221
Elijah's Violin	206-207
Elisha	50
Eliyahu Hanavi	207
Elul	29-30, 31
End of Days	260-261
Ephraimites	45
Esau	102-104
eShofar	208
Esther	273
Et Sha'arey Ratzon	144, 147
Europäisches Musikfest Stuttgart	235
Exodus	263
Ezekiel	33-35
Ezra	184
Ezra ben Solomon of Gerona	84, 90, 102
false prophecy	178-181

Famous Funnies	281
Fantastic Four	268
Feldstein, Al	277
Felstiner, John	232, 234, 235
Fertile Crescent	37
Festive Horns	177
Fight Comics	278
First Temple	18, 33-36, 50-51, 53
Fischman, Rajmil	191-192
Flash	268
Flash Gordon	281
Fleisher, Robert	176-177
Flood	273
Folkway Records	6
For Julian	205
Forbes	271
Former Prophets	41
Forms of Prayers for the New Year	147, 152
Foss, Lukas	176
Freier, Recha	178
Friedman, Jay	188
Gabriel	292-295
Gächinger Kantorei	236
Gaines, Maxwell Charles	269-273, 276
Gaines, William	276-277, 280
Galil	44
Garden of Eden	191
Geba	45
Geonic period	132, 133-134, 135, 136
Gevurah	90, 100
Gibeon	46
Gideon	17, 43-45, 267, 275-276
Gihon Spring	49
Gluck, Bob	207-209
Godspell	252
Goehr, Alexander	178-181
Golden Calf	23

Goldsmith, Jerry	9, 252-260, 261, 263-264
Golijov, Osvaldo	188-190
Goor, Joel	201-202
Goren, Shlomo	191
Graham, Lorenz	281
Green Arrow	289
Green Goblin	290
Green Lantern	268, 289
Guardian	292
Gwen Stacy	290
Hajdu, Andre	177
halakhah	2, 20, 21, 57, 64, 69, 132, 133
Hammurabi's law code	52
Handel, George Frideric	168
Harvey, Jonathan	192
ḥatzotzerah	12-13, 14, 18, 19, 22, 223
The Haunt of Fear	277
Hausdorff, David M.	6
The Hawk and the Dove	289, 291
Hayom Harat Olam	143, 162
Hebron	222, 223, 224, 245
ḥesed	100
Heston, Charlton	252-253
Hinduism	192
Hirsch, Samson Raphael	153
Hoffman, Melchior	180
Holocaust	167, 177, 184-190, 209
Hör	9, 221, 230-245
Hornblower	292-293
Hosea	38-39
Hoshana Rabbah	29, 31, 48
House of Jacob	11, 39, 62
House of Jehu	41
House of Omri	50
Humanistic Judaism	158
Iberian Peninsula	106, 115, 127

Idelsohn, Abraham Z.	6, 200, 249
"In Dat Great Gettin' Up Mornin'"	294
Inner Sanctum Mysteries	277
Isaac	11, 22, 65-67, 73, 95-96, 102, 105-106, 115-116, 118-127, 139, 145-147, 155, 273
Isaac Arama	80-81
Isaac ben Jacob ha-Kohen	78, 95-97, 103
Isaac Emmanuel	131
Isaac Luria	137, 140
Isaiah	39, 76
Islam	117, 127, 192, 193, 293, 295
Israel Museum	7
Israeli nationalism	167, 190-193
Israfil	293
Ithamar	35
Jacob	11, 100, 102, 105
Jacob ben Jacob ha-Kohen	94-95
Jaeger, August	224, 228-229
Jehoiakim	33
Jehoram	50
Jehu	50
Jeremiah	35-38
Jericho	3, 16-17, 40, 42, 47-49, 267, 273-275, 283-284
Jerubbaal	43
Jerusalem	22, 35-36, 37, 38, 50, 54, 64, 115, 136, 155, 176, 178-179, 188, 191, 224-225, 230, 244, 248
Jerusalem Sephardic practice	118-119
Jesus	97, 222-225, 228, 244, 247, 249, 252, 281, 294
Jewish Encyclopedia	5, 169-170, 225-226
Jewish Theological Seminary (Breslau)	131

Jewish Theological Seminary (New York)	26
The Jewish War	231
Jewish Images in the Comics	268
Jezreel Valley	44
Joab	46, 49
Joash	43
Job	40
Joel	18, 77
John the Baptist	252
Johnson, Blind Willie	262
Johnson, Robert	262
Jolly, Don	272
Jonathan	45
Jordon Valley	42
Joseph	11
Joseph ben Abraham Gikatilla	104-106, 109, 112
Joseph of Hamadan	106, 109
Josephus	231
Joshua	47-48, 249, 250, 275, 282-283
Joshua ibn Shu'eib	86
Josiah ben Amon	36
Jubilee	1, 15-16, 52-53, 61, 68, 100, 107, 199
Judah b. R. Nahman	72
Judah haNasi (R. Judah)	19, 63, 67, 68
Judas	171
Kaddish (prayer)	129, 186
Kaddish (album)	206
Kaddish for Terezin	186
Kaddish Symphony	175-176
Kaplan, Mordecai	161
kavanot	148
Kedemites	43-45
Keele University	191
Kefauver, Estes	280
Kennedy, John F.	175
Kerioth	39
Kid Flash	291

King Edward VII	229
The Kingdom	168, 172, 229
Klein, Earl	153
Klingons	256-260, 264
Kohanim	13, 15, 16, 24, 30
Kol Bo	151
Kol Haneshamah	159, 162
Kol Ha'Shofar	6
Kol Nidrei	175
Koren Rosh Hashana Maḥzor	156-158
Krakauer, David	189, 201
Kramer, Lawrence	170-171
Kubowitzki, Avraham Tzvi	207
Küng, Hans	192
Laban	11
Laderman, Ezra	191
Lafargue Clinic	279
Le danze del Re David	173-174
Le Sacre du printemps	255
Le Shofar	7
Lees, Benjamin	185
Leeser, Isaac	146-148
Legion of Super-Heroes	285, 287
Lehti, John	281-282
Leibowitz, Jack	270
leshem yiḥud	154
Let the Trumpet Sound	177
Lev Shalem	159-160, 162
Leviathan	53
Levin, Neil	186, 202
Levites (Levi'im)	4, 13, 15, 16, 24
Leviticus Rabbah	2, 72-73
Lewandowski, Louis	186
Lewis, Carroll	253
Livnat, Arik	201
Lockwood, Jeremiah	201
Lot	12
lulav	3, 268
MacDowell Colony	194

MacFarren, George	168-169, 227
Machzor Vitry	142
MacMillan, James,	172-173
MAD	280
Madsen, Catherine	178
Maḥta	3
maḥzor	2-3, 9, 139-164
Mahzor Ori Veyishi	153
Maḥzor Qol Yehudah	153
Maimonides	23, 78, 95, 105, 153, 195
Mal Duncan	291-295
Malkhiyot (Malkhuyot)	25-28, 81, 133, 135-136, 143
Malkhut	90, 91, 92, 93, 104, 108
Manasseh (Manassites)	43, 44, 45
Marvel Comics	284, 290
Mary	247
Mary Magdalene	171, 222
Mayer, Sheldon	270
McClure newspaper syndicate	269-270
Mechaye Hametim	184-185
Meditations	176-177
Mediterranean	23
Mediterranean compositional style	185
Mendelssohn, Felix	221
menorah	3, 51, 268
Mesopotamia	37
Metatron	94
Metropolitan Synagogue	201
Mi Yodea	200
Michael	293
"Michael, Row the Boat Ashore"	294
Midianites	17, 43-45, 275-276
Miller, Malcolm	199-200
Mills College	187
Milton, John	293
Mishkan Hanefesh	140, 159, 162

Mishneh Torah	23
mitzvah	84, 135, 162, 235
Mjolnir	268
Moabites	39, 42-43
Montagu, Jeremy	248-249, 253
Moore, Jerrold Northrop	226
Moses	11, 12, 14, 19, 51, 94, 99, 234, 250, 252
Moses, Stéphane	234
Moses ben Shem Tov de León	87, 91, 99-104, 109, 110, 111
Moses und Aron	180, 250
Moshe ibn Ezra	116
Mostel, Raphael	188, 201
Mount Moriah	96, 105, 127
Mount Sinai	11, 12, 22-23, 30, 51, 94, 105, 234, 250, 267
musaf	25-26, 27-28, 63, 64, 67, 81, 128-130, 132-136, 143, 145
Music Memorial from Auschwitz	189
The Musical Quarterly	227-228
mysterium tremendum	240-243, 245
Naftali	44
Nahmanides	91-94, 100, 106
Nathan	49
Nation of Islam	295
National Organization for Decent Literature	273
Negro spirituals	293-294
Nehemiah	18
New Grove Dictionary of Music and Musicians	169
New Moon	19, 30, 54, 62, 74, 106, 109, 168, 267
Night and Dawn (Nacht En Dageraad)	188
Norse mythology	268
North, Sterling	279
"O die Schornsteine"	177
Obadiah the Proselyte	178
objets d'arts	7

Olat Tamid	161
O'Neil, Denny	289
opera	181-184
Orchestra Hall (Chicago)	188
Orthodox Judaism	9, 19, 141, 144, 145-158, 203
Otto, Rudolf	240-241, 243
Panufnik, Roxana	192-193
Paradise Lost	293
Parsifal	171
The Passion of the Christ	262
Pecker, Talia	236
Pesaḥ (Passover)	22, 30, 61, 200
Pesiqta deRav Kahana	2, 72-76
Pesiqta Rabbati	76-77
Peter	171
Pharaoh	11, 250
Pharaoh Necho	36
Philips, A. Th.	152
Philistines	45-46
Phineas	35
Picture Stories from the Bible	268, 269-276, 281
Planet of the Apes	9, 252, 256, 260
Poling, Daniel A.	281
Portugal	127
Prayers for the New Year	147
Preludes for Organ on a Theme of Bruto Sen.	174
priests	12-13, 16-17, 18, 24, 35-36, 47-48, 249, 274-275, 283
Prophecy for the End of Days	192
Prophet or King	192
Pumbedita	132, 134
Punch Comics	278
Punisher	290
Rabbi Abbahu	22-23, 27, 65-66, 70, 73, 80
Rabbi Isaac	67, 78
Rabbi Isaac Emmanuel	131

Rabbi Ishmael	222
Rabbi Judah b. Bathyra	222
Rabbi Levi	68
Rabbi Nathan	24, 64-65
Rabbi Simeon ben Gamliel	23-24
Rabin, Yitzhak	190
Rahab	275
raḥamim	93, 96, 105, 110, 112
Ran, Shulamit	181-182
Rashi	28, 78
Rav Ahai	132-133
Rav 'Amram	28
Recanati, Menahem	84-85
Reconstructionist Judaism	158-159, 161, 207
Reed, William	229
Reform Judaism	131, 140, 158-160, 202
Requiem of Reconciliation	9, 221, 236, 241-242, 243
ribbon olamim	156-157
ribbono shel olam	148, 150, 152, 153-154
Ricca, Gus	278
Richter, Hans	226
Rilling, Helmuth	236
The Ring	171
Robin	280, 291
Roman period	3
Rose of the Winds	189
Rosenbaum, J.	152
Rosh Hashanah (New Year)	1, 2, 3, 5, 8, 14, 15, 16, 22, 24, 26, 30, 31, 55, 57, 58, 60, 62, 63, 64, 68, 74, 76, 80, 88, 95, 103, 105, 106, 109, 123, 127, 128, 139, 141-142, 150, 157-158, 163, 165, 189, 198, 202, 207, 248
Rosh Ḥodesh	30, 74
Royal Concertgebouw Orchestra Brass Ens.	188

Rozakis, Bob	292
Rózsa', Miklós	247, 250
Rubin, Emmanuel	177
Saadia Gaon	23, 25-26, 78, 146
Sachs, Nelly	177, 185
Sacks, Jonathan	156-158
sacrifice	5, 13, 30
Safed	136
St. John the Baptist	168-169, 227
Salonika	131, 132
Samael	96, 103-104
Samson	251, 273, 285-288
Samuel	45-46
Samuel ben Yahya ben al Maghribi	178
šapparu	6, 33, 41
Sarah	115, 119-120, 124-125, 126
Satan	59, 66-67, 71, 77, 78-80, 96, 97, 103, 134-135, 140, 143, 146, 149, 150, 154, 155-156, 162, 261
Saul	40, 45-46, 251
Saul	168
Schaffner, Franklin J.	252
Schelomo	174-175, 259
Schlomo ben Dugi	179
Schoenberg, Arnold	180, 250
Scholem, Gershom	87-88
Schuster, Leo	229
Schwartz, Julius	292
Schwartz, Stephen	251-252
Second Temple	4, 5, 13, 14, 21-22, 50-51, 134, 222, 225, 228, 248
Seduction of the Innocent	279-280
Sefer ha-Orah	94
sefirot (sefiroth)	86, 87, 112
Selihot	30

Senator, Ronald	186
Sensation Comics	272-273
Sephardic customs	8, 9, 28, 29, 108, 115-137, 142-144, 146-148, 150, 152-154
Sermon on the Mount	222
Seven Angels	172
Sforno	155
Sha'arei Tsedeq	103, 105
Shabbat (Sabbath)	2, 21-22, 29, 31, 132, 231
Shalom Al Yisrael synagogue	3
Shatin, Jusith	206-207
Shearmur, Edward	262-263, 264
Sheba	46
sheḥita	23
Sheiltot	132
Shekhinah	87, 92, 107, 109, 110-112
Shem MiShmuel	156
Shemini Atseret	29
Shene Luhot HaBerit	136
shepherd's horn	4, 12, 285-286
Sheriff, Noam	184-185, 190-191
shevarim	25-28, 64, 69, 70, 71, 80-82, 90, 128, 133, 164, 169, 177, 189, 196, 197, 199, 203, 223, 239, 251, 253, 257, 258
Shiloh	35
Shin Far Shofar I	205
Shlomo ben Aderet	79
Shofar (Gluck)	208
Shofar (Stern)	177-178
Shofar for Instruments and Electronic Sounds	188
Shofar on the Temple Mount	7
Shofar Rags	7, 205
Shofar Service	202-203

Shofarot	25-28, 133, 135-136, 143, 163
Shostakovich, Dmitri	185
Shulḥan Arukh	78, 135-136
Siddur (Seder) Rav Amram Gaon	133, 142
Siddur Rashi	142
Siftey Tzadiqim	147
Silver Streak Comics	278
Silverman, Morris	161
Simeon b. Laqish	72
Simeon bar Yohai	109
Simḥat Torah	29, 31
A Single Voice	191
Six-Day War	191, 230
The Skeleton Key	262-263
Smith, Ruth	168
Smithsonian Institution	5
Softley, Iain	262
Solomon	18, 35, 49-50, 174
Solomon ibn Adret	86
"Someone Blew a Shofar"	185
Sonata about Jerusalem	178-180
Song of Songs	176
Spain	116-117, 127, 132
Spider-Man	268, 284, 290
Ssshofar	208
Star Trek: The Motion Picture	9, 252, 256-258, 260
Star Trek V: The Final Frontier	259-260
Star Wars	257
Stern, Max	192
Stern, Robert	177-178
Stevenson, Ronald	175
The Story of Jesus	281
The Story of Ruth	250
Strauss, Richard	257
Stravinsky, Igor	255
Strömberg, Fredrik	268
Sukkot	22, 29, 30, 31, 48, 61
Superman	270, 280, 283, 284,

	287-288, 289
Superman's Pal Jimmy Olsen	269, 270, 283-288, 291, 295
Sura	134
Swan, Curt	285
The Sway Machinery	201
Syrian Jews	16
Takis, John	255
Tales from the Crypt	277
Tales from the Great Book	268, 276, 281-283
Tarzan	281
te'amim	26, 89
Teen Titans	269, 288, 290-295
teḥinot	144
tefillin	21
Tekeeyah (A Call)	193-198
Tekoa	37, 39
Tekyah	188-189
Temple Mount	230-231, 233
Ten Commandments	52, 234
The Ten Commandments	250-251, 252, 281
teqi'ah	2, 21, 22, 25-27, 28, 63, 71, 80-81, 90-91, 102, 133, 142, 164, 168-169, 170, 173, 176, 177, 179-180, 189, 196, 197-198, 203, 204, 207, 208, 222, 223, 224, 231, 239, 243, 250, 252, 253
teqi'ah gedolah	28, 57, 186, 189, 198, 199, 203, 204, 207, 259
teqi'ot me'umad	142-143
teqi'ot meyushav	142
Terezin	186

teru'ah	1-2, 14-15, 17, 25-27, 28, 29, 59, 60, 61-62, 63, 67, 69, 70-71, 72, 80-81, 82, 90-92, 93, 98, 102, 106, 133-134, 135, 137, 156, 164, 169, 173, 174, 175, 177, 179, 180, 189, 196, 197, 199, 203, 204, 207, 208, 223, 237, 239, 254
Teruah	207
teru'ah gedolah	17, 28, 29, 57, 129, 137
Teru'ah haMelech	177
Teshuva	75
"There's a Star in the East"	294
Thesaurus of Hebrew Melodies	200
Three Paths to Peace	192-193
Thor	268
Tibetan Singing Bowl Ensemble	201
tiferet	90, 91, 93, 100, 101, 104, 107, 108
tikkun olam	193, 210
Tisha B'Av	188
Tishri	31, 55, 62-63
T'kiatot	203-204
Todros ben Joseph ha-Levi Abulafia	96-97, 99, 112
Toledano, Eliezer	153-154
Tom Corbett, Space Cadet	281
Torah Haminḥa	79-80
Tosafot	78
Towering Inferno	206
The Tree of Knowledge Still Bears Fruit	191-292
Triptych	178
TRT (*teqi'ah, teru'ah, teqi'ah*)	128-129, 133, 135-136
TSRT (*teqi'ah, shevarim, teru'ah, teqi'ah*)	128-129, 133, 135-136
TST (*teqi'ah, shevarim, teqi'ah*)	128-129, 133, 135-136
tumtum	24-25

Tur	28
Tzadik Records	7
Union Prayer Book	202
Vanished Voices	186
Venice Haggadah	4
Vienna Jewish Music Week	206
Viet Nam War	289
Vilna	151
Wagner, Richard	171, 254, 257
Warshauer, Meira	193-198
Water Libation	22, 23
Waxman, Franz	250-251, 263, 264
Weird Science	277
Weisgall, Hugo	203-204
Weisinger, Mort	283-284
Weltethos	192
Wertham, Frederic	279-280
West Side Story	176
Western Wall	188, 191
Widmann, Jörg	182-184
Williams, John	256-257
Williams, Ralph Vaughn	257
Wise, Robert	252
The Witch's Tale	277
Wolverine	290
Wonder Girl	291
Wonder Woman	272, 280
Wycliffe, John	293
Wyler, William	247
Ya'aqov ben Asher	28
Ya'aqov ben Moshi Levi Moelin	28
Yaakov ben Hananel of Sikily	79
yael	15
Yavneh	134
Yehi ratzon	149, 150, 151, 153, 155, 157, 158
Yehudah ben Shemuel ibn Abbas	116-117, 127
Yehudah Al-Harizzi	117
Yehudah HaLevi	116

Yeshayahu HaLevi Horowitz	136-137
yevava	64, 69, 70
Yiddish	20, 26, 184, 185, 235
Yitzhak bar Yosef	134
Ynys Lochtyn	225
yom teru'ah	55, 59, 61, 69, 248
Yom Kippur	5, 15, 28-29, 31, 53, 55, 61, 68, 76, 100, 107, 241, 248
Yosef Karo	135-136
X-Men	284
Zadok	35
Zadokite priest	33-34
Zebulun	44
Ze'ev Wolf of Zhitomir	163
Zeitlin, Leo M.	258
Zikhronot	25-28, 133, 135-136, 143
Zorn, John	7

www.ingramcontent.com/pod-product-compliance
Lightning Source LLC
Chambersburg PA
CBHW021800220426
43662CB00006B/127